The *Trotula*

THE MIDDLE AGES SERIES

Ruth Mazo Karras, General Editor
Edward Peters, Founding Editor

A complete list of books in the series
is available from the publisher.

The *Trotula*

An English Translation of the
Medieval Compendium
of Women's Medicine

Edited and translated by
Monica H. Green

PENN

University of Pennsylvania Press

Philadelphia

Copyright © 2001, 2002 University of Pennsylvania Press
Printed in the United States of America on acid-free paper

10 9 8 7 6 5 4 3 2 1

Published by
University of Pennsylvania Press
Philadelphia, Pennsylvania 19104-4011

Library of Congress Cataloging-in-Publication Data

The Trotula : an English translation of the medieval compendium of
women's medicine / edited and translated by Monica H. Green.
    p. cm. — (The Middle Ages series)
  Includes bibliographical references and index.
  ISBN 978-0-8122-1808-4 (pbk. : alk. paper)

  1. Gynecology—Early works to 1800. 2. Obstetrics—Early works to
1800. 3. Women—Health and hygiene—Early works to 1800. 4. Medicine—Italy—Salerno—History. 5. Medicine, Medieval. I. Green, Monica
Helen. II. Series.

RG61 .T74 2002
618'.09'02—dc21

                                                        2001057397

Ilā bintayya al-'azīzatayn
Malaika wa Kanza

Contents

Note on the Paperback Edition

The following translation of the *Trotula* standardized ensemble is based on my edition of the Latin text (published in hardcover by the University of Pennsylvania Press in 2001). In that volume, the Latin text appears opposite the English translation, with full critical apparatus for those who wish to consult it. The present paperback edition omits the Latin text with its accompanying descriptions of the manuscripts. The annotations to the translation conflate and condense separate annotations to the Latin text and the English translation in the hardcover edition. Finally, I have omitted the comprehensive list of medieval Latin terms, substituting a simple list of *materia medica* alphabetized according to English common name. Aside from a few minor corrections, the Introduction and translation presented here are unaltered via-à-vis the hardcover edition.

Illustrations

Preface

In histories of women as in histories of medicine, readers often find a passing reference to a mysterious person called Trotula of Salerno. "Trotula," for whom no substantive historical evidence has ever been brought forth, is said by some to have lived in the eleventh or twelfth century and is alleged to have written the most important book on women's medicine in medieval Europe, *On the Diseases of Women* (*De passionibus mulierum*). She is also alleged to have been the first female professor of medicine, teaching in the southern Italian town of Salerno, which was at that time the most important center of medical learning in Europe. Other sources, however, assert that "Trotula" did not exist and that the work attributed to her was written by a man.

Any figure who could generate such diametrically opposed opinions about her work and her very existence must surely be a mystery. Yet the mystery of "Trotula" is inevitably bound up with the text "she" is alleged to have written. The *Trotula* (for the word was originally a title, not an author's name) was indeed the most popular assembly of materials on women's medicine from the late twelfth through the fifteenth centuries. Written in Latin and so able to circulate throughout western Europe where Latin served as the *lingua franca* of the educated elites, the *Trotula* had also by the fifteenth century been translated into most of the western European vernacular languages, in which form it reached an even wider audience.[1]

Surprisingly, for all its historical importance, no modern printed edition of the Latin *Trotula* was available for the use of students and scholars until the Latin-English edition and translation I published in 2001.[2] Prior to that, the Latin *Trotula* had been edited for publication only once, in the sixteenth century, under the title *The Unique Book of Trotula on the Treatment of the Diseases of Women Before, During, and After Birth*,[3] and the only previous modern translations were based on this same Renaissance edition.[4] While these modern translations have had some utility in keeping alive the "Trotula question," they have in another sense perpetuated the confusion, since they have passed on to new generations of readers the historical distortions of the Renaissance edition, a work which is in fundamental respects a humanist fabrication.

The Renaissance editor, undoubtedly with the best of intentions, added what was to be the last of many layers of editorial "improvements." These intrusions had, over the course of the four-hundred-year life of the *Trotula*, almost thoroughly obliterated all indications that this was not one text but three. True, they were all probably of twelfth-century Salernitan origin, but they reflected the work of at least three authors with distinct perspectives on women's diseases and cosmetic concerns. The first and third of these texts, *On the Conditions of Women* and *On Women's Cosmetics*, were anonymous. The second, *On Treatments for Women*, was attributed even in the earliest manuscripts to a Salernitan woman healer named Trota (or Trocta). Each of the texts went through several stages of revision and each circulated independently throughout Europe through the end of the fifteenth century, when manuscript culture began to give way to the printed book. But the texts also had a second, parallel fate. By the end of the twelfth century, an anonymous compiler had brought the three texts together into a single ensemble, slightly revising the wording, adding new material, and rearranging a few chapters. This ensemble was called the *Summa que dicitur "Trotula"* (The Compendium Which Is Called the "Trotula"), forming the title *Trotula* (literally "little Trota" or perhaps "the abbreviated Trota") out of the name associated with the middle text, *On Treatments for Women*. The appellation was perhaps intended to distinguish the ensemble from a general, much longer medical compilation, *Practical Medicine*, composed by the historical woman Trota. The *Trotula* ensemble soon became the leading work on women's medicine, and it continued to be the object of manipulation by subsequent medieval editors and scribes, most of whom understood *Trotula* not as a title but as an author's name.[5]

By 1544, when the ensemble came into the hands of the Renaissance editor, Georg Kraut, generations of scribes and readers had come to believe that they were dealing with a single text or, at most, two texts on the same subject by a single author.[6] It is, then, quite understandable that Kraut saw his task as merely to clean up a messy, badly organized text. He rewrote certain passages, suppressed some material and, in his most thorough editorial act, reorganized all the chapters so as to eliminate the text's many redundancies and inconsistencies (due, we know now, to the fact that several authors were addressing the same topics differently). There is no way that a reader of this emended printed text could, without reference to the manuscripts, discern the presence of the three discrete component parts. Hence when some twenty years later a debate over the author's gender and identity was initiated (and it has continued to the present day), it was assumed that there was only one author involved.[7]

Medieval readers were coming to the *Trotula* texts with urgent questions about how to treat women's diseases or address cosmetic concerns, or perhaps with more speculative questions about the workings of the female body or the processes of generation. For them, the texts were a vital fund of information. Questions of authorship or textual development were of minimal importance.[8] For modern students of medical history or the history of women, however, it is imperative to understand the processes by which the *Trotula* ensemble was compiled if we are to answer such questions as: What do these texts show us about the development of medieval medical theories concerning the workings of the female body? What can they reveal about the impact of the new Arabic medicine that began to infiltrate Europe in the late eleventh century? Is there, in fact, a female author behind any of the texts and, if so, what can she tell us about medieval women's own views of their bodies and the social circumstances of women's healthcare either in Salerno or elsewhere in Europe? Answering these questions calls for close textual analysis that pulls apart, layer by layer, decades of accretion and alteration. Such analysis shows us not simply that there are three core texts at the heart of the *Trotula* but also that the ensemble became a magnet for bits and pieces of material from entirely unrelated sources. We cannot, for example, attribute the neonatal procedures described in ¶¶124-27 to local southern Italian medical practices but must recognize them instead as the work of a ninth-century Persian physician named Rhazes. Such analysis shows us, in other words, that the *Trotula* ensemble is a patchwork of sources. There is no single author and no single text. There is, consequently, no single (or simple) story to be told of "Trotula" or women's medicine at Salerno.

Knowledge of the multiplicity of the *Trotula* may resolve certain questions (about the redundancies and inconsistencies that so troubled the Renaissance editor Georg Kraut, for example), but it raises others. Particularly, if the texts are so protean (a total of fifteen different versions of the independent texts and the ensemble can be identified in the medieval manuscripts),[9] how do we choose any single version to study? Obviously, the authors of the three original, independent works had their own unique conceptions of the content and intended uses of their texts. On the basis of my reconstructions of these original forms of the texts, I describe in the Introduction their more distinctive medical theories and practices; I also summarize what is now known about the medical practices of the women of Salerno—including, most important, Trota. Nevertheless, the three original twelfth-century works often bore only an oblique resemblance to the text(s) that later medieval readers would have had in front of them. The *Trotula* ensemble, ragged patchwork though it is, has a historical importance in its own right, since it was this version of the texts that the largest proportion of medieval readers would have seen, and it was this assembly of theories and remedies (whatever their sources or however incongruous the combination originally may have been) that would have been most commonly understood throughout later medieval Europe as the authoritative Salernitan teachings on women and their diseases.

One of the several versions of the ensemble was particularly stable in form and widespread in circulation: this is what I have called the "standardized ensemble," which, with twenty-nine extant copies, ranks as the most popular version of the Salernitan texts in any form, circulating either independently or as a group. The standardized ensemble is a product of the mid-thirteenth century (whether it was produced at Salerno itself I cannot say) and it reflects the endpoint of what had been an active first century of development for the three texts.[10] Since it was also the version most closely associated with university circles (and so the version most likely known to medieval commentators, both medical and lay), I felt that this was the version best suited for use by modern scholars and students who are interested in medieval medical and intellectual history and the history of women.

The following translation of the *Trotula* standardized ensemble is based on my edition of the Latin text. For the Latin edition, nine manuscripts from the second half of the thirteenth century or the early fourteenth century were collated. The base text was a manuscript from the mid- or late thirteenth century composed in Italy and now owned by the Universitätsbibliothek in Basel (see fig. 10). The other eight manuscripts come from Italy, northern France, Montpellier, and Germany, and show the breadth of circulation of the text throughout Latinate Europe.

This translation, like all such endeavors, is merely an attempt to recapture a physical world and a conceptual world-view in many ways foreign to modern readers, especially those who function within the western biomedical paradigm. Inevitably, many nuances—anatomical, nosological, and botanical—can never be adequately articulated.[11] As translator, therefore, I in no sense wish to authorize the efficacy of any of the following remedies. Many more questions remain regarding Trota and the *Trotula*, but it is my hope that this edition of these important and influential texts will offer a foundation for future debates and, in the process, enhance our understanding of women's healthcare in medieval Europe.

Note on Abbreviations and Pronouns

For reasons of space, when quoting in the Notes from the original *Trotula* treatises I refer to them by abbreviations of their Latin titles:

TEM = *Tractatus de egritudinibus mulierum* (*Treatise on the Diseases of Women*, the "rough draft" of the *LSM*)

LSM = *Liber de sinthomatibus mulierum* (*Book on the Conditions of Women*)

DCM = *De curis mulierum* (*On Treatments for Women*)

DOM = *De ornatu mulierum* (*On Women's Cosmetics*)

All quotations come from working drafts of my editions of the independent texts. For complete descriptions of the manuscripts, please see my published handlists.[12]

I have employed the same system of enumeration for component paragraphs of all the different versions of the *Trotula*, whether in their original independent form or when combined into the ensemble, as laid out in my essay "The Development of the *Trotula*."[13] Paragraphs identified with a simple arabic numeral will refer to material that is found in the standardized ensemble (the version of the text translated here) as well as in earlier versions. Hence, for example, when I refer to ¶45 in the first version of *Conditions of Women* (*LSM 1*), this refers to the same section on uterine suffocation, *mutatis mutandis*, as ¶45 in the present edition. Since many passages from the original texts were moved or deleted during the first century of the texts' development, however, I have also employed subordinate alphanumerics so that readers may understand where these now-lost sections were located. So, for example, ¶305f, a detailed procedure for vaginal hygiene, had appeared in early versions of *Women's Cosmetics* in the position after ¶305 as found in this edition. Readers may refer to the concordances of the *Trotula* texts in my above-mentioned essay for full comparisons of all the different versions of the texts.

Finally, my employment of pronouns should be explained. As noted earlier, the gender of the author(s) of the *Trotula* has been a central concern in scholarship to date and will, no doubt, be of prime interest to many readers of the present edition precisely because gender—whether of the authors, scribes, practitioners, or patients—is central to larger historical questions surrounding women's healthcare and roles in medical practice. Although it is not my objective to settle all these questions here, I have employed gendered pronouns to indicate where I think the gender of the author (or, for that matter, the patient) is clear and where it is not. Thus, I believe the authors of *Conditions of Women* and *Women's Cosmetics* to be male and so use the masculine pronoun. *Treatments for Women*, however, represents what I believe to be a palimpsest, with a female author's voice overwritten by another (or oth-

ers) of uncertain gender.[14] For that text and for other situations where there
is still ambiguity or doubt about a historical actor's gender, I have employed
the inclusive forms s/he, her/his, her/him.

* * *

This book had three beginnings. In 1981, John F. Benton, of the California Institute of Technology, was asked to write a new introduction for a
planned reprint of Elizabeth Mason-Hohl's 1940 English translation of the
Renaissance edition of the *Trotula*. In checking the translation, Benton soon
became aware of many significant problems with Mason-Hohl's work and so
began a new translation of his own (again based on the Renaissance text). He
also began a study of the manuscript tradition in order to clarify the question
of authorship, collecting microfilms of many of the several dozen copies he
had identified. In the course of that research, Benton discovered the three-
text origin of the *Trotula* ensemble, which immediately demolished any question of single authorship. Equally important was his discovery in a Madrid
manuscript of a completely different text, the *Practical Medicine According to
Trota* (*Practica secundum Trotam*), which he identified as the authentic work
of a Salernitan woman healer named Trota, whose historicity could now for
the first time be established. These initial findings were published in 1985 in
an article in the *Bulletin of the History of Medicine*.[15] Unfortunately, at his
death in 1988 Benton had not yet made the final revisions of his new translation and commentary on the Renaissance *Trotula*.

My own involvement with the *Trotula* treatises began simultaneously
with Benton's and resulted in my Ph.D. dissertation, which surveyed the history of early medieval gynecological theory up through the creation of the
Trotula in the twelfth century.[16] Benton and I carried on a lively correspon-
dence about the *Trotula* for several years, and my postdoctoral work on the
pre-Salernitan Latin gynecological corpus complemented his study of the
manuscript tradition of the *Trotula* texts. Since the history of the *Trotula* was
vitally important for the overall history of medieval gynecological literature, I
found it necessary to see that Benton's pioneering work did not die with him.
In 1989, Elspeth Benton very graciously granted me permission to take over
the *Trotula* project and make use of all the materials her late husband had collected. It very quickly became apparent, of course, that John Benton's own
discoveries had made yet another translation of the Renaissance edition irrelevant, so I decided it was time for a proper edition of the medieval texts.
While I am thus solely responsible for the form and content of the present
work, it is to John and Elspeth Benton that I owe not simply profoundest

thanks but also acknowledgment that it is because of them that the present edition came into being at all.

Thanks are also due to the late Robert Benson and to Rosie Meiron, John Benton's literary executor and secretary, respectively, for facilitating transfer of his materials; to Richard Rouse, Patricia Stirnemann, and Theresa Webber whose paleographical expertise, generously and repeatedly offered, allowed me to ground my study of the manuscripts of the *Trotula* in historical space and time; to Michael McVaugh, for innumerable conversations that helped me think through this project in its early phases; to Klaus-Dietrich Fischer, who turned his keen philologist's eye on a draft of the edition; and to Montserrat Cabré i Pairet, Joan Cadden, Luke Demaitre, Florence Eliza Glaze, and Ann Ellis Hanson, whose copious comments on earlier incarnations of this book helped me find a sense of direction. Francis Newton was my Virgil who led me through the depths of Latin darkness, while Patricia Skinner introduced me to a wealth of scholarly literature on southern Italian history. Mary Jane Morrow deserves a special *kudos* for her efficient handling of the illustrations. Henrietta Leyser and Kathleen Shelton many times took me in off the streets of Oxford and London, and Susan Thorne made sure the manuscript got to the post office. Thanks as well to my former students at Duke University for beta-testing the introduction and translation for classroom use.

Dozens of libraries throughout Europe and North America allowed me to make use of their holdings. Many thanks to all of them, especially to those that have granted permission to publish material in their collections. I wish especially to thank the Öffentliche Universitätsbibliothek in Basel, which not only has granted permission to use material from two of its manuscripts, but also responded with efficiency and generosity to my many requests. Closer to home, the staffs at Duke University's Perkins and Lilly Libraries, as well as that of the University of North Carolina at Chapel Hill's Davis Library, were indefatigable (and cheerful!) in pursuing all my requests. Financial support for this project came from the Josiah Charles Trent Memorial Foundation, the Institute for Advanced Study, the National Endowment for the Humanities, and the Duke University Arts and Sciences Research Council.

To all these individuals and institutions—and to the many others who have contributed to the enormous collaborative effort that stands behind this book—I would like to express my gratitude for their patience over the years it took to bring this study to fruition. I wish also to express my gratitude to my family, both local and extended, whose enormous collaborative effort has always stood behind me.

Figure 1. Southern Italy and north Africa.

Introduction

Why have different societies, at different times, seen diseases that we no longer see? Why did they interpret physiological processes differently from the way we do? Why did they employ therapeutic techniques that seem to us inexplicable? These questions are at the heart of any history of medicine. A strictly biological approach would search for genetic alterations, changing patterns in interactions between human hosts and microbial predators, or alterations in the environment. These kinds of physical changes no doubt occurred and profoundly affected the morbidity and mortality of medieval women. Yet from what little we know about the general afflictions of women in medieval Europe, we find no evidence of conditions radically different from those already documented in modern times such as diseases brought on by nutritional deficit (e.g., rickets, which is caused by a lack of vitamin D), by infection (leprosy, plague, etc.), or by naturally occuring degenerative processes of the body.[1] Rather than looking through the lens of modern biology, a history of medicine—and not merely of disease—tries to explore medical systems of the past on their own terms. These societies saw a different body than we do, not necessarily because the physical body itself differed significantly, but because their intellectual structures of explanation and their social objectives in controlling the body differed. The task of the history of medicine is to reconstruct an image of the world that they saw, a sensation of the body as they experienced it.

When seen through the lens of intellectual history, the systems of thought and practice embodied in the *Trotula*—the disease categorizations, the therapeutic techniques, the pharmaceutical lore—are found to belong to larger systems of thought and practice that, sometimes in dynamic tension, characterized medieval medicine. Similarly, when seen through the lens of social history, both the genesis and the later uses of the *Trotula* are shown to be intimately tied to the milieus that shaped the production of medical knowledge and the delivery of healthcare in twelfth-century Salerno and in medieval Europe more broadly. These milieus—most important, those that structured medieval gender systems—also left their imprint on the texts. It is in recapturing this interplay between text and context that we can best make sense of the genesis of the *Trotula* in twelfth-century Salerno and its components' later success throughout medieval Europe.

The three treatises that make up the *Trotula* ensemble—the *Book on the Conditions of Women*, *Treatments for Women*, and *Women's Cosmetics*—are, each in its own way, remarkable witnesses to a veritable explosion in medical thought and writing that occurred in southern Italy in the eleventh and twelfth centuries. The rise of formal medical writing in the Lombard and later Norman territory of Salerno was part of what has been called the "twelfth-century Renaissance," which manifested itself in the areas of law, theology, literature, and architecture between the mid-eleventh and thirteenth centuries.[2] The flourishing of medical writing at Salerno was at once a rebirth, a rediscovery of ancient medical texts and theories, and a new departure, a new synthesis of indigenous European practices with the much more formal, more philosophically sophisticated medicine only recently beginning to enter Latin Europe from the Arabic-speaking world.

Medieval Europe was by no means lacking in medical literature before the Salernitans. Prior to the twelfth century, texts of Roman origin, late antique translations from the Greek, and even a few Latin compositions from the Carolingian period continued to be copied and adapted by scribes both within and outside the main centers of literate culture, the courts and monasteries. The "twelfth-century Renaissance" in medicine had in fact begun in the middle decades of the eleventh century, when a handful of writers began to compose new texts out of late antique Latin or contemporary Greek sources. The most important prelude to Salerno, however, was the series of translations from Arabic into Latin made between the 1070s and 1090s at the monastery of Monte Cassino, some 120 kilometers northwest of Salerno. Within fifty years of their composition these new works were circulating widely north of the Alps. But it was the Salernitan enterprise that was to make this new Arabic medicine[3] truly functional in the West by fusing it with the older Latin texts and traditional empirical practices, and by developing techniques of commentary that sought to elucidate the deeper truths embedded within the texts. Although a second circle of translators from the Arabic in later twelfth-century Spain was to produce a new corpus of texts that ultimately proved more influential in university curricula of the thirteenth and fourteenth centuries, the contributions of twelfth-century Salerno—whether tracts on diet, urines, fevers, pharmacology, or general medicine—were to serve as standard handbooks of introductory teaching and practice until the end of the Middle Ages.

The *Trotula* texts participated both in the characteristics of this new medicine and in its popularity throughout later medieval Europe. Together, they represent the varying degrees to which Salernitan medicine might have come out of either bookish or empirical traditions. The two gynecological texts conformed to some degree to the general precepts of Galenic, humoral medicine, which was very quickly being adopted as authoritative in the new formal medical writings of the twelfth century. *Conditions of Women* (later to be called the *Trotula major*) is an essentially bookish composition based on the *Viaticum*, one of the more important of the medical texts translated at Monte Cassino, to which were added select remedies from a handful of Latin texts that had been available in Europe for several centuries. *Treatments for Women* (later to be called the *Trotula minor*)[4] was, in contrast, a disorganized collection of empirical cures with only a thin theoretical overlay; most of the cures were presented as the practices "we" perform, though it also on occasion refers to the proven remedies of a few named Salernitan practitioners.[5] It bears only a few signs of direct influence from the new translations of Arabic medicine and none of the philosophical concerns with explaining Nature's creation that we find in *Conditions of Women*. Its therapeutics are not entirely novel, yet neither do they show the same direct textual dependence on earlier materials as does *Conditions of Women*. The genesis of *Treatments for Women* is thus, like that of *Conditions of Women*, rooted in its southern Italian context, though in this case it is a more local, perhaps marginally literate one. Finally, *Women's Cosmetics*, probably the first medieval Latin text of its kind,[6] reflects the strictly empirical side of Salernitan medicine. It describes in head-to-toe order how to beautify women's skin, hair, face, lips, teeth, and genitalia. Offering no theories of dermatological conditions or their causes, it simply lists and describes in detail how cosmetic preparations are to be made and applied. *Women's Cosmetics* thus reflects not so much a formal, textual Arabic influence as the regular personal interactions between Christians and Muslims living side-by-side in southern Italy and Sicily.

To varying degrees, then, the three *Trotula* texts give us evidence of not simply how the diseases of women were formally theorized by medical writers eager to assimilate the new Arabic texts but also how local Salernitan practitioners, with or without formal training, conceptualized and treated the medical conditions of women. The specific characteristics of twelfth-century Salernitan culture thus form a necessary prelude to a detailed analysis of the *Trotula* texts.

Salerno

In trying to explain the efflorescence of medicine in eleventh- and twelfth-century Salerno, scholars have often wondered why this explosion in medical thought and writing happened here and not someplace else.[7] Europeans north of the Alps were willing to travel hundreds of miles to seek out the healing treatments of this southern Italian town or accept the ministrations of itinerant Salernitan practitioners traveling north, so much so that Salernitan physicians became stock figures in twelfth- and thirteenth-century literature.[8] Definitive explanations are not yet forthcoming, though when they are they will probably hinge in no small part on Salerno's fortuitous position as an entrepôt of Mediterranean cultures. For our purposes, it is necessary to understand why Salerno offered fertile ground for exchange between these cultures, and how women's social status in Salerno may have played a role in the formation of women's medicine.

THE CITY

Between 1169 and 1171, a Spanish Jew named Benjamin toured through southern Italy, describing the communities in which he found co-religionists. Of Salerno, "where the Christians have schools of medicine," he said "It is a city with walls upon the land side, the other side bordering on the sea, and there is a very strong castle on the summit of the hill."[9] Benjamin's dry physical description does little to suggest the wealth and prosperity of this vibrant community on the edge of a vast network of international trade. A Muslim traveler, al-Idrisi, writing a decade or two before Benjamin, had called Salerno "an illustrious city, with flourishing merchants, public conveniences, wheat and other cereals."[10] The Christian historian William of Apulia, writing just before the turn of the twelfth century, was even more effusive:

> Rome itself is not more luxurious than this city;
> It abounds in ships, trees, wine and sea;
> There is no lack here of fruit, nuts, or beautiful palaces,
> Nor of feminine beauty nor the probity of men.
> One part spreads out over the plain, the other the hill,
> And whatsoever you desire is provided by either the land or the sea.[11]

"Opulent Salerno" (as eleventh-century princes called it on their coins)[12] was well established as a center of trade and agricultural production by the late eighth century. Founded as a Roman colony in the second century B.C.E., Salerno had contracted into an insignificant settlement in the early Middle Ages. It was essentially refounded by the Lombards, who gradually built up the city from the harbor all the way to the top of the hill (fig. 2). Aside from

LA CITTA DI SALERNO CAPITALE DEL PRINCIPATO ULTERIORE NEL REGNO DI NAPOLI

Figure 2: The city of Salerno as depicted in an eighteenth-century engraving. Reproduced from Arcangelo R. Amarotta, *Salerno romana e medievale: Dinamica di un insediamento*, Società Salernitana di Storia Patria, Collana di Studi Storici Salernitani, 2 (Salerno: Pietro Laveglia, 1989), p. 12.

intermittent Arab raids in the ninth and early tenth centuries, it continued to prosper through the twelfth century. Involved in Mediterranean trade, especially with Muslim North Africa, which bought its grain, lumber, and linen cloth, Salerno was one of the wealthiest Italian cities of its day. Although not on the regular trade routes of Jewish or Arab merchants in the eleventh or twelfth century, Salerno is occasionally mentioned as a destination in merchants' accounts coming out of Egypt.[13] In any case, Salernitans needed to look no farther than nearby Sicily to obtain the spices, resins, minerals, and other items of *materia medica* (some of local manufacture, some imported from the East) that were to become integral parts of their medical system.[14]

Salerno's port had been built up in the eleventh century, which broadened the city's capacity to engage in maritime trade. The "very strong castle on the summit of the hill" that Benjamin of Tudela had described began its existence as a simple church at the end of the tenth century. A tower was added in the fifth decade of the eleventh century and then, between 1062 and 1076 under the threat of Norman invaders, it was transformed into a real fortress. Salerno's cathedral, still famous for its mosaics, marbles, and bronze doors, was constructed under the supervision of Archbishop Alfanus and dedicated in 1085. The city had at least two dozen churches and nine monasteries, three of which were female houses.[15] The Benedictine convent of San Giorgio was a very wealthy community that left a large record of its property transactions. One of the earliest documents we have records the gift of a vineyard whose profits are to be used to support the monastery's infirmary; the intent is that the sick nuns will pray for the donor's soul.[16]

The culture of water in Salerno symbolizes both the relative wealth of the city and the kind of concern for care of the self we find in the medical and cosmetic sections of the *Trotula*. Three aqueducts, originally constructed in Roman times and later restored by the Lombard princes, brought water to the city; these waters were supplemented by spring water coming down from the hills, plus wells and cisterns (to collect rainwater) in private courtyards.[17] Salerno's "opulence" was also seen in its many public fountains in the eleventh and twelfth centuries and, as well, in the availability of public baths which in other parts of the former Roman world had become rare.[18] Even in Salerno, however, the habit of bathing publicly seems to have diminished, for those few who could afford it built their own private bathhouses. The nuns of San Giorgio had such a bathhouse, and while we do not have specifics about its construction, documents from the male house of Santa Sofia suggest what it may have looked like. The latter seems to have been a substantial establishment, with at least two levels, furnaces and bronze cauldrons for providing hot water, and a pool. It was so luxurious, in fact, that contracts were drawn up allowing monastics from other houses (male and female) and secular clerics to come bathe there as well.[19] The frequency with which medicinal and cosmetic baths are prescribed in the *Trotula* suggests that both public and private baths in Salerno would have been put to extensive use.[20]

Salerno was just one of several flourishing urban communities in eleventh- and twelfth-century southern Italy. Naples, on the Tyrrhenian coast north of Salerno, and Bari, on the eastern coast of the peninsula, were larger;[21] nearby Amalfi was a more important center of international trade. The whole region of southern Italy shared in a relative bounty of grains, fruits, nuts, and other foodstuffs,[22] with increasing surpluses of raw materials and textile goods to export to other lands. Still, there were several respects in which Salerno stood out. It was made the capital of the newly created Lombard principality of Salerno in 847. The city's fortunes immediately took off, for it became the main supply center for the Amalfitan merchants, whose own hinterland was insufficient to feed them and whose port was inadequate to sustain traffic in the heavy goods they exported from southern Italy to north Africa.[23] Salerno's status also changed vis-à-vis its neighbors in 1076 when it was captured by the Norman Robert Guiscard, duke of Apulia (1057–85). Norman pilgrims passing through southern Italy at the end of the tenth century had been asked to aid the city of Salerno in repelling an attack of Muslim invaders. Hired as mercenaries (by Christians as well as Muslims) during subsequent years, these Norman knights gradually became invaders themselves and bit by bit expanded their control over several southern Italian duchies. Their extended siege of Salerno in 1076 took its toll on the city, but Robert Guiscard immediately made it the capital of the newly united Norman duchy of Apulia and Calabria. In 1130, when the Normans consolidated most of the fragmented Norman duchies into a single kingdom, they moved their capital to Palermo, in Sicily, which they had seized from Muslim control. Even so, Salerno remained an important city in the mainland kingdom. It had become an archepiscopal see in the mid-980s, and so was of some importance for local ecclesiastical administration.[24]

Southern Italy was already ethnically mixed when the first Normans arrived. The Lombards, a Germanic people who had immigrated into the area in the late sixth century, controlled the duchies of Benevento, Capua, and Salerno up through the eleventh century, and they remained numerically dominant in the population afterward. There were also enclaves of Greek-speaking communities in southern Italy, and whole principalities (such as Gaeta, Naples, and Amalfi) continued to follow Byzantine (Roman) law throughout this period. In the far south, Byzantium had reconquered Calabria, Lucania, and Apulia in the ninth century, and these remained under loose Byzantine authority until the Normans began to wrench control away in 1041. Contact with Byzantium remained frequent even after its political control faded, and individuals such as Archbishop Alfanus of Salerno are known to have traveled to Constantinople.[25] There were also many Jews in the area; Salerno's community of six hundred Jews (as reported by Benjamin of Tudela) was the largest in southern Italy. Although there were no resident Muslim communities on the southern Italian mainland during the eleventh and twelfth centuries, commercial interchange with Sicilian, North African, and other Muslim merchants throughout the period would have kept southern Italians aware of Muslim culture.

All of these communities, of course, had their respective notions of how the genders should function and what rights and responsibilities they had. Most of the Normans who came were male, and they quickly intermarried with local Lombard women.[26] These women would have continued to live according to traditional Lombard law, which had been codified as early as the seventh century. Lombard women spent their whole lives under the guardianship (*mundium*) of a male: their father was their guardian until they married, then their husband, and then (if widowed) their adult sons, brothers, or other male relatives. Women could not alienate property without the permission of their guardian.[27] Also, unlike Roman law (under which some women of nearby territories and even a few Salernitan women lived), Lombard law did not allow daughters to automatically inherit even a portion of their father's property, as did sons.[28] Women often received some kind of dowry and trousseau from their natal family and were normally granted a quarter of their husband's landed possessions at the time of marriage (the "morning gift"). Nevertheless, even though wives technically retained their right over alienating this property (always, of course, with the permission of their guardian), charter evidence suggests that they more often merely consented to their husband's actions than initiated such transactions themselves.[29] Lombard women seem to have been less likely than other women in southern Italy to acquire literacy,[30] and at the moment there is little evidence to suggest Salernitan women's engagement in trades or other commercial activity. There were important class differences among Salernitan women, to be sure. Salernitan society has been characterized as having "an acute consciousness of nobility or aspirations to noble status,"[31] a sensitivity that manifests itself in *Women's Cosmetics* as well as in the medical writings of other Salernitan practitioners.[32] Irrespective of class, though, it seems that for most Lombard women of Salerno, if they did not opt for religious seclusion, their lives were expected to consist of marriage and maternity (and perhaps widowhood), always dependent on the support of male relatives or guardians.[33] To what extent life differed for the several hundred Jewish women in Salerno has not, to my knowledge, yet been studied.

There may have always been some level of awareness among Christian women in southern Italy of the differing cultural practices of Muslim women; a Muslim slave woman is listed as part of a Christian woman's dowry in Bari in 1065,[34] and it is likely that there were others.[35] It was probably only after the Norman conquest of Sicily in 1092 and the transference of the Norman capital to Palermo in 1130, however, that interaction with Muslim women became common. The Spanish Muslim historian Ibn Jubayr, who described his travels through the Mediterranean in 1184-85, noted with some surprise how eagerly Christian women in Palermo adopted the customs of local Muslim women: "The Christian women of this city follow the fashion of Muslim women, are fluent in speech, wrap their cloaks about them, and are veiled. They go forth on this Feast Day [Christmas] dressed in robes of gold-embroidered silk, wrapped in elegant cloaks, concealed by coloured veils, and shod with gilt slippers. Thus they parade to their churches, or (rather) their dens, . . . bearing all the adornments of Muslim including jewellery, henna on the fingers, and perfumes."[36]

Women's Cosmetics provides confirmation of precisely this sort of exchange between Muslim and Christian women when it acknowledges the "Saracen" origin of various preparations. Indeed, the attribution of a certain cosmetic preparation to Muslim *noble*women suggests Christian women's turning to this neighboring culture for any symbols that would help secure their own class aspirations.[37] It would be a mistake, of course, to characterize southern Italy as a *convivencia*, that harmonious coexistence of Christian, Jew, and Muslim that allegedly characterized medieval Spain.[38] Muslims and Jews were subject to Christians; Lombards and Greeks were subject to Normans. Yet the exchanges between these cultures were as real as their mutual antagonisms. The recognition by Christians that the Muslims had intellectual goods to offer as valuable as their spices and perfumes is at the heart of what made Salernitan medicine unique.

MEDICINE

In 1075 or early in 1076, the Salernitan writer Alfanus reminisced that in his youth "Salerno then flourished to such an extent in the art of medicine that no illness was able to settle there."[39] Alfanus's claim was hardly objective, since besides serving as archbishop of Salerno from 1058 to 1085, he himself was an important medical writer and practitioner. At the time he made his claim, many other parts of southern Italy were richly supplied with practitioners; indeed, the neighboring city of Naples was particularly notable for its large number of lay healers.[40] Yet there was more than a kernel of truth in Alfanus's boast, for already before the beginning of the eleventh century Salerno had acquired a reputation that reached beyond the Alps for the skill of its medical practitioners.[41] That reputation would only increase during the next two centuries, as the same factors that made Salerno an important political and commercial center also made it an important hub in the circulation of medical ideas and pharmaceutical products in the Mediterranean basin. These features also contributed to the support of a population wealthy enough to afford the services of these increasingly sophisticated practitioners. Salerno's growing reputation, in turn, attracted visitors from distant lands, including a significant number of English people who themselves contributed to the further dissemination of Salernitan medicine.[42]

In referring to the "School" of Salerno in the twelfth century, historians actually mean an informal community of masters and pupils who, over the course of the twelfth century, developed more or less formal methods of instruction and investigation; there is no evidence of any physical or legal entity before the thirteenth century.[43] Obviously, even before the twelfth century there must have been traditions of teaching that passed empirical lore down from master to pupil; moreover, the fact that so many of the practitioners whom we know of from the eleventh century were clerics suggests their literacy and hence their ability to make use of the rich variety of medical texts then circulating in southern Italy. But it is only in the second quarter of the eleventh century, in the figure of a physician by the name of Gariopontus, that we find the beginnings of the intellectual transformation that would not simply give shape to the distinctive teachings of Salernitan masters but would also serve as the foundation for medical instruction throughout all of western Europe for the next several centuries. Gariopontus, apparently frustrated with the disorganized and often indecipherable texts then circulating in southern Italy, decided to rework them into usable form. His resulting compilation, the *Passionarius*, would become a popular resource for physicians both near and far and initiate the first teaching glosses and commentaries that marked the revival of medical pedagogy in early twelfth-century Salerno.[44]

Alfanus, working a couple of decades later, would likewise play a critical role—or rather, two roles—in the turn toward theory at Salerno. Sometime before the mid-1050s, Alfanus translated Nemesius of Emesa's Greek *On the Nature of Man* into Latin; he also composed two medical works in his own right, at least one of which shows Byzantine influence.[45] His second, though undoubtedly more important contribution to medicine was his patronage of the immigrant Constantine the African (d. before 1098/99). Constantine came from North Africa, perhaps from Tunis, and was thus a native speaker of Arabic.[46] He may have been a drug merchant, for he clearly was well traveled and knew a good deal about medicine. Constantine arrived in Salerno around the year 1070 but soon, at the recommendation of Alfanus, moved to the Benedictine Abbey of Monte Cassino, with which Alfanus had intimate ties. Constantine became a monk and spent the rest of his life in the rich, sheltered confines of the abbey, rendering his valuable cache of Arabic medical texts into Latin. He translated at least twenty works, including the better part of Alī ibn al-ʿAbbās al-Majūsī's *Pantegni* (a large textbook of general medicine) plus smaller, more specialized works on pharmaceutics, urines, diets, fevers, sexual intercourse, leprosy, and melancholy.[47] One of his most influential texts was his translation of a handbook of medicine meant, as its title described it, as a "Provision for the Traveler and Sustenance for the Settled" (*Zād al-musāfir wa-qūt alḥāḍir*); it was, in other words, a concise summary of all the basics of medicine that the traveler or the home-bound yet physicianless individual needed to have at hand. Written by a physician from Qayrawān (in modern-day Tunisia) named Abū Jaʿfar Aḥmad b. Ibrāhīm b. Abī Khālid al-Jazzār (d. 979 C.E.), the *Viaticum* (as it was known in Latin) did indeed live up to its name, providing in seven books a basic survey of etiology and therapeutics. Its sixth book was devoted to diseases of the reproductive organs and the joints, and it was upon this that the author of the Salernitan *Conditions of Women* would draw most heavily.[48]

Constantine's vast *opera* (which fill more than four hundred large pages in a Renaissance edition) were not immediately embraced in their entirety, nor is this surprising. Beyond their length, they had introduced into Europe a rich but difficult vocabulary, a wealth of new pharmaceuticals, and a host of philosophical concepts that would take medical thinkers years to fully assimilate. Yet ultimately, the availability of this sizable corpus of new medical texts would profoundly change the orientation of Salernitan medicine.

The medical writings of twelfth-century Salerno fall into two distinct categories. Embodying the dictum that "medicine is divided into two parts: theory and practice," twelfth-century Salernitan writings can be classified as either theoretical or practical. Salernitan medicine was distinguished by its emphasis on what can properly be called a "philosophical medicine."[49] This involved the basing of medical practice, and medical instruction, on principles of natural philosophy: the nature of the most basic components of the natural world (elements, humors, spirits, etc.) and the ways in which they functioned in living organisms to produce health or disease. A curriculum of basic medical texts to be used for introductory instruction seems to have formed just after 1100. Later to be called the *Articella* (The little art), this corpus initially comprised five texts, among which were Constantine's translations of Ḥunayn ibn Isḥāq's *Isagoge* (a short handbook that introduced the student to the most basic principles of medical theory) and the Hippocratic *Aphorisms* and *Prognostics*. Two additional works recently translated from Greek—Philaretus's *On Pulses* and Theophilus's *On Urines*—were also included.[50] What is most distinctive about Salernitan medicine, however, is not the mere collection of these texts but the creation of pedagogical and investigative techniques of exegesis to study them: analytical glossing, often word by word, of the meaning and significance of terms and concepts; the identification of *quaestiones*, select topics on which there was controversy;[51] and commentary. Gariopontus's *Passionarius* may have served as the first text to be subjected to this kind of intense analysis, though at least by the second or third decade of the twelfth century extended commentaries were being composed on the *Articella* as well.[52] In addition to this textual work, there developed a tradition of anatomical demonstrations; these were performed on pigs and were meant to help explicate the details of anatomical theory already espoused by Salernitan writers rather than foster new investigation.[53]

While pedagogic and speculative work was going on, many of these same writers also compiled their therapeutic lore: specialized texts on pharmacology, diagnosis by urines, how to prepare foods or administer medicines, how to let blood or perform minor surgery, how to behave when called to attend a patient.[54] These writers did not simply put their observations and practices down on parchment; they also took advantage of new techniques of textual organization to achieve both greater practical utility for their compilations and a higher level of analytical uniformity. The reintroduction of alphabetization for pharmaceutical texts, for example, made it possible for Salernitan writers to absorb some small portion of the wealth of pharmacological lore that Constantine had rendered into Latin.[55] The Salernitan texts *Circa instans* (a catalogue of medicinal herbs, minerals, and other natural substances) and the *Antidotarium Nicholai* (a collection of recipes for compound medicines) would become two of the most widely circulated and translated medical texts in western Europe.

The organizational benefits that written discourse provided were equally evident in the Salernitan masters' *Practicae*. These were veritable medical encyclopedias, usually arranged in head-to-toe order, encompassing all manner of diseases of the whole body. Copho in the first half of the twelfth century, Johannes Platearius in the middle of the century, and Archimattheus, Bartholomeus, Petrus Musandinus, Johannes de Sancto Paulo, and Salernus in the latter half of the century all wrote their own compendia of cures. These *practicae* replicated the Arabic encyclopedias in including sections on women's diseases (usually placed after diseases of the male genitalia), yet at the same time they showed considerable originality in devising their own therapeutic programs. None of these male writers, however, broke new ground in his categorization of gynecological disease.[56] Menstrual difficulties, uterine suffocation (to be discussed below), uterine prolapse, tumors and lesions, fertility problems, and assistance with difficult birth usually merit discussion in these texts, but there is no attempt to probe more deeply or specifically into the variety of ills of the female reproductive organs. Salernitan anatomical writers did devote considerable attention to the anatomy of the uterus and the "female testicles"; that these descriptions became increasingly more detailed over time owes not to inspection of women's bodies, however, but to the assimilation of bits and pieces of anatomical and physiological lore from a variety of other written sources.[57]

The male physicians who wrote these texts, and presumably their pupils, also drew from their Greek and Arabic sources notions of not simply how they should comport themselves but also what the rewards would be if they cultivated their professional identities successfully. Nicholaus, the author of the most important text on compound medicines, promised his readers that by dispensing the medicines described in his text, "they would have an abundance of money and be glorified by a multitude of friends."[58] Some of this was sheer rhetorical posturing, but it is also clear that fundamental shifts were occurring in the social status of the more learned male medical practitioners. These men began to style themselves as "healer and physician" (*medicus et physicus*) and later simply as "physician." It is also at this point that the traditional association of clerics and physicians begins to break down in Salerno; the majority of the known practitioners of the twelfth century were lay. Yet even as certain practitioners were able to enhance their social status through their learning, there continued to exist in Salerno traditions of medical practice that partook little or not at all in the new learned discourses. It is clear that religious and even magical cures continued to coexist alongside the rationalized practices of physical medicine. There were, moreover, as we shall see in more detail later, some women in Salerno who likewise engaged in medical practice; these women apparently could not avail themselves of the same educational privileges as men and are unlikely to have been "professionalized" in the same way as their male counterparts. There was, in any case, no regulation of medical practice in this period (licensing was still a thing of the future),[59] so to that degree the "medical marketplace" was open.

The context in which the three Salernitan texts on women's medicine came into being thus was quite expansive and open to a variety of influences and practices. These texts share to varying degrees the characteristics of "mainstream" Salernitan medical writings, *Conditions of Women* with its attempts to assimilate Arabic medicine, *Treatments for Women* with its collection of traditional local practices. *Women's Cosmetics* is most interesting as an example of how traditional empirical practices could be adopted by learned physicians and deployed as another strategy in re-creating the ideal of the ancient city physician whose success lay largely in the reputation he was able to cultivate. Clearly, women were among the patients whose patronage these practitioners wanted to earn. The Lombard princess Sichelgaita seems to have had her own personal physician, Peter Borda, in the 1080s,[60] and there is ample evidence that women regularly figured in the clientele of male practitioners. Nevertheless, as was noted above, gynecology and obstetrics were areas of medical practice that saw relatively little innovation by male medical writers. Male physicians clearly diagnosed and prescribed for gynecological conditions, and they recommended a wide variety of potions and herbs for difficult birth. But it is doubtful that they ever directly touched the genitalia of their female patients. This limitation of male gynecological and obstetrical practice left room for the existence of female practitioners whose access to the female body was less restricted.

Even if we cannot answer the larger question, "Why Salerno?" we can pose the more limited but equally important question, "Why *women's* medicine?" On the surface, there seems to be nothing we yet know about Salerno that would have favored the development of what would become the three most important specialized texts on women's medicine in medieval western Europe. As we have seen, women had no higher social position here and they may well have been less literate than women in neighboring areas. Nor did the Arabic inheritance favor this development. Few specialized texts on women's medicine existed in Arabic, and none were translated by Constantine.[61] Rather, the creation of the three Salernitan texts on women's medicine seems to have been due to the coincidence of at least two factors: a preexisting Latin corpus that set a precedent for specialized texts on women's medicine and the willingness (on the part of the compilers of *Treatments for Women* and *Women's Cosmetics*) to take seriously the empirical practices and knowledge of local women. The larger intellectual currents of Salernitan medicine—the concern to systematically analyze and explain, the eagerness to incorporate new pharmaceutical products, and, most important, the desire to capture all this new knowledge in writing—provided the spark that would make Salernitan women's medicine different from anything that had gone before it.

Women's Medicine

PRE-SALERNITAN GYNECOLOGY

Had it been possible to draw up an inventory of European medical writings on women in the third quarter of the eleventh century, that list would have included at least two dozen different texts.[62] These works ranged from simple receptaries (collections of brief recipes) like the *Book on Womanly Matters* and pseudo-Theodorus Priscianus, *To His Son, Octavius*, to small theoretical pieces like the *Letter on Virginity*, which prognosticated the future health of a woman depending on the age at which she began to menstruate, to such major works as the *Gynecology* of Caelius Aurelianus and Muscio, which offered technically sophisticated surveys of the whole range of gynecological and obstetrical disorders. But such an inventory would be insufficient to assess the varying importance of these texts, for even though copies might be found in this library or that, an individual text's usefulness may have been minimal, either because its Latin (often interlarded with Greek terminology) had been corrupted over the course of several centuries of copying or because its theoretical precepts were no longer adhered to or even understood.

The gynecological literature in western Europe prior to the late eleventh century represented two ancient medical traditions. First was the Hippocratic tradition, embodied in a corpus of anonymous Greek writings composed between the fifth and fourth centuries B.C.E. and often of inconsistent theoretical perspectives. From at least the second century B.C.E., these had circulated together under the name of the physician Hippocrates of Cos. The gynecological materials of the Hippocratic Corpus constituted as much as one-fifth of that vast collection of writings.[63] The two principal texts, the *Diseases of Women 1* and *Diseases of Women 2*, were translated, at least in part, into Latin in the late antique period, perhaps in North Africa or Italy. The abbreviated translation of *Diseases of Women 1* laid out the basic physiology of women (especially as it related to pregnancy), then moved on to alterations of the womb, impediments to conception, disorders of gestation, causes of miscarriage, difficulties of birth, and subsequent problems.[64] The Hippocratic *Diseases of Women 2* was translated at least twice. The longer version, called by its modern editor *On the Diverse Afflictions of Women*, addresses questions of etiology, diagnosis, and prognosis, as well as the more routine matters of basic pathology and therapy in its ninety-one subheadings. Three other texts (*Book on the Afflictions of Women*, *Book on the Female Affliction*, and *Book on Womanly Matters*) also derive from *Diseases of Women 2*; these are fairly brief and often redundant recipe collections rather than organized medical treatises. Just as influential in disseminating Hippocratic views of the female body were the *Aphorisms*, a collection of pithy verities about the nature of the physician's craft, the symptoms of disease, prognostic signs, and so forth. The fifth (or in some versions the sixth) of the seven sections of the *Aphorisms* was devoted primarily to women and their diseases; it was on occasion accompanied by an extensive commentary. Here, a reader would find such statements as "If the menses are deficient, it is a good thing when blood flows from the nostrils," or "If in a woman who is pregnant the breast suddenly dries up, she will abort."[65] Several other texts—such as the so-called *Gynecology of Cleopatra* or *On the Diseases of Women*—may also derive in part from the Hippocratic tradition; whatever their direct textual dependence on the ancient Greek writings, they are generally consistent with the Hippocratic tradition in the way they categorize women's diseases and how they go about treating them.[66]

The second major gynecological tradition in the early medieval Latin

West was the Soranic tradition. Soranus of Ephesus, a Greek physician from Asia Minor who practiced in Rome in the late first and early second century C.E., had written a massive gynecological text that applied his theories of "the Method" to women's diseases. "The Method" was a belief that the extensive speculations of many Greek physicians about anatomy, physiology, and the causes of disease were fruitless and unnecessary. All the physician needed to know was that there were three basic states of the human body: the lax, the constricted, and a combination of the two. Upon diagnosing which of the three states was manifest in any given case, the physician's therapeutic response was to treat by opposites: to relax the constricted, constrict the lax, and do both in mixed cases, treating the more severe symptoms first. Soranus's views of female physiology and pathology in particular seem to have been novel. He argued, for example, that menstruation, sexual activity, and pregnancy were harmful to women, in contrast to the Hippocratic tradition, which asserted (as we shall see in more detail later) that these three processes were not only salubrious but actually vital to women's health.

Soranus's Greek *Gynecology* was adapted into Latin several times in the late antique period, in every instance (though to varying degrees) being stripped of its more theoretical elements. The most influential of these Latin Soranian texts was the *Gynecology* of Muscio, who had deliberately abbreviated and simplified his translation of Soranus (using, he says, "women's words") so that he would not overburden the allegedly weaker minds of midwives, to whom the work was addressed. In its first book, Muscio's *Gynecology* set out in question-and-answer form basic information on female anatomy (originally with an accompanying diagram of the uterus), physiology, and embryology and described in detail how normal birth and neonatal care should be handled. The second book covered both gynecological and obstetrical pathological conditions and included a series of fetus-in-utero figures to show the midwife the various ways in which the fetus might malpresent. For all its simplifications and heuristic aids, however, there was much in the text that proved incomprehensible to later European readers; by the eleventh century, perhaps even earlier, the *Gynecology* was abbreviated into two shorter texts, both of which eliminated much of Muscio's technical vocabulary and his concepts of Methodism.[67]

Copies of all these texts, both Hippocratic and Soranic, are found in various locations throughout early medieval Europe, as are other medical texts that contained sections on gynecological matters.[68] Most of them can be situated at monasteries, all of which, notably, were male houses. Whether laymen or women also owned the texts is unknown.[69] The extant manuscripts show, nevertheless, that the medical literati of the ninth to eleventh centuries had a pronounced interest in gynecological matters. Gynecological texts were regularly grouped together, with the result that even a single manuscript could contain a substantial collection of material on women.[70]

Since many of these early medieval texts can also be documented in libraries of eleventh- and twelfth-century Italy, it is surprising how little influence they seem to have had on the Salernitan writings on women. The author of *Conditions of Women* made use of one of the Hippocratic texts, the *Book on Womanly Matters*,[71] and may have made a passing allusion to a section of Muscio's *Gynecology*,[72] but he was either ignorant of all the other texts or actively chose to ignore them. *Treatments for Women* exhibits no direct textual parallels at all with the pre-Salernitan works, while cosmetics, the topic of both large parts of *Treatments for Women* and *Women's Cosmetics*, was almost never combined with gynecological matters in early medieval medical writings. For all the wealth of the early medieval gynecological corpus, then, the new Salernitan writings on women are largely independent of the Latin works preceding them. Still, it seems likely that the author of *Conditions of Women* took the existence of some of these texts—and, perhaps, the rhetoric of at least one of them—as a spur to writing his own specialized text about an area of medicine that some were reluctant to speak about openly.[73]

THE TROTULA TEXTS

More important than the early medieval Latin gynecological corpus for the genesis of the *Trotula* were the new theories and practices from the Arabic world or, in the case of *Treatments for Women* and *Women's Cosmetics*, traditions that had developed locally in southern Italy. The former and, to a far lesser degree, the latter, have their origin in theories and practices developed in Greco-Roman antiquity. From the disease categories they envisioned to the therapeutic practices they deployed, the uniqueness of each *Trotula* text can best be seen by analyzing the content of the texts in relationship to the theories and practices from which they derived.[74]

Conditions of Women

The earliest version of *Conditions of Women* we have seems to have been a rough draft. Entitled, in its sole complete copy, *Treatise on the Diseases of Women* (*Tractatus de egritudinibus mulierum*), this first attempt to synthesize the new Arabic medicine employs a simplified, colloquial vocabulary to render technical concepts accessible. *Conditions of Women* proper reflects a greater confidence with the Arabic material and is a thoroughly revised version; for all intents and purposes, it can be considered a new text.[75] It is devoted solely to women's gynecological and obstetrical conditions, moving from menstrual problems to uterine conditions, control of fertility, and aid for complications in childbirth. A slightly later version (*Conditions of Women 2*) was to add aids for normal birth. Although we cannot be entirely certain that it was composed at Salerno, its strong philosophical and stylistic similarities to other Salernitan writings make a southern Italian origin likely.[76]

Conditions of Women is more conscientious in articulating physiological and etiological theory than most of its early medieval predecessors,[77] largely because it had adopted the more speculative, philosophical interests of Arabic medicine. Arabic medicine, in turn, was distinct from its early medieval Latin counterpart in its adherence to the philosophical principles of the greatest—or at least the most prolific—physician of antiquity, Galen of Pergamon (ca. 130-ca. 215 C.E.).

Galen, like his predecessor Soranus, was a Greek physician who left his native Asia Minor to seek out a career of medical practice in Rome. When he died in the early third century, Galen left behind a huge body of writings (well over three hundred individual titles).[78] Only one, a detailed exposition on the anatomy of the uterus, was devoted exclusively to women's medicine, so it is at first glance surprising that what we find in Arabic medical writings and (because of its derivation from the *Viaticum*) in *Conditions of Women* is a Galenic gynecology. Galen had addressed female physiology and disease intermittently in his general writings on physiology and pathology, using, for example, the female model paradigmatically in his discussion of bloodletting or the nature of the faculties.[79] What happened between Galen's death and the twelfth century was the gradual creation, by Byzantine and especially Arabic medical writers, of a gynecology that fused general Galenic principles of medicine, plus the bits and pieces of his scattered gynecological discussions, onto the substantive symptomatology and therapeutic material of other Greek gynecological writings, particularly that of Soranus.

Galen's medical writings, though philosophically sophisticated, were not only numerous but too often tedious, long-winded, and obtuse. Greek medical writers and teachers in late antiquity focused on only a handful of Galen's more concise and cogent works, using them as a basis for teaching in such centers as the school of Alexandria in Egypt. Other writers, such as Oribasius (326–403), compiled large, synthetic works of medical theory and practice. They drew for these works on a wide array of ancient Greek writers, of whom Galen was given pride of place. With the rise of Islam in the seventh century and the fall of the former Greek territories of Asia Minor and

North Africa to the Arabs, Greek medical learning passed to the Arabic-speaking world. Here, Galen's writings (at least 129 of which were translated into Arabic) again took precedence and led to newer, even grander synthetic works.

These Arabic medical encyclopedias included sections on women's diseases, based in their substance on the work of the Methodist physician Soranus. But their content was stripped of its overlay of Methodist theory, in whose place were substituted Hippocratic and Galenic principles of the workings of the elements (hot, cold, wet, and dry), the humors (blood, phlegm, yellow or red bile, and black bile), the temperaments (the actual elemental or humoral predominance that would characterize any given individual), the faculties (physiological processes we would today describe in terms of chemical or muscular action), and so forth. Whereas Soranus had argued that the Methodist physician need only know the three states—lax, constricted, or mixed—in a Galenic system disease must be distinguished according to which of the four humors predominates in the body (any imbalance in their proper proportion being itself a sign of disease). This fusion of Soranus's nosographies and therapies with Galenic theory resulted in the creation of a Galenic gynecology, which bore the distinctive stamp of its Arab and Muslim creators, not only for the increased philosophical rigidity of the humoral system (which Galen had never been so formal about), but also for the new, unique Arabic contributions to therapy and especially to *materia medica* (pharmaceutical ingredients). Thus, for example, when the North African writer Ibn al-Jazzār described the various possible causes of menstrual retention, he distinguished between the faculty, the organs, and the substance (of the menses themselves) as the causative agents, dialectically breaking down each of these three categories into their various subcategories.[80]

In Galenic gynecology, as in Hippocratic gynecology before it, the basic physiological process unique to the female body was menstruation. Whereas in modern Western medical thought menstruation is seen as a mere by-product of the female reproductive cycle, a monthly shedding of the lining of the uterus when no fertilized ovum is implanted in the uterine wall, in Hippocratic and Galenic gynecology menstruation was a necessary purgation, needed to keep the whole female organism healthy. The Hippocratic writers had been inconsistent on whether women were hotter or colder than men by nature. In Galenic gynecology, in contrast (which in this respect built on the natural philosophical principles of Aristotle), women were without question constitutionally colder than men.[81] The effect of this defect of heat—and a defect it was, for heat was the very principle of life, its absence or deficiency a sign of a less perfect life form—was that women were unable to concoct (literally, "cook") their nutrients as thoroughly as men. Men, moreover, were also able to exude those residues of digestion that did remain through sweat or the growth of facial and other bodily hair. Because (it was assumed) women exerted themselves less in physical labor even while they produced, because of their insufficient heat, a greater proportion of waste matter, they had need of an additional method of purgation. For if women did not rid their bodies of these excess materials, they would continue to accumulate and sooner or later lead to a humoral imbalance—in other words, to disease. This purgation was menstruation.[82]

When it came in normal amounts, at the normal times, the woman was likely to be healthy. When, too, she did not menstruate because of pregnancy or lactation, she was still healthy, for the excess matter—now no longer deemed "waste"—either went to nourish the child in utero or was converted into milk. When, however, in a woman who was neither pregnant nor nursing menstruation was abnormal, when it was excessive or, on the other hand, too scanty, or worse, when it stopped altogether, disease was the inevitable result. Nature, in her wisdom, might open up a secondary egress for this waste material; hence *Conditions of Women*'s suggestion that blood emitted via hemorrhoids, nosebleeds, or sputum could be seen as a menstrual substitute (§7). In modern western medicine, absence of menstruation in a woman of child-bearing age might be attributable to a variety of causes (e.g., low body fat ratio, hormonal imbalance, or problems of the pituitary gland), but in most instances amenorrhea would be considered a problem limited to the reproductive system. It might not even be deemed to merit therapeutic intervention, unless the woman desired to get pregnant. In Hippocratic and Galenic thought, absence of menstruation—or rather, *retention* of the menses, for the waste material was almost always thought to be collecting whether it issued from the body or not—was cause for grave concern, for it meant that one of the major purgative systems of the female body was inoperative. The necessary therapeutic response was simple: induce menstruation. It is for this reason that the largest percentage of prescriptions for women's diseases in most early medieval medical texts (which reflected the Hippocratic tradition only) were aids for provoking the menses.[83]

Conditions of Women reflects this same urgent concern with maintaining regular menstruation. Between the ages of fourteen ("or a little earlier or a little later, depending on how much heat abounds in her")[84] and thirty-five to sixty (upped to sixty-five in the standardized ensemble), a woman should be menstruating regularly if she is to remain healthy.[85] In fact, any irregularity of menstruation—either too little or too much—is a serious threat to overall health, for it can lead to loss of appetite, vomiting, cravings for unnatural foods, pain in the back, head, or eyes, acute fever, heart palpitations, dropsy, and painful urination. In overall length, the four sections on menstruation (¶¶3–7 on the general physiology and pathology of menstruation, ¶¶8–18 on menstrual retention, ¶¶19–28 on paucity of the menses, and ¶¶29–44 on excess menstruation) constitute more than one-third of the text of the original *Conditions of Women*.

Throughout these long sections on menstruation, the author is adhering closely to his sources: the *Viaticum* for overall theory and basic therapeutics and the *Book on Womanly Matters* for supplemental recipes.[86] There are, however, some interesting novelties. In ¶3, the author tells us that the menses are commonly called "the flowers" because just as trees without their flowers will not bear fruit, so, too, women without their "flowers" will be deprived of offspring. This reference to "women's flowers" has no precedent in the *Viaticum* (the source for the rest of this general discussion on the nature of the menses) nor in any earlier Latin gynecological texts, which refer to the menses solely as *menstrua* (literally, "the monthlies").[87] Yet *Conditions of Women* undoubtedly reflects what people in fact did say: "the flowers" was a common vernacular term to designate the menses in most of the medieval western European languages and, indeed, still is in many traditional societies throughout the world. The term "flower" (*flos*) had been used systematically throughout the *Treatise on the Diseases of Women* (the "rough draft" of *Conditions of Women*, which had employed frequent colloquialisms), and at least fourteen of the twenty-two different vernacular translations of the *Trotula* (including Dutch, English, French, German, Hebrew, and Italian) employ the equivalent of "flowers" when translating the Latin *menses*.[88] The contemporary German nun Hildegard of Bingen (1098–1179), despite the fact that she links menstruation to Eve's sin in Paradise, likewise employs the tree/flower metaphor: "The stream of the menstrual period in woman is her generative greenness and floridity, which sprouts forth offspring; for just as a tree flowers in its floridity and sends forth branches and produces fruit, so the female extrudes flowers from the viridity of the streams of menstrual blood and produces branches in the fruit of her womb. But just as a tree which lacks viridity is said to be unfruitful, so, too, the woman who does not have the viridity of her flowering at the proper age is called infertile."[89] These Western usages are, moreover, strikingly similar to a description of menstruation from the Beng ethnic group in Ivory Coast: "Menstrual blood is special because it carries in it a living being. It works like a tree. Before bearing fruit, a tree must first bear flowers. Menstrual blood is like the flower: it must emerge before the fruit—the baby—can be born."[90]

The positive view of menstruation found in *Conditions of Women* and Hildegard will stand in stark contrast to some later medieval European scientific attitudes, which, drawing on ancient traditions collected by the Roman encyclopedist Pliny, abbreviated by the second-century Roman writer Solinus, and transmitted to the Middle Ages by Isidore of Seville (d. 636) and others, represent menstruation as thoroughly poisonous or noxious.[91] These latter views would contribute substantially to the growing body of misogynistic views from the thirteenth century on.[92] It is notable, therefore, how largely immune the *Trotula* tradition remained to these influences.[93]

After abnormal menstruation, the next major gynecological condition in the Galenic system—a slightly modified inheritance from Hippocratic gynecology—was the disease entity known as uterine suffocation (*suffocatio matricis*). In the Hippocratic writings themselves, although there is discussion of suffocation caused by the womb, the actual term "uterine suffocation" (in Greek, *hysterike pnix*) is never used. It was only out of loose elements of Hippocratic disease concepts (which were always very vaguely defined and identified) that the etiological entity of uterine suffocation was created, probably sometime before the second century B.C.E.[94]

The most striking element of Hippocratic gynecology is the idea that the uterus is capable of movement throughout the body. Such movement was thought to be caused by retention of the menses, excessive fatigue, lack of food, lack of (hetero)sexual activity, and dryness or lightness of the womb (particularly in older women). When these conditions obtain, the womb "hits the liver and they go together and strike against the abdomen—for the womb rushes and goes upward towards the moisture . . . and the liver is, after all, moist. When the womb hits the liver, it produces sudden suffocation as it occupies the breathing passage around the belly." The arid womb might also move to the head, heart, ribs, loins, or bowels—in each case causing a unique cluster of symptoms. For example, when the womb strikes the liver or abdomen, "the woman turns up the whites of her eyes and becomes chilled; some women are livid. She grinds her teeth and saliva flows out of her mouth. These women resemble those who suffer from Herakles' disease [epilepsy]. If the womb lingers near the liver and the abdomen, the woman dies of the suffocation."[95]

Although it was possible for a variety of women to be afflicted with this violent disease (including pregnant women), widows and virgins were the most vulnerable, precisely because they had no recourse to the "moistening" properties of male semen deposited in their wombs. Multiple means of treatment were employed, including the recommendation that, when the womb moves to the hypochondria (the upper abdomen or perhaps the diaphragm), young widows or virgins be urged to marry (and preferably become pregnant).[96] But one procedure that stands out is odoriferous therapy. This was premised, apparently, on the belief that the womb was capable of sensing odors. Fetid odors (such as pitch, burnt hair, or castoreum) were applied to the nostrils to repel the womb from the higher places to which it had strayed, while sweet-smelling substances were applied to the genitalia to coax the uterus back into its proper position.

Not all the symptoms were listed every time uterine movement was mentioned by the Hippocratic writers, nor did all cases of *pnix* involve uterine movement.[97] *Hysterike pnix* seems to have only really coalesced as a fixed disease—with a more or less stable core of symptoms and susceptible groups—somewhat later.[98] For the second-century C.E. writer Soranus, the disease involved "obstructed respiration together with aphonia [inability to speak] and a seizure of the senses caused by some condition of the uterus. . . . When an attack occurs, sufferers from the disease collapse, show aphonia, labored breathing, a seizure of the senses, clenching of the teeth, stridor, convulsive contraction of the extremities (but sometimes only weakness), upper abdominal distention, retraction of the uterus, swelling of the thorax, bulging of the network of vessels of the face. The whole body is cool, covered with perspiration, the pulse stops or is very small."[99]

Soranus was adamant, however, that the womb did *not* wander. Critical to his views, and to all contemporary criticisms of the "wandering womb" (including Galen's, as we shall see in a moment) were the anatomical discoveries made at Alexandria in the third century B.C.E.—most important, those of Herophilus of Chalcedon.[100] Although Soranus in general dismissed anatomy as irrelevant, here he employed the Alexandrian anatomical findings to assert that the womb was firmly held in place by membranes that connected it to the other pelvic organs. The womb "does not issue forth like a wild animal from the lair" but is instead "drawn together because of the stricture caused by the inflammation" of these uterine ligaments.[101] Soranus also broke with Hippocratic tradition in rejecting the idea that women needed regular sexual activity to remain healthy (though illogically, given his claims that sexual abstinence was in fact salubrious, he included "long widowhood" as one of the predisposing conditions for uterine suffocation). Soranus also adamantly rejected the Hippocratic odoriferous therapy, or at least the part of it that employed foul-smelling substances.[102] This condition, which was a classic "constricted" condition, was to be treated by relaxing drugs and regimens. Yet for all his modifications, Soranus never questioned the disease category itself. On the contrary, his thorough engagement with it was to help render it canonical in almost all later gynecological texts up through the Renaissance.

Galen, active only a generation after Soranus, was more accommodating of traditional Hippocratic perspectives. Himself a highly experienced anatomist,[103] Galen no more than Soranus could accept the possibility that the womb actually wandered to various parts of the body since the diaphragm, if nothing else, absolutely prohibited movement to the thorax. He did not, however, question the by now traditional litany of symptoms, let alone the existence of the disease category. He, like Soranus, thought the womb could *appear* to be drawn up slightly because of inflammation of the ligaments. Yet to explain *apnoia hysterike* (difficulty of breathing caused by the uterus), Galen offered something of a compromise that would explain how the uterus, without moving to the upper parts, could still affect them. He posited a sympathetic poisonous reaction caused by either the menses or the woman's own semen being retained in her uterus. (He had kept "widows and women whose menstrual discharge is suppressed" as the primary victims.) Once retained, one or both of these substances gradually corrupted and turned into a noxious substance that could affect other, distant parts of the body in the same way the bite of a spider or a rabid dog could have wide-ranging effects. Notable here is Galen's shift in ideas about how semen and sexuality played into this disease: for Galen, it was not her lack of semen provided by a man that made the widow susceptible, but the buildup of her *own* seed. Despite these disagreements, Galen maintained elements of the traditional odoriferous therapy, though he complemented this with bloodletting, massage, and a host of other treatments.

Both Soranus and Galen represented the very highest theoretical traditions of Greek medicine, catering as they did to the elite, Hellenized urban classes of Rome. Their views never eradicated what were apparently deeply rooted popular beliefs that the womb did indeed wander. Early medieval Latin texts are strewn with references to uterine movement. Even Muscio, in the fifth or sixth century when he was rendering Soranus into Latin, slipped in the more than suggestive phrase "when the womb moves upwards toward the chest" when referring to uterine suffocation; as he repeated this several times, it seems that he, too, thought the womb capable of more than "distension caused by the ligaments."[104] The most graphic example of the persistence of the notion of the "wandering womb" is found in a variety of exorcisms. One is written into a blank space of a late ninth-century medical volume by a tenth-century hand. Having invoked the aid of the Holy Trinity, the nine orders of the angels, the patriarchs, prophets, apostles, martyrs, confessors, virgins, and "all the saints of God," the priest is to command the womb to cease tormenting the afflicted woman:

I conjure you, womb, by our lord Jesus Christ, who walked on the water with dry feet, who cured the infirm, shunned the demons, resuscitated the dead, by whose blood we are redeemed, by whose wounds we are cured, by whose bruise[s] we are healed, by him I conjure you not to harm this maidservant of God, [her name is then to be filled in], nor to hold on to her head, neck, throat, chest, ears, teeth, eyes, nostrils, shoulders, arms, hands, heart, stomach, liver, spleen, kidneys, back, sides, joints, navel, viscera, bladder, thighs, shins, ankles, feet, or toes, but to quietly remain in the place which God delegated to you, so that this handmaiden of God, [her name], might be cured.[105]

The introduction of Galenic medicine into the West seems to have modified these views only slightly. The chief vehicle for Galen's views in the twelfth century was, of course, Ibn al-Jazzār's *Viaticum*. In discussing uterine suffocation in book 6, Ibn al-Jazzār had echoed Galen in asserting that "the sperm increases, corrupts, and becomes like a poison." He added, however, the novel idea that rather than the sympathetic reaction between the womb and the upper respiratory organs that Galen had postulated, there was an actual physical transmission. Ibn al-Jazzār postulated that the putrefying menses and/or semen in the uterus produced "a cold vapor" that rose to the diaphragm. "And because the diaphragm is connected with the throat and with the places [of origin] of the voice suffocation occurs." He said nothing, however, to suggest that the womb itself wandered.[106]

Conditions of Women adheres essentially to Ibn al-Jazzār's views. Yet there is an underlying tension. In the main chapter on uterine suffocation (¶¶45–48), the author closely follows the *Viaticum* in laying out the standard litany of symptoms, recounting Galen's cure (from *On the Affected Parts*), and positing the same causation: corrupted semen (or menses) is turned into a "venomous nature," and it is this "cold fumosity" that ascends up to "the parts which are commonly called the *corneliei*, which because they are close to the lungs and the heart and the other organs of the voice, produce an impediment of speaking."[107] In a later chapter, however, we see the first signs of a conflict with traditional Latin views. This chapter (¶60) is drawn from the alternate source, the Hippocratic *Book on Womanly Matters*. In the "rough draft" of *Conditions of Women*, the *Treatise on the Diseases of Women*, it was stated very clearly that movement of the womb to the upper body was possible: "Sometimes the womb [moves] from its place, so that it ascends up to the horns of the lungs, that is, the *pennas* [feathers], and [sometimes] it descends so that it goes out of [the body] and then it produces pain in the left side. And it ascends to the stomach and swells up so much that nothing can be swallowed. And the belly is chilled and suffers cramping, and it rumbles."[108]

Conditions of Women inserts a negative, thereby rendering the passage somewhat differently: "Sometimes, however, the whole womb moves from its seat but neither is it lifted upward towards the respiratory organs, nor does it descend outside through the orifice [of the vagina]. The sign of this is that she feels pain in the left side, and she has distention of the limbs, difficulty swallowing, cramping, and rumbling of the belly."[109]

Far from denying that the womb rises to the respiratory organs, however, the author of *Conditions of Women* in fact perpetuates the belief that such movement is possible. What this change in phrasing from the first draft does is distinguish three nosological conditions: movement up to the respiratory organs (discussed in ¶¶45–50), prolapse downward, sometimes with complete extrusion (¶¶51–59), and this third intermediate condition where it goes neither up nor all the way down.

Conditions of Women's allusions suggest that the "wandering womb" was indeed part of the general belief structure in southern Italy at this time. The tension between, on the one hand, the Galenic/Arabic view of uterine suffocation as caused by either a sympathetic link between uterus and respiratory organs or the actual physical transmission of a noxious vapor and, on the other hand, the traditional Hippocratic idea of the "wandering womb" finds a graphic expression in the work of Johannes Platearius, another Salernitan writer working at perhaps the same time that *Conditions of Women* was composed. Johannes Platearius had interpreted Ibn al-Jazzār's reference to "fumes" as meaning that the fumes filled the uterus and caused *it* to move upward to the respiratory organs.[110] Although this view was not held by other Salernitan authors nor, indeed, by most medieval medical writers, as late as 1316 the Italian anatomist Mundino de' Luzzi (who produced one of the first textbooks in the Middle Ages based in part on human dissections) was still having to counter views that the womb actually wandered. Interestingly, he asserts that it is *women* who say they "have their womb in their stomach" or in their throat or at their heart.[111]

As the foregoing discussion has made clear, the disease of uterine suffocation was intimately associated with notions about sexuality. It was a general medical assumption throughout most of the medieval period that women needed regular sexual activity in order to remain healthy.[112] Although this idea had been rejected by Soranus (who thought sexual activity and pregnancy debilitating and virginity a preferable way of life), the several Latin renditions of his *Gynecology* seem to have had little effect in altering a view that could be traced back to the Hippocratics. Indeed, Soranus's distinctive views on sexuality were suppressed when Muscio's *Gynecology* was twice readapted to new uses in or before the eleventh century.[113] Ibn al-Jazzār kept the tight association between sexual abstinence and uterine suffocation, as did *Conditions of Women*. Johannes Platearius went farther than *Conditions of Women* in reincorporating the traditional Hippocratic recommendation of sex and marriage as suitable, even preferable cures: "If [the disease] occurs because of corrupt semen, let her know her husband. If she is a virgin or widow, counsel her to marry . . . ; if she maintains a vow of chastity or continence, let this remedy be prepared."[114] Platearius may be referring to vowesses (women, usually widows, who took an oath of chastity but did not join a formal monastic community) rather than nuns specifically. This is, nevertheless, one of the first acknowledgments by a medical writer of a category of Christian women who were chaste not by force of circumstance but by individual choice.[115] Notably, Platearius is reaffirming the traditional Hippocratic/Galenic view that sexual activity is a sine qua non for all women's health; while there are pharmaceutical remedies that can be employed if sex is not an option, continence is clearly seen as a perilous state.[116]

A fascinatingly enigmatic series of illustrations made in the late thirteenth or early fourteenth century paints what seems to be a picture of this disease (figs. 3–4). Although not produced at the same time as the *Trotula* text found within this manuscript, these images do offer vivid evidence of how medical theory and practice may have been played out.[117] Presumably, the artist had intended to write some descriptive text into the scrolls that the physician is holding in each frame; without this gloss, we can only infer the meaning of the images or, indeed, the order in which the frames are to be "read." If the images had originally been intended to be on a single leaf, then the two top images would have preceded the two bottom ones. First, on the top of the recto side of folio 33, we see the woman falling in a seizure; the dog with her signifies that she is of noble status, though it perhaps also indicates that she has only her pet to keep her company. In the upper half of the verso page, we see her as if dead, already laid out on a bier while her servants, apparently, mourn her death. The physician, however (as had Galen), suspects she is still alive. The bowl on her chest points to an amplification that Platearius made on the *Viaticum*'s text when he suggested that the woman's condition could be determined by either a flock of wool placed to the nose or a glass bowl placed on the chest. Just as the wool would move slightly with her breath, so the water in the bowl would, by its slight vibrations, show that she was still alive.[118]

Moving back to the bottom of the first page, we find the basic elements

Figures 3 and 4: Illustrations of a case of uterine suffocation from a late thirteenth-century English manuscript. Reproduced with permission from Oxford, Bodleian Library, MS Ashmole 399, f. 33r-v.

of the therapy: foul-smelling substances applied to the nose and fumigations of sweet-smelling substances to the genitals. The final frame depicts the kinds of women most susceptible to uterine suffocation: widows (note the prayer-book falling from the hand of the veiled woman) and virgins who have just reached the age of marriage. Here we also get an additional mode of treat-ment: the female attendant is holding a bone to the nose of the older woman. Although burnt bones were mentioned in neither *Conditions of Women* nor Platearius, various kinds of burnt substances–because of their stench–were usually recommended for application to the nose.[119]

As this example shows, the therapy employed for uterine suffocation (as for menstrual irregularities, too) differed little from that advocated in antiq-uity. Odoriferous therapy was still the basis of treatment for uterine suffoca-tion, and the associative links it had with the notion of uterine movement seem to have been strong. As we saw earlier, Soranus had vehemently reject-ed odoriferous therapy as nonsensical and harmful, and his views, even if somewhat attenuated, were carried into Latin in the late antique Latin trans-lations. Yet use of odoriferous therapy persisted in almost all other gyneco-logical texts in the early Middle Ages, so much so that it is not really surprising to find that the compiler who abbreviated Muscio's *Gynaecia* in the eleventh century or so put odoriferous therapy back into the text.[120] This same odoriferous therapy was used in reverse for uterine prolapse (¶53), and for the same reasons: to induce the womb to move upward toward the sweet smells applied to the nose and away from the foul smells applied to the geni-tals. The inclusion of odoriferous therapy for prolapse is particularly notable, since it was not found in the *Viaticum*. Indeed, the author of *Conditions of Women* thought it so important that, uncharacteristically, he situated it *before* the therapies offered by Ibn al-Jazzār.[121]

Of course, other elements of ancient therapeutics persisted in *Conditions of Women* as well. Theories on the utility of phlebotomy had developed around the third century B.C.E. and Galen, in the second century C.E., was still intensely engaged in these debates.[122] In the Middle Ages, there were two basic principles that determined where and in what amounts the phle-botomist should bleed. The notion of "revulsion" dictated that blood was to be drawn off from a vein quite distant from the affected part. The objective was to force the flow of blood in a direction in which it was not accustomed to flowing. "Derivation," in contrast, demanded that blood be drawn from the same general part of the body in order to route its flow back into its nor-mal direction.[123] These technical terms are never used in *Conditions of Women*, though the theory of derivation clearly underlies the recommendation of phlebotomy for menstrual retention (¶8), constipation (¶10), and uterine tumors (¶66). In all three cases, blood is drawn from the saphenous vein under the arch of the foot in order to reorient the body's bloodflow down toward the uterus, which is where it normally should flow. The employment of cupping glasses—used for excessive menstruation (¶35) and suffocation (¶48)—has a similar rationale as that of phlebotomy. In both cases, the suction created on the surface of the skin by the cupping glass pulls blood toward that area. In the first instance, however, cupping glasses are applied near the breasts in order to encourage bloodflow *away* from the uterus, since it is clearly in excessive abundance there. In the second case, cupping glasses are applied to the groin to encourage menstrual flow downward. Finally, scarification (the superficial incision of the skin) works on the same principle, though, like cupping glasses, it produces a less intensive effect than phlebotomy. It is mentioned only once in *Conditions of Women*, as an alternate therapy for menstrual retention (¶27).[124]

Another therapeutic procedure deriving from ancient practices was the application of fumigations to the genitalia. These were not simply used to direct odors to the vagina and womb, but were also a means of introducing medications for menstrual retention (¶26), a retained afterbirth (¶108), and uterine pain (¶112). The variety of fumigation pots and stools depicted in a fifteenth-century Dutch translation of the *Trotula* (fig. 5) gives us some indication of the equipment that women throughout western Europe may have used.[125] As for pessaries—tamponlike wads of cotton or some other material into which medications were wrapped or poured—these, too, derive from ancient therapeutic practices.[126] Indeed, we see in late antique texts (particularly the *Pessaria* of Muscio and pseudo-Cleopatra) the development of a whole armory of standardized types of pessaries. Again, the late medieval Dutch manuscripts are the only ones to offer us depictions of pessaries (fig. 6), but there can be no doubt that these were a mainstay of all medieval gynecological therapy. The late twelfth- or early thirteenth-century writer Roger de Baron gives a particularly well-articulated rationale for the use of pessaries: "Just as . . . clisters [enemas], suppositories and syringes ought to be used for conditions of the bowels, so ought pessaries be used for conditions of the womb. Nor should this be surprising. For to the degree that the former organs are remote from the organs of nutrition and to the degree that substances coming to the bowels are weakened in strength in proportion to their remoteness, not only by the length of the distance [they have to travel] but also by the narrowness of the passages, to that degree they have no efficacy."[127] Pessaries, in other words, offered a better mechanism for administering medicines to the uterus than orally consumed substances.

We have seen in this extended analysis of menstrual disorders and uterine movement all the main pathological and therapeutic characteristics of *Conditions of Women*. These same principles of physiology, pathology, and

anms finenards eppenfaet gaftin faet omander en alle hoete
onden en die ghefoden in wiin en dat ghefonken Nuut alle
hoete dinghen doen romt de vloet en alle ronde dinghen uer
gaethenfe Oft nemt bloet hoe qualeng wnst dien ghefoodt
en ghedronken met wiine int dbat oft ghefode en ghebode
onder den nauel oft ghefoden in wiin oor met
eenen cleynen halfe ghemaect aldus En ronde
men det met alle de wiuuf oude gherichten hoe
wone en dronken die fij hebben Een men fal de
hals vanden pottekens fteken In die poorte en ont
faen inden lichame Oft men maecht froden in eenen
widen pot den wolken es ghemaect aldus
En hier ouer falmen fitten al naect en late
die cleden der ouer hanghen tot der erden ende
ftappen alfe den wafem dat hm met wut en
ifa en op eenen ftoel met een gate falmen fitten Oft
fij fal den wafem ontfaen met eenen infromente dat fal
werden belonpelt met linen doeken aen
die pipe en dinftrament ghemaect aldus
En dit ghedaen In die matrice en die doen uer
warmen fij een gudne en dan al waerm gheleit
op den lichame dat doet comen die colore
Oft maect een vierant fackel
kijn en de fubftancie voorfz daer?
ghedaen al waerm ghefoden en die
ghelegt op den lichame Item noch hen ander mnt die
woortel vander medon wel ghefooct en ghebonde op die
wuflicheit doet come menftrua En es dan die moeder te
gro verfluet det die aderen met en moghen hebben hair
gane oft fijn fij te gro ueert faer nemt een dume cleedekn
en maect daer af een lang fackelkijn alfe lane als j.
comighen en dat ghewolt inj ghefoden locke

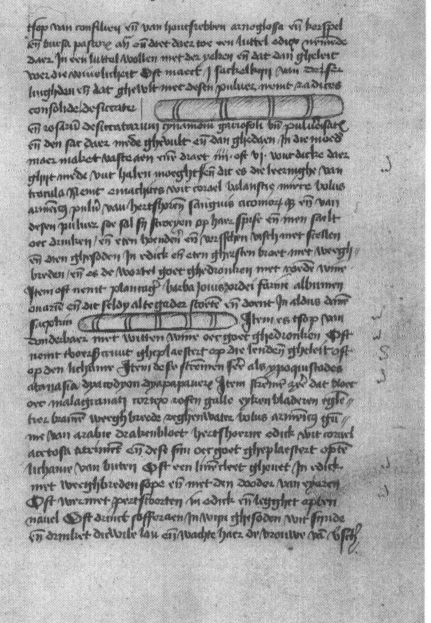

Figures 5 and 6: Depictions of fumigation pots and pessaries from a fifteenth-century Dutch translation of the *Trotula*. Reproduced with permission from Copenhagen, Det Kongelige Bibliotek, MS GKS 1657, ff. 29r and 32r.

appropriate therapeutic intervention guide the rest of the text. Aside from a brief discussion of excessive heat in the womb (¶64), the next group of chapters—swellings or tumors (apostemes) from various humoral causes (¶¶65–69), wounds of the womb and vagina (¶¶70–71), and itching of the vagina (¶¶72–73)—derive their substance from the *Viaticum*. Next comes the topic of infertility (¶74).[128] Either the man or the woman may be "at fault": the woman may be too thin or too fat, or her womb may be so slippery that the man's seed cannot be retained. The man's seed, in turn, may itself be too thin and liquidy, or his testicles may be so cold that he cannot generate seed. A test is then offered to determine whether the cause lies with the man or the woman (¶75). Interestingly, infertility in either partner is considered incurable; it is only if neither partner is found to be sterile that medical aids are deemed to be in order. Five recipes are then provided, sometimes for the woman alone, sometimes for the man and woman together.[129] One is explicitly said to be for the generation of males, and the three that follow may be as well. Neither here nor in the vast majority of medieval medical texts are there any explicit instructions on how to conceive females.[130]

On the topic of contraceptives, our author quotes the Benedictine monk Constantine the African to the effect that certain women ought not be sexually active because their anatomical limitations will make childbearing fatal (¶83).[131] But, our author adds, not all such women are able to be continent—a direct nod to the belief that women require sexual activity in order to remain healthy. Hence, these women need to be provided with contraceptives. Those that this author advocates, interestingly, all rely on amulets or sympathetic magic (¶¶84–87), which derive from the author's alternate source, the *Book on Womanly Matters*. It is notable that there is no reference here to any of the many herbs of presumed contraceptive or abortifacient properties described in a variety of readily available pharmacological texts.[132]

Next come several chapters on pregnancy and childbirth. From the *Viaticum* the author draws discussions of the causes of miscarriage (¶88), care of the pregnant woman (¶88a; ¶79 in the present edition), common disorders of pregnancy (¶¶88b and 88c; in the present edition, ¶¶80 and 81, respectively), followed by a brief statement on the process of birth itself (¶89), then aids for difficult birth (¶¶90–91). Then, perhaps referring to Muscio's *Gynecology*, the author adds the specific instruction that "the women who assist her ought not look her in the face, for many women are ashamed to be looked upon during birth" (¶92).[133] Detailed instructions for repositioning the malpresented fetus then follow (¶93). These, in turn, are followed by twelve remedies for extracting the fetus that has died in utero (¶¶94–103). Recipes for removing the afterbirth (¶¶104-5 and 107-11) and treating postpartum pain (¶112) follow, while a test to determine the sex of the fetus closes the text (¶¶ 113–14). Some of these obstetrical remedies derive from the *Viaticum*, though many of the rest reflect traditional practices, some of them magical, some strictly herbal. Notably, while an ancient pagan charm is included here (¶98; cf. fig. 7), there is no Christian element whatsoever.[134]

Figure 7: A SATOR AREPO charm from a fifteenth-century medical amulet (bottom row, left of center). The text in the circle surrounding the square reads: "Show this figure to a woman giving birth and she will be delivered" (*Hanc figuram mostra mulierem in partu et peperit*). Reproduced from Alphonse Aymar, "Contributions à l'étude du Folklore de la Haute-Auvergne: Le Sachet Accoucheur et ses mystères," *Annales du Midi* 38 (1926), 273-347, plate IV.

In the second version of *Conditions of Women* (*Conditions of Women 2*), a different editor added preventive measures for difficult birth caused by constriction (¶¶115–22). These consisted of both prenatal procedures and instructions for attendance at the birth itself. Sneezing is to be induced; potions are to be prepared; a magnet is to be held in the hand; coral is to be suspended from the neck; the white substance found in the dung of a hawk is to be drunk, as are the washings from the nest and a stone found in the belly of a swallow. Here, too, we find the explicit statement that "the womb follows sweet smells and flees foul ones." In order to induce the womb to move down and expel the fetus, fetid odors are applied to the nose, while aromatic substances should be applied to the vagina. And so the treatise ends.

The *Book on the Conditions of Women* is very much the offspring of Greco-Roman and Arabic medicine. Although by no means slavish in its adherence to the *Viaticum* or its other sources, the points on which it diverges from its textual models are for the most part themselves reflections of the survival of certain ancient medical notions (the concept of uterine movement being the most prominent) through a probable combination of oral and literate transmission. The only distinctive indication that *Conditions of Women* is the product of a Christian culture is the prologue (¶¶1–2). A recasting of the creation story of Genesis (2:20–25 and 3:16) into Galenic physiological terms, the prologue explains how woman's subjugation to man allows reproduction to take place, which in turn is the chief cause of illness in the female body. The author recasts Galen's original view of man as the perfect standard (from which women then deviate) into a case of equal divergence of both men and women from a temperate mean. Lest the man tend too strongly toward his natural state of hotness and dryness, God desired that the male's excess be restrained by the opposite qualities of the female, coldness and wetness. Heterosexual intercourse is, in effect, a tempering of extremes. The author nevertheless leaves no doubt that this mutual "tempering" is not really a balancing out of *equal* opposites: the man is "the more worthy person"; heat and dryness are "the stronger qualities." Moreover, the author likens the process of insemination to that of sowing seed in a field—a metaphor that, on the one hand, contradicts the text's own assumption that women, too, have seed, yet on the other firmly reifies the original Genesis dictum that the female is indeed subject to the male.

It is because women are in fact weaker than men that they suffer so greatly in childbirth and that they are more frequently afflicted by illness, "especially around the organs assigned to the work of Nature." The fragility of their condition, moreover, causes them to be ashamed, which in turn prevents them from revealing their illnesses to a (male) physician. It was out of pity for their plight–and, it seems, because of the influence of one woman in particular–that the author, laboring "with no small effort," was induced to "gather the more worthy things from the books of Hippocrates, Galen and Constantine, so that I might be able to explain both the causes of [women's] diseases and their cures."[135] The author of *Conditions of Women* has, of course, used neither "Hippocrates" nor Galen directly, yet his claim is not totally untrue. *Conditions of Women*, probably one of the first attempts to synthesize the Galenic framework of the new Arabic medicine with older Hippocratic traditions, offers, in effect, what will become the foundation for later medieval Latin views of female physiology and pathology.

Treatments for Women

That *Treatments for Women* could have come out of the same general social milieu as *Conditions of Women* is an indication of how diverse twelfth-century southern Italian medical culture was. Despite their shared general subject matter of women's medicine, *Treatments for Women* and *Conditions of Women* are surprisingly different in their theoretical outlook, their organizational structure, and their social-intellectual origins.

If *Treatments for Women* has any Arabic influence at all, it is only oblique. There are only a few vaguely Galenic elements of theory, and its use of the compound medicines that were apparently introduced into Italy by Constantine the African is likewise limited.[136] *Treatments for Women* in fact lacks virtually any organizing principle at all, being as it is a quite chaotic assembly of treatments for gynecological, andrological, pediatric, cosmetic, and general medical conditions. This is not to say that it has no medical theory that gives structure to its therapeutic precepts; on the contrary, there are several consistent principles of female physiology and disease that underlie this seemingly random string of remedies. *Treatments for Women* takes these theoretical precepts for granted, however, rarely articulating a physiological (let alone an anatomical) basis for the malfunctions of the female reproductive organs that it enumerates.[137] Its standard introductory formula, "Sometimes there are women who . . . ," is about as far as it goes in exploring the nature and causes of disease.

Treatments for Women makes its theoretical allegiances clear in its opening sentence: "So that we might make a succinct exposition on the treatment of women, it ought to be determined which women are hot and which are cold, for which purpose we perform this test."[138] The test that follows is perhaps the most graphic example imaginable of how the notion of "hot and cold temperaments" functioned as real physiological categories: "We anoint a linen cloth with pennyroyal oil or with musk oil, or with laurel oil or any other hot oil, and we place the cloth thus anointed into the vagina in the amount of the little finger when she goes to sleep at night, tying it with a strong thread to her thighs so that if, when she wakes up, it has been drawn inside, this is proof for us that she labors from frigidity. But if it is expelled, this is proof that she labors from heat."[139]

The remedies that follow for both conditions are fully consistent with the basic principles of elemental qualities. On the theory that "contraries are cured by their contraries," for a woman suffering from heat the author recommends several "cold" substances—roses, marsh mallows, and violets—to be placed in water and administered by means of a vaginal suffumigation. In calling these substances "cold," medieval medical theory did not mean that they were necessarily cold to the touch but that they induced a chilling effect on the body when used as medicines. Thus, one of the leading Salernitan texts on *materia medica*, the *Circa instans*, described roses as cold in the first degree (out of a possible four) and dry in the second; mallow was cold in the second degree and moist in the second; violets were cold in the first degree and moist in the second. Likewise, women suffering from cold are to be treated with "hot" substances: pennyroyal (warm in the third, dry in the third), laurel leaves (warm and dry, no degree being specified), and small fleabane (warm and dry in the third).[140] "Thus they will be found cleansed from this awful excess and ready for conception."[141] We can now understand the rationale for the initial test: the linen cloth is anointed with "any 'hot' oil." When placed in the vagina, this "hot" suppository will be drawn inside if the uterus is "cold" (opposites attract) or expelled if it is "hot" (like substances repel each other).

The notion of elemental properties is part of the rational if unarticulated framework of diagnosis and therapy that underlies other treatments in the text. In ¶142, "phlegmatic and emaciated" women and men who cannot conceive because they are too cold are treated with a bath of the "hot" herbs juniper, catmint, pennyroyal, spurge laurel, wormwood, mugwort, hyssop, "and other hot herbs of this kind." This bath is to be followed by a suffumigation of hot, aromatic herbs for women, and for men the application (external, we presume) of similar substances. For uterine prolapse and induration caused by the excessive size of the male member during coitus (¶150), a rag is to be anointed "with some hot oil, either pennyroyal or musk or walnut," and placed in the vagina. This is to be fastened with a ligature "so that the womb recedes on its own and is made warm." Such hot herbs are similarly to be used for women who, because of their excessive frigidity, emit a sanious flux instead of menses (¶161), while women who urinate involuntarily due to paralysis of the urethra (a condition of frigidity) should be fomented with hot herbs (¶168), as should women who have fleshy growths in their wombs (¶170).

Finally, pain in the womb can be caused by miscarriage or by menstrual retention, and this can be due either to cold or, more rarely, to excessive heat. If cold is the cause (¶225), the symptoms will be pain and stabbing sensations in the left side; if hot (¶226), a condition that itself is due to sexual activity, which dries out and heats up the womb, the signs will be great heat in the genital area. The therapy is accordingly constituted of "hot" herbs for a cold cause and "cold" herbs for a hot cause. The one exception seems to be the use of marsh mallow, a cold substance, to treat menstrual retention caused by frigidity. Here we may assume that the rationale was that all the other "hot" substances effectively negated the minor cooling action of the mallow, thus allowing one of its secondary properties—that of provoking the menses—to come into play.

In contrast to the attention paid to the elemental qualities "hot" and "cold," humoral theory per se receives scant attention in *Treatments for Women*. Aside from the passing reference to "phlegmatic" thin women in ¶142, a humoral causation is ascribed to only one condition, dysentery (¶169). Here, dysentery is differentiated into that caused by phlegm and that caused by bile; the therapies differ accordingly.

In defining "the diseases of women," *Treatments for Women* includes most of the same categories as had *Conditions of Women*: menstrual irregularities, uterine prolapse, problems of fertility, difficulty of birth. But there are many differences, too. Some are matters of nuance; others are more substantively distinctive conceptions of what kinds of problems women really have. Of principal concern to the author of *Treatments for Women* is the promotion of women's fertility. We see this emphasis already in the opening lines, quoted above, on the necessity of distinguishing hot women from cold. Heat and cold are of concern because they are impediments to conception; as stated explicitly in ¶134, by use of the prescribed suffumigation women "will be found cleansed of this awful excess [of cold] and [will be made] ready for conception." Many of the subsequent prescriptions in *Treatments for Women* are likewise intended to aid conception, whether by provoking the menses (¶¶135 and 213),[142] restraining excessive menstruation (¶¶136–38 and 216), or plumping up thin women or slimming down fat ones (¶¶142-43).[143] The connection between menstruation and fertility is seen especially clearly in ¶¶160 and 162: for some women there is no point in attempting to induce menstruation, since they are permanently sterile. Here we see more of *Conditions of Women*'s notion of menstruation as "woman's flower"—that is, the necessary prelude to conception—than the view that it is a purgation vital in and of itself for women's health. Given this continual emphasis on promoting fertility, it is perhaps not surprising that *Treatments for Women* nowhere mentions contraceptives.[144]

This last omission may seem to fit poorly with the kinds of concerns we would expect twelfth-century women to have had, but the rest of *Treatments for Women* continually evinces a greater distance from "bookish" traditions than does *Conditions of Women* and a greater sensitivity to the ways in which women in the patriarchal culture of medieval southern Italy might have experienced the biological "facts" of their existence. This is apparent in the text's attitude toward sexuality. A chapter devoted to the effects of sexual abstinence (¶141) says that continent women—vowed women, nuns, and widows—will incur "grave suffering" if they are not able to sate their desire.[145] At first glance, this might seem to be yet another incarnation of traditional theories of uterine suffocation, in which lack of heterosexual activity led to disease. Unlike *Conditions of Women* and every other Salernitan textbook of the period, however—where uterine suffocation is a regular feature of the canon of gynecological diseases—*Treatments for Women* employs the term "uterine suffocation" just once, and this only in passing in a completely different context. The latter is an almost aphoristic statement: "Certain girls seem as if they are suffering from the falling sickness, which comes about from uterine suffocation compressing the respiratory organs" (¶203).[146] The identification of young unmarried women as likely victims and the comparison with epilepsy ("the falling sickness") are standard features of the nosography of uterine suffocation, yet there is here no direct description of the disease nor any recommended therapy. The passage just quoted immediately follows an assertion that the breast pain that some young women experience occurs upon eruption of the menses (i.e., at menarche). This might suggest an association of suffocation with menstruation, yet none of the three chapters devoted to menstrual retention (¶¶135, 213, and 225–26) mentions suffocation. Likewise, the metaphorical description of the womb in another chapter (¶140, on postnatal uterine pain and displacement) as being "as if it were wild . . . wandering" certainly seems reminiscent of the traditional "wandering womb," yet there is no mention here of suffocation nor of the remedies most commonly prescribed for it.[147]

Treatments for Women does not, it is true, entirely reject traditional views of female sexuality: that is, that women need regular (hetero)sexual activity to remain healthy. This view of sexuality is, after all, implicit in ¶141 when it identifies abstinence as a possible prelude to disease. Yet there is equal acknowledgment that heterosexual activity might be painful in and of itself, or that it can lead to other disorders. According to ¶150, prolapse of the uterus can be caused by the excessive size or length of the penis; ¶196 suggests that the vagina can swell up because of coitus. In ¶226, one of many remedies for pain in the womb, it is suggested that sexual activity is capable of desiccating the womb and heating it to an inordinate degree. One chapter (¶170) specifically implicates retained semen as the culprit in a certain disorder: a piece of flesh hanging from the womb. This occurs not from the woman's own seed being retained due to lack of intercourse but rather "because women do not clean themselves *after* coitus," thereby allowing the semen (whose is unspecified) to be retained and trapped within the uterus.[148]

Treatments for Women is, in fact, silent on the question (later to be hotly contested by medieval natural philosophers) of whether or not women produce seed,[149] nor is its existence presumed in ¶141 with its discussion of vowesses, nuns, and widows. In ¶141, the author of *Treatments for Women* acknowledges the cause of the discomforts of sexual abstinence not as retained or corrupted semen but as physical and perhaps even emotional desire itself: "Such women, when they have immoderate desire to have intercourse and they do not do so, if they do not satiate the desire they incur grave suffering." This acknowledgment that such women have desire is decidedly different from the traditional, mechanical view that semen simply builds up inside women who are not sexually active. The therapy advocated by *Treatments for Women* is traditional in that it employs "sweet-smelling" substances to be applied to the vagina (laurel or musk oil, or the compound medicine *trifera magna*—made of opium, cinnamon, cloves, etc.). The intended effect, however, is neither to lure the uterus back into place nor to expel the collected and corrupted menses or seed; rather, the text says unambiguously that "this constrains the lust and sedates the pain." The less "bookish" of the two gynecological *Trotula* texts seems, then, to be less influenced by traditional notions surrounding the disease concept of uterine suffocation and less grounded on strictly mechanical views of female sexuality.

With its concern about chastity, ¶141 may, in fact, have more to do with social "realities" than medical theory. When s/he spoke of "some widows who are not permitted to take a second vow,"[150] the author of *Treatments for Women* may have been referring to the fact that, in Salerno in this period, widows living under traditional Lombard law would have been under special pressure, more so than women living under Roman law, to keep their late husband's bed "chaste." Although remarriage was not uncommon,[151] husbands sometimes stipulated in their wills that their wives could retain usufruct of the husband's property (remember that wives usually only received one-fourth of the property as their wedding gift) only on condition that they did not remarry. Given that remarriage would have threatened a woman with loss of her property and perhaps guardianship of her children as well, maintenance of chastity may well have been a pressing concern.[152]

Another topic for which *Treatments for Women* recognizes the pragmatic needs of women is that of "restoring" virginity. Five recipes are given as a group (¶¶190–91 and 193–95),[153] with a sixth comment on the subject later (¶231). The main group of remedies opens with a straightforward and non-apologetic statement: "A constrictive for the vagina, so that women may be found to be as though they were virgins, is made in this manner." It may be that some of these constrictives were meant only to tighten the vagina to enhance the friction of vaginal intercourse, not necessarily to produce a fake bloodflow of "defloration"; in other words, they may have been intended as aids to sexual pleasure within marriage.[154] The fifth recipe (¶195), however, is explicit in stating that the point of the procedure—the use of leeches to induce bloodflow—is indeed to deceive the man.

The third recipe (¶193) shows that not every kind of deception was approved: "There are some filthy and corrupt prostitutes who desire to be found more than virgins. They make a certain constrictive for this, but they are ill advised for they render themselves bloody and they wound the male member. They take glass and natron and reduce them to a powder and place them in the vagina."[155]

By its very juxtaposition next to the other, nonmoralizing recipes, this explicit condemnation of "filthy and corrupt prostitutes" shows the implicit approval of other mechanisms of virginal simulation.[156] In fact, even while condemning the practice it transmits the illicit information. The desire of women, "honest" or "dishonest," to "restore" their virginity suggests acknowledgment by at least some medical practitioners that women's honor in this Mediterranean culture, to a degree that would never have been true for men, was bound up intimately with their sexual purity. If successful, these recipes may well have made the difference for some women between marriage and financial security, on the one hand, and social ostracization and poverty, on the other.[157] That sense of desperation may also account for the presence of a similar prescription in the writing of a male Salernitan practitioner later in the century.[158]

Treatments for Women demonstrates this same level of pragmatism and attention to a broad spectrum of women's medical concerns throughout. From recognition of difficulties of bladder control (a common affliction of older women, exacerbated by frequent childbearing, ¶168) to cracked lips caused by too much kissing (¶184) to breast pain during lactation (¶200) to instructions for cutting the umbilical cord (¶217), we sense the mundane but nonetheless pressing concerns of women. Care of obstetrical problems, especially those consequent to birth, is a particularly frequent concern (¶¶140, 146–49, 189, and 227–31).[159] The chapter on repairing the torn perineum (¶149) has, with one exception, no parallel anywhere else in Salernitan medical writings,[160] and there is similar attention to physical detail in recommendations such as the warning that women should avoid foods that induce coughing when they are recuperating from uterine prolapse.[161] Surprisingly, *Treatments for Women* provides even less information on management of normal births than does *Conditions of Women*. Here, the only recommendations are to bathe, fumigate, and offer sternutatives (substances that induce sneezing) to women giving birth (¶139) and to give a potion and fumigate with vinegar to aid birth and help expel the afterbirth (¶232). This absence is perhaps to be explained by the author's belief that childbirth in and of itself is not pathological. It does not, in other words, demand the attention of a medical practitioner; what needs to be known about aiding labor is already part of the common knowledge of the women (relatives and neighbors) who would normally attend the birth.[162]

This assumption of common knowledge does not, however, obtain with respect to matters of hygiene and dermatological conditions, which are thoroughly integrated into *Treatments for Women*.[163] Again, in chapters ranging from care of the skin to that of the hair and teeth, we sense that this material is coming out of the real-life concerns of local women. In ¶167, for instance, we find "a very useful unguent for sunburn and any kind of lesions, but especially those caused by the wind, and for the blemishes on the face which Salernitan women make [while mourning] for the dead."[164] Exactly this habit of self-mutilation is recorded in William of Apulia's description of the Lombard princess Sichelgaita, who mourned her dying husband, the Norman Robert Guiscard, in 1085. Having realized that her husband had reached the end of his life, she delivered an impassioned speech of grief, all the while "ripping her cheeks with her nails and tearing at her disheveled hair."[165] *Treatments for Women*'s reference to these facial "blemishes" suggests that such self-mutilation was a normative practice among Salernitan women.[166]

One perhaps surprising element of *Treatments for Women* is the inclusion of several remedies for men's disorders. To the extent that these are mostly uro-genital and other conditions of the pelvic region that men share with women—infertility caused by obesity or emaciation (¶¶142–44), hemorrhoids (¶152),[167] kidney and bladder stones (¶¶157–59), and intestinal pain (¶155)—their presence is understandable. Yet the author not merely mentions that men have these same disorders but (with the exception of two cases, where the therapy is not differentiated) s/he provides full details of the differing treatments needed for men. Moreover, there are two remedies exclusively for men: ¶154 on swelling of the penis and lesions of the prepuce and ¶223 on swollen testicles. The inclusion of this material probably reflects more than the mere categorical affinity of gynecological and andrological diseases. In his mid-twelfth-century compendium of medical practices, the Salernitan physician Johannes Platearius credited "Salernitan women" with a remedy for pustules of the penis very similar to that described in ¶154. I will have more to say about the Salernitan women momentarily; here it should simply be noted that Platearius's citation suggests that it was not considered problematic for female practitioners to treat both men's and women's reproductive complaints.[168] A larger culture of sharing is also suggested by the inclusion in *Treatments of Women* of four references to male Salernitan physicians. Copho is credited with the statement that sneezing can aid obstructed birth by rupturing the "cotyledons" (¶139). He is also mentioned as the "author" of a special powder used for treatment of impetigo (a skin condition).[169] A cure for bladder stone (with accompanying recipe, ¶159) is credited to Master M. F. (Mattheus Ferrarius), while Master J. F. (Johannes Furias or Johannes Ferrarius?) is credited with a remedy for chapped lips (¶186).[170]

The two Salernitan gynecological texts, *Conditions of Women* and *Treatments for Women*, are in basic agreement with each other on several fundamental points of female physiology and etiology. Both place greatest stress on maintaining (or attempting to maintain) regular menstruation;[171] both are concerned to remedy displacements and lesions of the uterus; both offer suggestions for aiding difficult childbirth. In this respect, it is quite understandable that the two texts should have been brought together at the end of the twelfth century and ultimately ascribed to a single author (see below). Yet there is also a certain irony in the texts' later fate. While *Conditions of Women* is thoroughly bookish, having little material beyond what the author has found in other tracts (which he readily admits in his prologue), *Treatments for Women* ranges more broadly, covering well over twice as many gynecological disease entities as its counterpart, not to mention its considerable material on cosmetics and other topics. Despite their differences, both texts are equally representative of twelfth-century Salernitan medicine, though of two clearly different varieties. While *Conditions of Women* embraces the new Arabic medicine and reflects the more learned, literate direction that Salernitan medical writing began to take in the early and middle decades of the twelfth century, *Treatments of Women* reflects an alternate, practical and probably largely oral tradition. It advocates a medicine that depends upon access to the international trade routes that brought into the Mediterranean basin spices and other expensive substances like cloves and frankincense,[172] and in its references to the treatments or theories of certain Salernitan masters it shows itself aware of a larger realm of medical discourse and practice. Yet on many other levels it is sui generis, independent of the growing theoretical and pharmaceutical sophistication embraced by contemporary authors. There were, these texts suggest, at least two distinct subcultures of medicine in twelfth-century Salerno. The third of the three *Trotula* texts, *On Women's Cosmetics*, reflects a point of intersection between them.

Women's Cosmetics

Women's Cosmetics does not participate in any theoretical system of explanation. Though often very detailed in its therapeutic prescriptions, listing down to the finest detail how to prepare this or that mixture, how to test when it is ready, and how to apply it, the text's sole organizing principle is to arrange the recommended cosmetics in head-to-toe order.[173] First come general depilatories for the overall care of the skin. Then there are recipes for care of the hair: for making it long and dark, thick and lovely, or soft and fine. For care of the face there are recipes for removing unwanted hair, whitening the skin, removing blemishes and abscesses, and exfoliating the skin, plus general facial creams. For the lips, there is a special unguent of honey to soften them, plus colorants to dye the lips and gums. For care of the teeth and prevention of bad breath, there are five different recipes. The final chapter is on hygiene of the genitalia: "There are some women who because of the magnitude of their instrument [i.e., their vagina] and its severe odor are oftentimes found unpleasant and unsuitable for sexual intercourse, with the result that they engender such great distaste in the men with whom they are having sex that, having begun the deed, they [the men] leave it unfinished, nor do they desire to approach them anymore."[174] A prescription said to be used by Muslim women then follows, describing a redolent water mixture that constricts the vagina and represses the odor. The author gives detailed instructions on how to apply the water just prior to intercourse, together with a powder that the woman is to rub on her chest, breasts, and genitalia. She is also to wash her partner's genitals with a cloth sprinkled with the same sweet-smelling powder.[175]

Like *Treatments for Women*, *Women's Cosmetics* relies on both local ingredients (numerous herbs and animal products) and imported substances (frankincense, cloves, cinnamon, nutmeg, galangal). It also employs a variety of mineral substances: orpiment (a compound of arsenic), quicklime, quicksilver, sulfur, natron, and white lead.[176] In laying out the desired objectives of cosmetic manipulation, it gives us a sense of the physical aesthetic of some southern Italian women. White or rosy skin (or both together),[177] black or blonde hair seem equally prized. The concern with whole-body depilatories is particularly interesting. As the figure of the bathing woman in a late

Figure 8: A private bath for a woman. The portable cauldron is reminiscent of equipment in the bathhouse of the Salernitan monastery of Santa Sofia, while the covered box and bag no doubt hold unguents or cosmetics. From a late twelfth-century copy of the Salernitan *Antidotarium magnum*; reproduced with permission from Basel, Öffentliche Bibliothek der Universität, MS D.III.14, f. 58r.

twelfth-century copy of a Salernitan pharmaceutical text shows (fig. 8), and, indeed, as we have already seen in the private bathhouses of Salernitan monastics, bathing could be an elaborate affair.[178] The detail with which the author of *Women's Cosmetics* describes the baths–even to the point of making allowance for women who have to substitute makeshift steambaths for formal baths–suggests the continued importance of bathing practices in the twelfth century.[179]

The author of *Women's Cosmetics* introduces several of the remedies as being the practices of Muslim women: a depilatory used by noble Muslim women (¶245),[180] a tried-and-true recipe for dyeing the hair black (¶251), a lead-based preparation named for its Muslim origin (¶280b),[181] a marine plant that the Muslims use to dye skins violet (¶296), and the redolent water to cleanse the genitalia just mentioned. One therapy the author even claims to have witnessed himself: "I saw a certain Saracen woman in Sicily curing infinite numbers of people [of mouth odor] with this medicine alone."[182] Muslims are the only named source for any of the cosmetics in this Latin text. What we have here in *Women's Cosmetics*, it seems, is confirmation of Ibn Jubayr's observation of Christian women's adoption of Muslim cosmetic practices in Sicily. It was, in fact, precisely the *Women's Cosmetics* author's recognition of this demand for knowledge of cosmetics that (by his own account) induced him, a male physician, to strengthen his account "with the rules of women whom I found to be practical in practicing the art of cosmetics." As he explained in his prologue (later lost from the *Trotula* ensemble and so not found in the present edition), the author's goal was that "to whatever noble or even common woman who seeks from me something of this art I should offer counsel appropriate to her status and means, so that I might succeed in obtaining fame and she would succeed in obtaining the longed-for result."[183] *Women's Cosmetics* is thus a witness both to the contemporary hygienic needs of women in southern Italy in the twelfth century and to their own cosmetic practices, for as this author himself admits, his sources of information have been women "practical in practicing the art of cosmetics."

The Women of Salerno

The traditional attribution of the whole ensemble of *Trotula* texts to a woman author has tantalized and teased modern readers with the possibility that they were reading what a woman thought about women's bodies and how a woman, with a woman's knowledge, would have gone about caring for women's diseases.[184] Although, as I have already mentioned, one of the

Trotula texts is probably and another certainly of male authorship (*Conditions of Women* and *Women's Cosmetics*, respectively), the possibility of female authorship is not in and of itself far-fetched, as there is plenty of evidence to suggest that women practiced medicine in eleventh- and twelfth-century Salerno. Two Anglo-Norman writers of the twelfth century, Orderic Vitalis and Marie de France, each tell different stories of a Norman (or, in Marie's case, possibly English) traveler journeying to Salerno and finding there a woman very learned in medicine.[185] Local evidence from Salerno itself likewise shows women who are credited for their medical skill. The necrology of the cathedral of Salerno lists a woman healer (*medica*) named Berdefolia, who died in 1155. The mother of Platearius (one of several members of a veritable medical dynasty of that name) is said to have cured a certain noblewoman of uterine suffocation. Moreover, several male medical writers of the twelfth century who either taught or studied at Salerno refer frequently to the medical practices of the *mulieres Salernitane*, the "Salernitan women." These references mention, for example, how "the Salernitan women" make a fumigation from olive leaves for children suffering from paralysis or other cerebral problems, or how, as the moon is leaving the house of Jupiter, they take sowbread, place it on the afflicted spleen of a patient, and perform a ritual of sympathetic magic whereby what is done to the sowbread will happen to the spleen as well. In all, more than five dozen such references to the Salernitan women can be found in medical texts of the twelfth and early thirteenth centuries.[186]

When taken together these references show a variety of writers reporting practices they had either witnessed or heard about. What these references also show, however, is a limited picture of the Salernitan women's practices. While their therapies are not confined to any specific area of medicine (they are credited with therapies for gastrointestinal disorders, skin problems, etc., as well as with gynecological and pediatric remedies), there is nothing in any of these references to suggest that the Salernitan women speculated about the causes of disease, let alone other, more abstract aspects of medicine or natural philosophy. They are credited with no medical writings, nor are they referred to as teachers. The Salernitan women, to judge from all these references, are empirical practitioners: they know the properties of plants and are even credited on occasion with finding new uses for them, but they seem to participate not at all in the world of medical theory or medical books.

Set against this background, the phenomenon of Trota is all the more remarkable. Trota is the only Salernitan woman healer whose name is attached to any extant medical writings.[187] Trocta (or less frequently, Trotta) was a common woman's name in southern Italy from the late eleventh century well into the thirteenth.[188] We have no way of knowing which (if any) of the many Troctas who appear in Salernitan documents in the twelfth century was the famed healer whose name is associated with the *Trotula* texts. Nevertheless, there can be no doubt that such a healer existed.

Trota and her medical practices are attested by three distinct textual sources. First, there is the *Practical Medicine According to Trota* (*Practica secundum Trotam*). Now extant in only two manuscripts, this is a compendium of seventy-one different remedies for gynecological and obstetric conditions, cosmetic problems, hair lice, burns, cancer, frenzy, eye problems, sprained foot, excessive sweat, snakebite, toothache, scrofula, spleen problems, depilatories, hemorrhoids, and fevers.[189] It is very likely that this text is just an abbreviated version of what was once a much larger work. The extent of this larger text is hinted at by a second witness to Trota's medical writings, a compendium called *On the Treatment of Illnesses* (*De egritudinum curatione*). Made in the second half of the twelfth century, this massive compilation draws together excerpts from seven leading Salernitan medical writers. Trota is among them, and the excerpts attributed to her here demonstrate her considerable expertise in the fields of gastrointestinal disorders and ophthalmology.[190] *Practical Medicine* and the excerpts in *Treatment of Illnesses* have, all together, more than two dozen passages in common, confirming that they both derive from a single source.

A third piece of evidence for Trota's medical practice is found within one of the *Trotula* texts themselves. About a third of the way into *Treatments for Women* (¶151), we find a story of how Trota cured a young woman suffering from gas or flatulence in her uterus (*ventositas matricis*).[191] The woman was at first diagnosed as having some kind of intestinal rupture and was about to be operated on. Trota, however, was called in "as a master" and was astonished by what she found. Doubting the initial diagnosis, she took the young woman home with her and there realized that she had "wind" (*ventositas*) in her uterus. She treated her with a combination of baths and external applications, and so effected a cure.

The inclusion of this anecdote—which refers to Trota consistently in the third person—suggests, of course, that she is not the author of *Treatments for Women*. Yet in attributing *Treatments for Women* to Trota, early scribes were claiming not so much that Trota was the text's sole author as that she was the authority who stood behind it. Much of the material does indeed derive from Trota's work. Trota's *Practical Medicine* and *Treatments for Women* have fifteen remedies that overlap directly. There are, moreover, additional similarities in theoretical character, *materia medica*, and the practical therapies employed. The attribution of *Treatments for Women* to Trota thus reflects both Trota's reputation and her "maternity" of the collected wisdom on women's diseases and other cures assembled in this text. It may well be that *Treatments for Women* reflects a transcript of Trota's cures as she orally recounted them to a scribe, who then added further elements of his/her own choosing.[192]

This scenario of a palimpsest—one layer of composition on top of another—may help explain one final puzzle that surrounds the genesis of *Treatments for Women*. Given its associations not simply with Trota but with the southern Italian city of Salerno, it is surprising that three times in the earliest versions of the text we find *vernacular English* synonyms for diseases or herbs.[193] As we have seen, English visitors to Salerno are documented from at least the late eleventh century, by which point, of course, the area had come under Norman control, as had England itself in 1066. It may, indeed, be precisely the shock of an outsider at seeing the dramatic and violent mourning practices of the Salernitan women that caused this author to specify that it was *Salernitan* women (rather than, say, "our women" or simply "women") who rip up their faces in mourning.[194] It is likely, therefore, either that *Treatments for Women* represents the appropriation of traditional Salernitan cures by such a visitor or that it reflects the interpolations of an English speaker who had access to it very early in its transmission.

Trota's relation to the *Trotula* texts thus at last becomes clear. The close relations between the *Practical Medicine According to Trota* and *Treatments for Women* confirm that Trota is directly associated with *Treatments for Women*, whether or not she authored all the parts of the text as it now exists. Either way, it is in no way inappropriate to consider her the text's principal source. The more we learn about the characteristics of Trota's authentic work, however, the less plausible it seems that she could have been directly connected with either *Conditions of Women* or *Women's Cosmetics*. Both *Conditions of Women* and *Women's Cosmetics* circulated anonymously and seem not to have been associated with Trota's name until they were brought into juxtaposition with *Treatments for Women*.[195] Their very different styles and use of sources confirm that they are not the work of the same author who compiled *Treatments for Women*, which has (unlike *Conditions of Women*) no substantive Arabic influence or high medical theory, nor (unlike *Women's Cosmetics*) any rhetorical elegance or organizational structure.

We still and may forever lack much of the information we should like to have about Trota: when, exactly, she lived, who her family was, how she was trained, whom she taught. More particularly, we should like to know how she came by her literacy in Latin and for whom she believed she was writing. There is nothing in *Practical Medicine* or *Treatments for Women* to suggest any direct connection with the Church.[196] While these elements of mystery may continue to surround Trota, the combined evidence of the *Practical Medicine According to Trota*, the Salernitan compendium *Treatment of Illnesses*, and *Treatments for Women* shows that Trota has as much claim to existence and authorship as do many of her contemporary male Salernitan writers, for whom we likewise have no more tangible evidence than ascriptions in the manuscripts and chance references. That Trota was not the author of the *Trotula* texts in their entirety does not detract from her achievement. She clearly was the source for many if not most of the therapies in *Treatments for Women*, and when some later editor attributed *Conditions of Women* and *Women's Cosmetics* to her as well, s/he did so, I believe, as an acknowledgment of Trota's fame.[197] The only thing truly mysterious about Trota is why the prosperous southern Italian town of Salerno could produce one such prolific female medical author but, apparently, no others.

The Fate of the *Trotula*

The 126 extant manuscripts of the Latin *Trotula* reflect only a fraction of the total that must once have circulated throughout Europe from the late twelfth century to the end of the fifteenth century.[198] Given their adherence to basic Galenic theory—which by the late twelfth century had become the dominant medical tradition in western Europe—it is quite understandable why *Conditions of Women* and *Treatments for Women* were to render their early medieval predecessors virtually obsolete within a century of their creation.[199] The attractions of Galenism had nothing to do with the popularity of *Women's Cosmetics*, of course (which, as we have seen, lacked any theoretical basis), but as a well-ordered summary of personal hygiene and beautification it had no peer. The three texts, moreover, also had the cachet of the Salernitan association, and they circulated most frequently with other Salernitan writings.

The reasons for the popularity of the *Trotula* are therefore not that difficult to understand. A more peculiar aspect of their history, however—and the one that has generated the most confusion among modern scholars—was their fusion into a single compendium, the *Trotula* ensemble. Perhaps the best way to understand these medieval transformations is with a very modern analogy. An ironic effect of the late twentieth-century computer revolution is that it has made us more comprehending of the extraordinary instability of medieval texts as they circulated in manuscript. Just as a computer file or Web page can be changed from day to day, deletions or additions made with bewildering ease from iteration to iteration, so too could

medieval texts be modified by any scribe or editor who wished to do so as
s/he labored to produce each new manuscript. Whereas we may be concerned about intellectual property rights, medieval scribes and "editors" were
more concerned with creating for themselves books that retained the authoritative essence of the texts but also answered their own immediate needs for
utility. Medieval scribes were not completely undisciplined in how they
intervened in these texts, of course. Six distinct versions of the *Trotula*
ensemble can be identified and, given the ease with which alterations
(whether deliberate or accidental) *could* have been made to these texts, it is
remarkable how stable they usually were. Nevertheless, the *Trotula* proved an
attractive locus in which to insert additional recipes on gynecology, obstetrics, or, most commonly, cosmetic concerns. This "magnet effect" suggests
not a lack of concern for the integrity of the texts but, rather, recognition of
the encyclopedic wealth they were seen to possess.

THE *TROTULA* ENSEMBLE

As with so many aspects of the history of the *Trotula* texts, the creation of the
original *Trotula* ensemble can be neither precisely dated nor attributed to an
identifiable individual.[200] Nor can we even be sure where this later editorial
work was done. The three individual texts had gone through several stages of
independent revision by the end of the twelfth century (fig. 9): in addition to
its original "rough draft," *Conditions of Women* existed in three different versions,[201] *Treatments for Women* in two, and *Women's Cosmetics* in two.[202] A
desire to bring together material on women seems to have manifested itself
already at this early stage when the third version of *Conditions of Women* and
the second version of *Women's Cosmetics* were first linked together. These
were both abbreviated versions of the texts: *Conditions of Women 3* omitted
the contraceptives and the following paragraph on the development of the
fetus (¶¶83–88); *Women's Cosmetics 2* abbreviated the text throughout, mostly
by omission of the detailed instructions for preparations.[203] The two texts
appear together in three manuscripts, two of which are among the earliest
extant copies of any form of the treatises.

The *Trotula* ensemble proper was probably first created in the late
twelfth century, for we find manuscripts of it from the turn of the thirteenth
century. The compiler of this proto-ensemble, whoever he or she was, combined the already-paired *Conditions of Women 3* and *Women's Cosmetics 2* with
a copy of *Treatments for Women 2*. Although this editor made no major revisions of the texts, s/he did introduce several substantive additions and

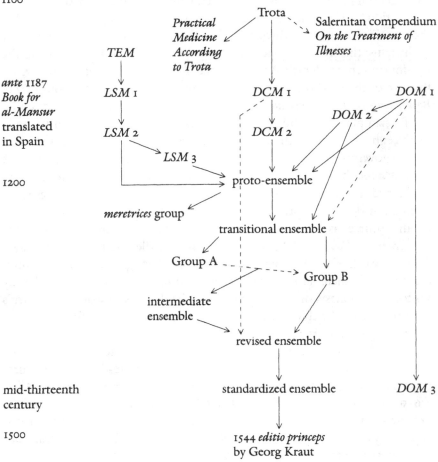

ca. 1070–1080
Constantine
translates
Viaticum

1100

ante 1187
*Book for
al-Mansur*
translated
in Spain

1200

mid-thirteenth
century

1500

Trota

*Practical
Medicine
According
to Trota*

Salernitan compendium
*On the Treatment of
Illnesses*

TEM

LSM 1   DCM 1   DOM 1

DOM 2

LSM 2   DCM 2

LSM 3

proto-ensemble

meretrices group

transitional ensemble

Group A   Group B

intermediate
ensemble

revised ensemble

standardized ensemble   DOM 3

1544 *editio princeps*
by Georg Kraut

KEY:

TEM = *Tractatus de egritudinibus mulierum* (Treatise on the Diseases of Women)
LSM = *Liber de sinthomatibuis mulierum* (Conditions of Women)
DCM = *De curis mulierum* (Treatments for Women)
DOM = *De ornatu mulierum* (Women's Cosmetics)
⟶ direct line of textual development
- - -> text used for selected readings only

Figure 9. The development of the *Trotula* ensemble.

rearrangements that transformed the ensemble into something more than a simple linking of the three original Salernitan texts. This compiler first compared *Conditions of Women 3* with a copy of *Conditions of Women 2* in order to check certain readings and fill in lacunae, particularly the deleted contraceptive section.[204] The compiler then added several more chapters to the end of the text. First was ¶123, which describes the month-by-month development of the fetus; this was excerpted from an embryological work attributed to the late-fourth-century North African writer Vindician. Paragraphs 124–27, on the care of the newborn and choice of a wet nurse, were drawn out of *The Book for al-Mansur* (*Liber ad Almansorem*), a large medical compendium by the Persian physician Abū Bakr Muḥammad ibn Zakarīyā' ar-Rāzī (d. early tenth century, known in the Latin world as Rhazes), which had been written for the governor of Rayy, Manṣur ibn Isḥāq ibn Aḥmad ibn Asad. *The Book for al-Mansur* had only recently been translated from Arabic into Latin in Spain, and its use by the *Trotula* compiler is one of the first witnesses to its circulation.[205] The chapter on pustules in children (¶128) came from yet another source (as yet unidentified). The last three sections of the expanded *Conditions of Women*, ¶¶129–31 on male and female infertility, were drawn from the work of the Salernitan writer Copho. Though they did not contradict the other material in *Conditions of Women*, these new chapters slightly shifted the emphasis of the original, from the diseases of women (women's sufferings being the chief concern) to procreation (the successful production and rearing of children).

With *Treatments for Women*, the compiler of the proto-ensemble excised the chapters on hair and skin care and placed them instead within the third, cosmetic section of the newly constructed text (in the present edition, ¶¶254, 256–59, 261–71, 286–88, and 290). The surviving manuscripts show that the proto-ensemble was left incomplete: the compiler never finished what was apparently a planned integration of all the cosmetic chapters from *Treatments for Women* with those of *Women's Cosmetics*.

Perhaps the most important feature of this first version of the ensemble is that it was here that "Trotula" first came into being. Tro(c)ta, as I have already noted, was a popular woman's name in late eleventh- and twelfth-century southern Italy; "Trotula" (which literally means "little Trota") has thus far been documented only twice, and in one case it is clearly used as a child's name.[206] "Trotula" as used in connection with these medical texts originally functioned as a title. Both *Conditions of Women* and *Women's Cosmetics*, as we have seen, were anonymous, while *Treatments for Women* was regularly ascribed to Trota. The compiler of the proto-ensemble probably thus had only the name of Trota to associate with the three works.[207] In a fashion that was not uncommon with other medical texts, the compiler dubbed the collection "the *Trotula*," that is, forming a title out of the presumed author's name, Trota. Thus we find early forms of the ensemble with the title "The Trotula of Women" (*Trotula mulierum*) or "The Book Which Is Called the *Trotula*" (*Liber qui dicitur Trotula* or *Summa que dicitur Trotula*). Already by the early thirteenth century, however, the title "Trotula" was misunderstood as the author's name—an author who, moreover, was responsible not just for one text but for the whole ensemble. From this point on, even though many scribes continued to differentiate between the *Trotula major* (i.e., *Conditions of Women*) and the *Trotula minor* (usually *Treatments for Women* and *Women's Cosmetics* viewed as a single text), the dominant textual traditions were to view "Trotula" as an author, some scribes stressing her status as a master of medicine (*magistra*) and her Salernitan origin. The internal reference to Trota in ¶151 was also changed to "Trotula," very few scribes or readers bothering to puzzle through why the work's author should describe one of her own successful cures in a distant third person rather than with the proud "I" of the first person.[208]

Later versions of the ensemble (each probably the work of a different editor) incorporated minor revisions into the text, adding the occasional new recipe here and there and introducing variant readings. In the "transitional" ensemble, an editor went back to *Women's Cosmetics 2* and incorporated it in full (together with his/her own substantive revisions), thus finally completing the third section of the ensemble. This editor also inserted some new material, such as two cosmetic practices that the early thirteenth-century author Bernard of Provence had attributed to the Salernitan women.[209] In the "intermediate" version, we find the fullest form of the *Trotula* ensemble: in the cosmetics section, it adds recipes for treating fistula, signs for distinguishing pregnancy from dropsy, symptoms of a fetus that has died in the womb (all of which, of course, are out of place here), and some additional cosmetics. This, then, is the magnet effect of the *Trotula*, attracting all manner of miscellaneous recipes on women's medicine.

Some time before the middle of the thirteenth century, yet another form of the ensemble emerged. Using copies of both the transitional and the intermediate ensembles as a base, the editor of this "revised ensemble" went back to manuscripts of the three original independent treatises in order to establish a purer form of the texts. In *Conditions of Women*, for example, the editor noticed that a group of recipes (here ¶¶107–9) had been omitted from the section on aids for difficult birth. The editor of the revised ensemble copied the abbreviated section as s/he found it, then added the missing recipes from *Conditions of Women 1*.[210]

Likewise in *Treatments for Women* this editor reintroduced occasional readings from the original text. In the opening sentence (¶132), for example, s/he clarified that the subsequent test was for differentiating "hot" women from "cold" in order that they might be properly aided in conception. (Earlier versions of the ensemble had said more vaguely that "it ought to be seen which cause dominates.") In ¶141, on the problems of sexual continence in vowesses, widows, and nuns, the editor reinserted a final passage which explained the anatomical reason why a pessary should not be used for this condition.

The editor of the revised ensemble also suppressed several recipes, such as the treatments for impetigo (a skin condition), worms in infants, and snakebite in *Treatments for Women*, as well as many of the cosmetics and obstetrical chapters that had closed *Women's Cosmetics* in the intermediate ensemble (including the chapter on sexual hygiene discussed above). Only one recipe is new in the revised ensemble: ¶222, which offers an additional remedy for deafness.

Sometime around the middle of the thirteenth century, the "standardized ensemble" first appeared. The last major version of the ensemble (and that presented here), the standardized ensemble offers no substantive additions or deletions; the content of the text is entirely identical to the revised ensemble. Rather, this version adds stylistic niceties and minor amplifications. Its editor chose to replace the assertion that Nature wished "to recuperate" women's defective heat by the more poetic phrase "to temper the poverty of their heat" (¶3). This editor had a particular taste for synonymy, that is, introducing a second term to more fully convey breadth of meaning: the veins of the womb are both "wide and open," not simply "open" (¶29); pain occurs in the "more prominent" or the more anterior part of the womb (¶64). This editor was also not averse to what apparently passed for ethnic humor in the thirteenth century: s/he was responsible for the suggestion that the language of Lombards is particularly noxious to the newborn (¶124).[211] This editor (or an early copyist) also introduced some new errors and redundancies, such as the repetition of the plantain root passage in the recipe for an infusion in ¶35 or that of the remedy for cankerous gums in the *Women's Cosmetics* section (¶¶300 and 304). Finally and more positively, to this editor can be attributed regularized chapter divisions and rubrics. True, there should have been quite a few more chapter headings than were actually added. For example, in the *Treatments for Women* section, the chapter on cancer of the nose is followed immediately by one on provoking the menses (¶¶212 and 213), with no chapter division to signal the separation of two such obviously distinct topics. Still, the addition of the regularized rubrics undoubtedly increased the utility of the text for reference purposes. Perhaps the most important of these rubrics was the opening one: "On the Diseases of Women According to Trotula" (*De passionibus mulierum secundum Trotulam*), yet another reinforcement of the attribution of this wide-ranging collection of texts on women's medicine to the single author "Trotula."

Readers of the present edition will now understand how far distant the standardized ensemble is from the three original Salernitan texts on women's medicine. Many of the changes that the texts underwent between their composition and the mid-thirteenth century were subtle and insignificant for the works' actual theoretical or therapeutic content. Some changes might be considered real improvements: the transposition of several of *Treatments for Women*'s cosmetic chapters into the *Women's Cosmetics* section rendered them more accessible, while additions like the precise instructions for the preparation of starch (¶274) must have been genuinely helpful. But some changes were not calculated emendments but accidental errors that crept into the texts. The loss of the negative in the opening sentence of ¶160 in *Treatments for Women*, for example, had the result of encouraging treatment of old women suffering from a sanious flux, whereas the original text had said it was pointless to treat them because they were already incapable of bearing children. Similarly, the occasional misreadings caused changes in ingredients (e.g., the recommendation in ¶190 of egg whites as a vaginal constrictive instead of alum) or changes in therapeutic procedure (e.g., in ¶232 the placement of vinegar into the woman's vagina instead of into a pot beneath her).

Many errors or corruptions, of course, would not have been obvious to readers without multiple copies of the texts at hand. Yet the failure of later scribes or readers to correct some of the more glaring errors must give us pause when imagining how actively the standardized ensemble in particular might have been used in any kind of clinical setting. Not a single reader of the extant standardized ensemble manuscripts seems to have noticed, for example, the obvious logical inconsistency within a recipe in *Women's Cosmetics* for reddening the skin and lips, where an accidental misreading changed a prescription to use a violet dye into one for a green dye (¶296).[212] Nor did anyone notice the obvious redundancy of ¶¶106 and 111 or ¶¶300 and 304, where because of editorial or scribal error the text was duplicated. And one wonders how even the most dedicated occultist could have made sense of the garbled magical passages in ¶¶98 and 100. It is likely, however, that the standardized ensemble became the preferred version of the *Trotula* texts, not because it was scrutinized in detail for every possible remedy for women's conditions (there are, after all, more than three hundred different prescribed therapies), but because it could serve a more general function as a basic reference work on fertility–a subject on which there was increasing concern from the thirteenth century on.[213] While it is clear that their popularity was not solely dependent on their association with the name of the famous Salernitan woman healer Trota (after all, when circulating independently both *Conditions of Women* and *Women's Cosmetics* were anonymous yet nonetheless highly popular), it is also clear that, once the Trota/"Trotula" association became attached to the whole ensemble, for some readers the apparent imprimatur of this female author assured them that they were reading "authentic" women's medicine.

LATER DISSEMINATION

The standardized ensemble is today found in twenty-nine manuscripts from all parts of Latinate Europe.[214] Its popularity peaked around the turn of the fourteenth century, when almost half of the extant copies were produced. In the fifteenth century, even though other forms of the texts were still being transcribed in many parts of Europe, the standardized ensemble seems to have been rarely copied in Italy, England, or even in France, where the text had earlier achieved its greatest popularity. Most of the extant fifteenth-century manuscripts come from central and eastern Europe. The standardized ensemble seems always to have been closely associated with university circles and in this context manuscripts preserved their utility as reference texts for years after their initial composition. By the mid-fourteenth century, for example, the library of the Sorbonne in Paris had three copies of the *Trotula*. It is not clear which version was kept chained in the library's reference section, but the other two manuscripts (both of which are extant) were copies of the standardized ensemble: one given by the theologian Gérard of Utrecht, and the other by Jacques of Padua, a master of arts and medicine and a doctor of theology.[215] Copies of the standardized ensemble are also found continuing to circulate in private hands. A manuscript produced in 1305 at one of the leading medical centers of the early fourteenth century, Montpellier, was owned a century later by Bertrand Cormerii (fl. 1435), who was a student of medicine at Paris. He, in turn, sold it to Jean Caillau (d. after 1472), who also was trained at Paris and who later served as physician to Charles, duke of Orléans. Caillau then gave the manuscript to his patron the duke in exchange for another book.[216] A final indication of the standardized ensemble's utility was its translation in the fifteenth century into the vernacular, once into Dutch, once, perhaps twice into French, and twice into German.[217]

Throughout this period, the standardized ensemble remained remarkably stable in form. Copy after copy reproduced the text with hardly any variation, in stark contrast to earlier versions, which copyists often felt free to abridge or emend as they liked. There were, of course, some exceptions. One scribe reinterpreted the title as "The Good Treatise Which Is Entitled 'The Old Woman on the Sufferings [of Women].'"[218] Another oddly attributed the text to both "Trotula" and the famous early fourteenth-century Catalan physician Arnald of Villanova.[219] More substantively, two copyists independently restructured the standardized ensemble by interweaving the *Conditions of Women* and the *Treatments for Women* chapters into a more logical order, moving from uterine conditions to fertility, pregnancy, childbirth, and finally care of the child. (Both copyists deleted the cosmetic material in its entirety.)[220]

Though it is likewise based on the standardized ensemble, the 1544 Strasbourg printed edition is unrelated to either of these last-mentioned reconstructions, reflecting instead the unique alterations of its editor, a German humanist physician from Hagenau named Georg Kraut. Kraut's major editorial innovation was to reorganize all the material from the ensemble into one smoothly ordered *summa*, rearranging the ensemble's disparate parts into sixty-one chapters.[221] Gone now were the redundancies and chaotic ordering of the three original texts of the ensemble. Gone, too, of course, were any remaining hints that the *Trotula* was a concretion of a variety of sources from a variety of different authors. While in general Kraut seems to have been concerned to preserve most of the material he found in the standardized ensemble, humanist that he was he could not refrain entirely from tidying up the text. He suppressed the two references to magical practices to aid birth in *Conditions of Women* (¶¶98 and 100), he clarified that the contraceptives were to be used only if out of fear of death the woman did not dare conceive,[222] and he apologized for the inclusion of mechanisms to "restore" virginity, saying that he would not have included them were they not necessary to aid in conception.[223] Even with this disclaimer, Kraut still felt uncomfortable with the topic; he included only two of the ensemble's nine recipes for vaginal constrictives.[224] He recommended that in case of difficulties of birth, one should first call upon God's aid before attempting other remedies, later adding that the procedure of bouncing a woman on a sheet to induce labor (¶145) would work if God were willing.[225]

For the most part, Kraut refrained from rewriting; aside from a few obvious errors, most readings are unchanged from the text edited here.[226] Of those passages he did alter, the most notable was the prologue to *Conditions of Women*, including the author's statement of his/her reasons for writing (§2). Kraut was apparently motivated by the desire to make both the femininity and the originality of "Trotula" more apparent. Whereas neither the original *Conditions of Women* nor the standardized ensemble had offered any direct hint of the author's gender, Kraut, presuming the *whole* of his newly unified text to be the work of a single feminine author, altered the preface to stress her gender. He also omitted the names of Hippocrates and Galen and even the author's clear admission that the work was a compilation of excerpts from other writings. Kraut's artificial text with his artificially unified and gendered author proved to be authoritative; all subsequent Renaissance editors reprinted this humanist fabrication rather than returning to the medieval manuscripts. Kraut's edition thus occluded the medieval history of the texts from view, with the result that most of the modern controversy about the authoress "Trotula" has produced little more than idle speculation.[227]

* * *

Habent sua fata libelli: books have their own fortunes and their own histories. The *Trotula* texts, whoever their authors may have been, were very real and very influential throughout Europe for nearly half a millennium. Whatever their relationship to Trota or the other women of Salerno, the *Trotula* were one of the pillars on which later medieval culture was built, being present in the libraries of physicians and surgeons, monks and philosophers, theologians and princes from Italy to Ireland, from Spain to Poland. When Latinate physicians or surgeons (such as the anonymous surgeon who owned a manuscript now in Laon) wanted a handbook on women's medicine, they used the *Trotula*. When medieval translators looked for gynecological material to render into the vernacular, it was to the *Trotula* texts that they most frequently turned. Of ten gynecological texts composed in Middle English between the fourteenth and fifteenth centuries, for example, five are renditions of the *Trotula*.[228]

The need for vernacular translations raises the question of women's access to the texts. The Latin texts probably only rarely made their way into women's hands in the early years after their composition, perhaps not at all after the thirteenth century. The Laon manuscript just mentioned, for example, passed from that anonymous male surgeon into the holdings of the cathedral of Laon, where it was annotated and used by the canons of the cathedral for the rest of the Middle Ages. Every other manuscript whose provenance is known is similarly found passing exclusively through the hands of men. A late thirteenth- or early fourteenth-century manuscript now in Glasgow is, however, an intriguing case. Its early provenance is not known, but it has the distinction among the Latin *Trotula* manuscripts in being the smallest codex, a handbook less than six by four inches in size. It also contains only one other text: a brief tract on useful and harmful foods, which could, conceivably, be used for self-medication by controlling diet. There are no contemporary annotations to confirm ownership by a woman, but its small size (similar to that of the books of hours owned by many upper-class women in this period) and the absence of any other, more technical medical literature may suggest use by a layperson and so, perhaps, by a woman. It is also therefore intriguing that the one manuscript it most closely resembles textually is one now in Poland, which though not as small is likewise unusual in having the *Trotula* as a separate pamphlet.[229]

From the thirteenth century on, female readers tended more and more to use the vernacular, so in this respect it is not surprising that seven of the twenty-two known medieval translations of the *Trotula* address themselves directly to female audiences. The author of the earliest English translation, writing in the late fourteenth or early fifteenth century, went so far as to demand of any male reader who happened upon the text that "he read it not in spite nor [in order to] slander any woman nor for any reason but for healing and helping them."[230] Even with these translations, however, we know of no identifiable female owners, and it is clear that most if not all of the other later medieval translations were intended for male readers. It seems, then, that relative to their widespread popularity among male practitioners and intellectuals, it was only very infrequently that the *Trotula* found their way into the hands of women. Despite the recognition by the author of *Conditions of Women* that women often did not want to turn to male physicians, the *Trotula* seem to have functioned as a prime tool by which male practitioners did, in fact, come to have significant control over the practice of gynecology and cosmetics.[231]

The *Trotula* did not represent the only medieval medical view of women, of course, as many other later medieval authors discussed the physiology and pathological conditions of the female body, often with no reference at all to the *Trotula*.[232] But the fact that they should have been continually copied, adapted, and translated right up through the end of the fifteenth century (and indeed, the fact that Kraut's edition should have been reprinted eleven times in the course of the sixteenth century) shows that long after the apogee of Salerno, the *Trotula* retained their power to both advise and inform.

Note on This Translation

Paragraph division of the text is editorial. It is meant not only to indicate the obvious grammatical and topical breaks but also to reflect the original component parts of the texts. Thus, strings of recipes will often be separated except in those instances (such as ¶124) where they all come uninterrupted from a single source.[233] The headings and subheadings in the text translate the original rubrics; in a few instances I have added in square brackets additional headings when necessary. In order to distinguish those parts of the texts that are original (that is, those that were found in the three independent Salernitan texts) and those sections that are later additions, I have flagged the latter with an asterisk (*) at the head of the paragraph. More detailed information on when, exactly, this material entered the ensemble and on internal transpositions of material within the texts can be found in my 1996 essay on the subject.[234]

In translating the text, I have aimed for clarity above all. I have retained the grammatical voice of most instructions—that is, I have rendered passive constructions passively and active actively. Although admittedly this results in a somewhat uneven text, it has the virtue of reflecting some remnants of the distinctive tone of address of the three original texts.[235] I have resisted the temptation to "diagnose" the conditions described and have preferred to replicate the sometimes loose phrasing of the Latin rather than offer more precise readings that presume the ideological framework of modern Western biology and medicine. Readers can decide for themselves if, for example, they wish to interpret infertility accompanied by dry lips and incessant thirst (¶129) as a description of diabetes. The annotations to the translation discuss particular aspects of medieval medical theory or therapeutics and comment on other issues of historical interest. In several instances where textual corruption or alteration affects the sense of the translation, I have flagged these problems in the notes. Additional information on historically significant deviations of the standardized ensemble from earlier forms of the texts can be found in the Latin edition.

The translation of pharmaceutical ingredients is the most vexing aspect of working with texts such as these, since all identifications carry a certain amount of imprecision. On the one hand, the names used by the authors of the original *Trotula* texts in twelfth-century southern Italy often became deformed in transmission (I have flagged only the major deviations in the notes to the edition), or they may have referred to several different plants. Some species may now be extinct or their chemical properties may have changed slightly over the past eight hundred years. On the other hand, there are instances when multiple Latin names seem to refer to the same plant, for example, *altea, bismalua, euiscus, malua*, and *maluauiscus*, all of which seem to refer to marsh mallow (*Althaea officinalis* L.). Having said this, I also feel my objective as translator is to attempt to bring a world long since disappeared back to life for the reader. This, it seems to me, can best be accomplished by attempting to identify plants, animals, and other *materia medica* by signifiers we use today. Since I am neither a botanist nor a phytopharmacologist, I have availed myself of the work of linguists and historical botanists in translating the medieval Latin terms with modern English common names. (For the sake of readers whose native language may not be English, I have also cross-identified the English common names with their Linnaean classifications in the list of *materia medica* at the end of the book.)[236] These scholars often disagree among themselves, of course, and I have not attempted to resolve their disputes, nor even to list all the possible identifications that have been proposed.[237] I intend this translation merely to give an approximation of the botanical and zoological world these texts attempted to exploit. *Any investigators, either historical or pharmaceutical, who wish to use these texts as the basis for scientific research should refer to the Latin text.* Needless to say, I can in no sense endorse the therapeutic use of these prescriptions.

The names of compound substances (e.g., *Trifera magna*) are for the most part untranslatable, and so I have left them in Latin. The Appendix provides full descriptions of their ingredients and preparations as described in the major twelfth-century Salernitan collection of compound medicines, the *Antidotarium Nicholai*. As for weights and measures, I have not attempted to modernize them. The description in the *Antidotarium Nicholai* can serve for the present purposes: "The following are the weights or measures which are used in the medicinal art and through subtle, ingenious, and clever study we have ordered them with the greatest diligence for the needs of those wishing to study the medical art. . . . Let us begin with the scruple. A scruple is the weight of twenty grains;[238] two scruples equal forty grains, and three scruples equal sixty grains. Three scruples collected together equal one dram. . . . Eight drams make one ounce. And 108 drams make one pound."[239]

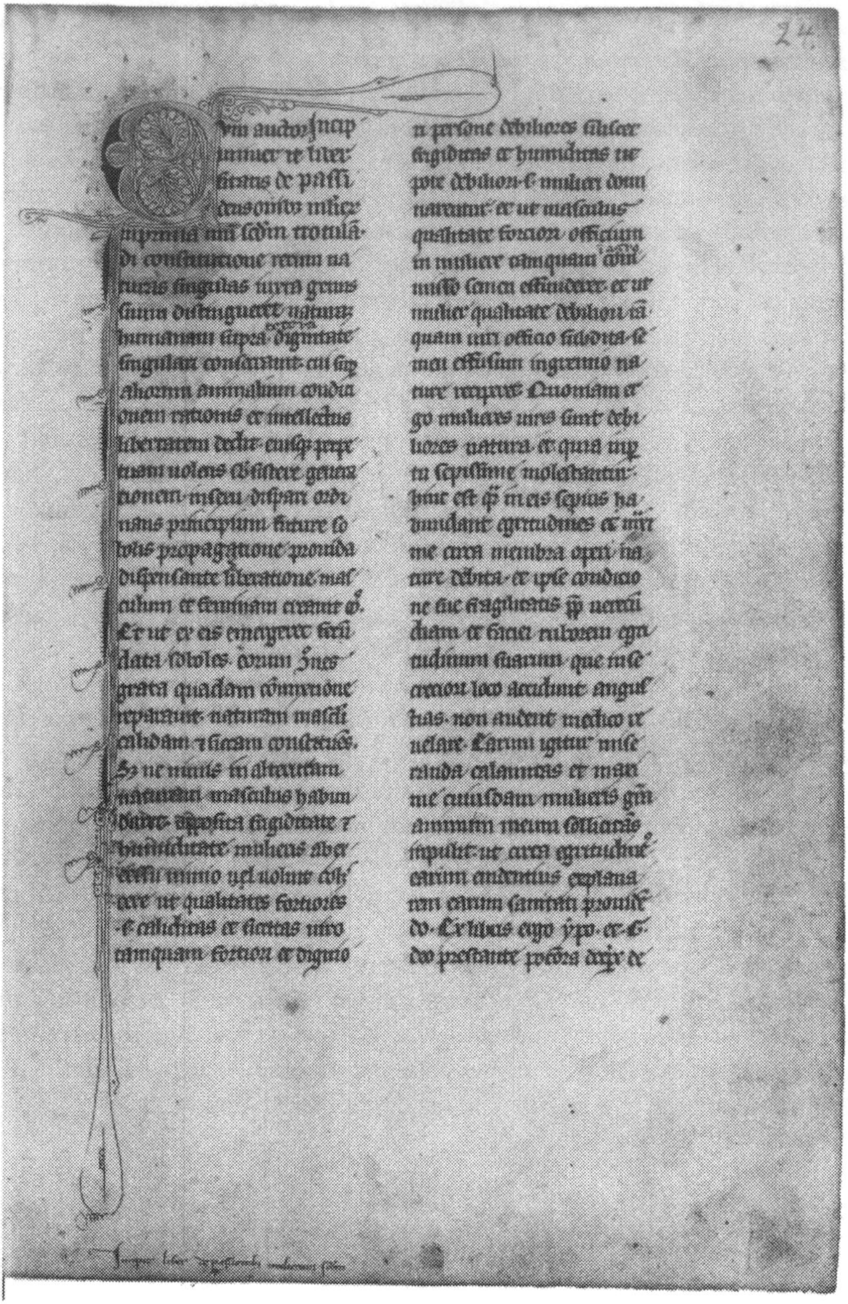

Figure 10: Opening page of the *Trotula* standardized ensemble. Reproduced with permission from Basel, Öffentliche Bibliothek der Universität, MS D.II.17, f. 24r.

[Book on the Conditions of Women]

Here Begins "The Book on the Diseases of Women According to Trotula"[1]

[1] When God the creator of the universe in the first establishment of the world differentiated the individual natures of things each according to its kind, He endowed human nature above all other things with a singular dignity, giving to it above the condition of all other animals freedom of reason and intellect. And wishing to sustain its generation in perpetuity, He created the male and the female with provident, dispensing deliberation, laying out in the separate sexes the foundation for the propagation of future offspring. And so that from them there might emerge fertile offspring, he endowed their complexions with a certain pleasing commixtion, constituting the nature of the male hot and dry. But lest the male overflow with either one of these qualities, He wished by the opposing frigidity and humidity of the woman to rein him in from too much excess, so that the stronger qualities, that is the heat and the dryness, should rule the man, who is the stronger and more worthy person, while the weaker ones, that is to say the coldness and humidity, should rule the weaker [person], that is the woman. And [God did this] so that by his stronger quality the male might pour out his duty in the woman just as seed is sown in its designated field, and so that the woman by her weaker quality, as if made subject to the function of the man, might receive the seed poured forth in the lap[2] of Nature.

[2] Therefore, because women are by nature weaker than men and because they are most frequently afflicted in childbirth, diseases very often abound in them especially around the organs devoted to the work of Nature. Moreover, women, from the condition of their fragility, out of shame and embarrassment do not dare reveal their anguish over their diseases (which happen in such a private place) to a physician.[3] Therefore, their misfortune, which ought to be pitied, and especially the influence of a certain woman stirring my heart, have impelled me to give a clear explanation regarding their diseases in caring for their health. And so with God's help, I have labored assiduously to gather in excerpts the more worthy parts of the books of Hippocrates and Galen,[4] so that I might explain and discuss the causes of their diseases, their symptoms and their cures.

[3] Because there is not enough heat in women to dry up the bad and superfluous humors which are in them, nor is their weakness able to tolerate sufficient labor so that Nature might expel [the excess] to the outside through sweat as [it does] in men, Nature established a certain purgation especially for women, that is, the menses, to temper their poverty of heat. The common people call the menses "the flowers," because just as trees do not bring forth fruit without flowers, so women without their flowers are cheated of the ability to conceive.[5] This purgation occurs in women just as nocturnal emission happens to men. For Nature, if burdened by certain humors, either in men or in women, always tries to expel or set aside its yoke and reduce its labor.

[4] This purgation occurs in women around the thirteenth year, or a little earlier or a little later, depending on the degree to which they have an excess or dearth of heat or cold. It lasts until the fiftieth year if she is thin, sometimes until the sixtieth or sixty-fifth year if she is moist. In the moderately fat, it lasts until the thirty-fifth year.[6] If this purgation occurs at the appropriate time and with suitable regularity, Nature frees itself sufficiently of the excess humors. If, however, the menses flow out either more or less than they ought to, many sicknesses thus arise, for then the appetite for food as well as for drink is diminished; sometimes there is vomiting, and sometimes they crave earth, coals, chalk, and similar things.

[5] Sometimes from the same cause pain is felt in the neck, the back, and in the head. Sometimes there is acute fever, pangs of the heart, dropsy, or dysentery. These things happen either because for a long time the menses have been deficient or because the women do not have any at all. Whence not only dropsy or dysentery or heart pangs occur, but other very grave diseases.

[6] Sometimes there is diarrhea on account of excessive coldness of the womb, or because its veins are too slender, as in emaciated women, because then thick and superfluous humors do not have a free passage by which they might break free. Or [sometimes menstrual retention happens] because the humors are thick and viscous and on account of their being coagulated, their exit is blocked. Or [it is] because women eat rich foods, or because from some sort of labor they sweat too much, just as Ruphus and Galen attest: for in a woman who does not exercise very much, it is necessary that she have plentiful menses in order to remain healthy.

[7] Sometimes women lack the menses because the blood in their bodies is congealed or coagulated. Sometimes the blood is emitted from other places, such as through the mouth or the nostrils or in spit or hemorrhoids.[7] Sometimes the menses are deficient on account of excessive pain or wrath or

agitation or fear. If, however, they have ceased for a long time, they make one suspect grave illness in the future. For sometimes women's urine turns red or into the color of water in which fresh meat has been washed. For the same reason, sometimes their face changes into a green or livid color or into a color like that of grass.

On Retention of the Menses

[8] If therefore the menses are deficient and the women's body is emaciated, bleed her from the vein under the arch of the inside of the foot,[8] the first day from one foot, the following day from the other, and let the blood be drawn off according to what her strength demands, for in every illness one ought generally be cautious and circumspect that the patient is not excessively debilitated.

[9] Galen tells of a certain woman whose menses were lacking for nine months,[9] and she was drawn and emaciated in her whole body, and she almost entirely lacked an appetite. [Galen] drew blood off from her from the aforementioned vein for three days: one pound of blood from one foot on the first day, one pound from the other foot on the second day, and eight ounces from the first foot on the third day. And so in a brief time her color and her heat and her accustomed condition returned to her.

[10] Also, very frequently [a woman's] belly is constipated, and then you should take five pills of any suitable medicine. Then intensify it to the degree that she is able to sustain its intensity, and give it to her. Afterward, bleed her from the saphenous vein.[10] Then let her be bathed, and after the bath let her drink some calamint or catmint or mint cooked in honey so that there are eight parts of water and a ninth of honey. This bath ought to be repeated frequently. And after the bath let her drink one denarius of *diathessaron* or two denarii with honey and water.

[11] *Diathessaron* is made from four plants, that is, mint or myrtleberry, felwort, birthwort, and laurel berry; an equal weight of each should be prepared with cooked honey. Let her take this, just like *hierapigra* or *hieralogodion*.[11]

[12] All diuretic substances are good for her, such as fennel, spikenard, wild celery, cumin, cowbane, caraway, parsley, and similar things. All these herbs together or individually are useful when cooked in wine or drunk with honey.

[13] Galen teaches as follows: mugwort ground with wine and drunk is

very good, or it helps when it is cooked in wine and drunk. In the bath, it helps not a little if catmint is drunk, or cooked in the bath itself. Or let it be tied, fresh and pounded, upon the belly either below the navel or upon the navel, or let it be cooked in a pot and let the woman set a perforated chair over it and let her sit there covered all over and let the smoke come out through a reed, so that the smoke is received inside penetrating through the reed up to the womb.

[14] Mugwort is also very good when mixed with these herbs: deadly carrot, sermountain, sage, oregano, cumin, cowbane, savin, balm, pennyroyal, dill, betony, anise, summer savory, lovage, either all of these or some of them cooked in water. And let one little sack be filled with finely carded wool in the manner of a cushion and let it be dipped in this water and placed warm on the belly. Let this be done frequently.

[15] Likewise, chickweed cooked in an earthenware pot and placed over [the belly] provokes the menses.

[16] Likewise, an excellent powder for provoking the menses: take some yellow flag, hemlock, castoreum, mugwort, sea wormwood, myrrh, common centaury, sage. Let a powder be made and let her be given to drink one dram of this with water in which savin and myrrh are cooked and let her drink this in the bath. And let her be given one dose of one scruple.[12]

[17] But if the womb becomes so indurated that with these aids the menses are not able to be drawn out, take gall of a bull or another gall or powder of natron, and let them be mixed with juice of wild celery or hyssop. And let carded wool be dipped therein, and then let it be pressed so that it is hard and rigid and long so that it can be put into the vagina. And let it be inserted.

[18] Or let there be made another pessary in the shape of the male member, and let it be hollow, and inside there let the medicine be placed and let it be inserted.

On Paucity of the Menses

[19] If women have scant menses and emit them with pain, take some betony or some of its powder, some pennyroyal, sea wormwood, mugwort, of each one handful. Let them be cooked in water or wine until two parts have been consumed. Then strain through a cloth and let her drink it with the juice of fumitory.

[20] If, however, the menses have been deficient for a long time, take two drams of rhubarb, one dram each of dry mugwort and pepper, and let

there be made a powder and let her drink it morning and evening for three days, and let her cover herself so that she sweats.

[21] Likewise, take one handful each of mint, pennyroyal, and rue; three drams of rock salt, one plant of red cabbage, and three heads of leek. Let all these be cooked together in a plain pot, and let her drink it in the bath.

[22] In another fashion, take Florentine iris, lovage, catmint, colocynth, fennel, and rue. Let them be cooked in wine and let this be given to drink.

[23] Another. Let savin, wild celery root, fennel, parsley, lovage, and catmint be cooked in wine, and let this be drunk.

[24] Likewise, take tansy, clover, mugwort, fry with butter, and place upon the navel.

[25] A certain physician made this in the region of France.[13] Take ginger, laurel leaves, and savin. Pound them and place them together in a plain pot on live coals, and let the woman sit upon a perforated seat, and let her receive the smoke through the lower members, and thus the menses will return. Let this be done three or four times or even more often. But for the woman who frequently makes applications of this kind, it is necessary that she anoint her vagina inside with cold unguents lest she becomes excessively heated.

[26] Also good for the above-mentioned conditions is a fumigation of cumin, fennel, dill, calamint, mint, nettle—all these mixed together or individually.

[27] Scarification also works well for the same condition, and coitus likewise. Phlebotomy from the hand, however, is harmful.

[28] If she has no fever, let her eat leeks, onions, pepper, garlic, cumin, and fishes with scales. Let her drink strong wine if she has no pain in the head nor any nervous disorder nor any fever, because wine is harmful in any fever.

On Excessive Flux of the Menses

[29] Sometimes the menses abound beyond what is natural, which has happened because the veins of the womb are wide and open, or because sometimes they break open and the blood flows in great quantity. And the flowing blood looks red and clear, because a lot of blood is generated from an abundance of food and drink; this blood, when it is not able to be contained within the vessels, erupts out. Or sometimes this has happened on account of the excessive heating of the blood caused by bile pouring out from the gall bladder, which makes the blood boil to such an extent that it is not able to be contained in the veins. Or [this has happened] because salty phlegm is mixed with the blood and thins it and makes it erupt out of the veins.

[30] If the blood which flows out turns into a yellowish color, bile is the cause. If into a whitish color, phlegm. If into a reddish color, blood. Illnesses of this kind emerge on account of corrupt humors within, which corruption Nature refuses to sustain. Sometimes it has happened on account of ulceration,[14] from which death very often follows. From these conditions the woman is discolored and she wastes away, and if it last for a long time, it easily changes into dropsy, for the substance of the liver is chilled on account of the subtraction of food through which the organs ought to be preserved in their natural heat. Or sometimes it has happened on account of a defect of heat which is incapable of digesting the abundance of fluids and which is not strong enough to alter the humors in the customary fashion.

[31] The cure. If, therefore, the blood is the cause, let it be bled off from the hand or the arm where the blood is provoked upward. Any sort of gentle cathartic ought also to be taken.

[32] If bile flowing out from the liver is the cause, let *trifera saracenica* and *rosata novella*[15] be given with juice of violets and prickly lettuce.

[33] If it happens from an abundance of phlegm and black bile, let any of the *hieras*[16] be given with warm water (or with wine, according to some people),[17] and let her drink it. After the purgation, there ought to be applied some sort of constrictive both externally and internally. Let her drink, therefore, water in which are cooked the bark of pomegranate, pomegranate skin, roses, oak apples, nutmeg, oak leaves, eglantine, bramble, agrimony, and great plantain. All these mixed together or individually help. After eating or during meals, let there be given to them to drink powder of hematite stone mixed with rainwater, or a powder of coral and gum arabic, pomegranate, myrtleberry seed, and purslane, Armenian bole, and powder of buck's-horn plantain, great plantain, knotgrass, dragon's blood,[18] burnt elephant bones, and quince seed.

[34] Let her eat hens cooked in pastry, fresh fish cooked in vinegar, and barley bread. Let her drink a decoction made from barley, in which great plantain root is first cooked, and boil it with the decoction and it will be even better. And afterward boil [the root] in seawater until it cracks and becomes wrinkled, and let vinegar be added and let it be strained through a cloth and let it be given to drink. Let her drink red wine diluted with seawater. And if great plantain root is boiled with the decoction, so much the better.

[35] And let burning cupping glasses be placed between the breasts so that they draw the blood upward.[19]

[36] Let juice of great plantain be inserted by means of a pessary.

[37] Juice of houseleek is also good if it is drunk with white wine.

[38] Also, juice of pellitory-of-the-wall works well when drunk with wine.

*[39] Likewise, juice of willow-weed works well when applied upon the belly.[20]

[40] Likewise, take two wide slabs of salted bacon, and let powder of coriander together with its seed be sprinkled on top, and powder of wormwood. And let one slab of bacon be tied upon the navel and the other upon the loins.

[41] Also, let two plasters be made from wormwood with animal grease and let them be tied upon the loins and the belly.

[42] And if tender leaves of myrrh that have been ground are applied, it will be even better. And if leaves of elm are applied with them, it will be even better.[21]

[43] In another fashion, take shells of walnut and make a powder and give it in a drink with seawater. Then make a plaster of the dung of birds or of a cat [mixed] with animal grease and let it be placed upon the belly and loins.

[44] Or make a powder of eggshells and give to drink for three days with warm water however much you can lift up with two fingers.

On Suffocation of the Womb

[45] Sometimes the womb is suffocated, that is to say, when it is drawn upward, whence there occurs [stomach] upset and loss of appetite from an overwhelming frigidity of the heart. Sometimes they suffer syncope, and the pulse vanishes so that from the same cause it is barely perceptible. Sometimes the woman is contracted so that the head is joined to the knees, and she lacks vision, and she looses the function of the voice, the nose is distorted, the lips are contracted and she grits her teeth, and the chest is elevated upward beyond what is normal.

[46] Galen tells of a certain woman who suffered thus and she lost her pulse and her voice and she was as if she had expired, because no exterior sign of life was apparent, though around her heart Nature still retained a little bit of heat. Whence certain people judged her to be dead. But Galen put some well-carded wool to her nose and mouth, and by its motion he knew that she was still alive. This [disease] happens to women because corrupt semen abounds in them excessively, and it is converted into a poisonous nature.[22]

[47] This happens to those women who do not use men, especially to widows who were accustomed to carnal commerce. It regularly comes upon virgins, too, when they reach the age of marriage and are not able to use men and when the semen abounds in them a lot, which Nature wishes to draw out by means of the male. From this superabundant and corrupt semen, a certain cold fumosity is released and it ascends to the organs which are called

by the common people the "collaterals," because they are near to the heart
and lungs and the rest of the principal instruments of the voice.23 Whence an
impediment of the voice generally occurs. This kind of illness is accustomed
to originate principally from a defect of the menses. And if both the menses
are lacking and the semen is superabundant, the illness will be so much the
more menacing and wide-ranging, especially when it seizes the higher
organs.

[48] The best remedy is that the hands and feet of the woman be rubbed
moderately with laurel oil and that there be applied to the nose those things
which have a foul odor, such as galbanum, opoponax, castoreum, pitch,
burnt wool, burnt linen cloth, and burnt leather. On the other hand, their
vaginas ought to be anointed with those oils and hot ointments which have a
sweet odor, such as iris oil, chamomile oil, musk oil, and nard oil. For these
things attract and provoke the menses. Let cupping glasses be applied on the
inguinal area and the pubic area. The women ought also to be anointed
inside and out with oils and ointments of good smell. Likewise, in the
evening let her take *diaciminum*24 with the juice of wild celery or with a syrup
of calamint or catmint, or with juice of henbane or juice of catmint. Or take
one dram each of castoreum, white pepper, costmary, mint, and wild celery,
let them be ground, and let them be mixed with white or sweet wine. And
give one dram of it in the evening.

[49] The physician Justianus25 prescribed for this illness that cumin be
dried and given in a potion [in the amount of] one dram or two spoonfuls.
He also prescribed that the penis of a fox or roebuck be taken and made into
a powder and inserted by means of a pessary.

[50] Oribasius ordered that root of common germander and fenugreek
be ground, or linseed, and that their juice be inserted, also juice of danewort.
He also says that what works very well for the same [condition] is root of
lovage cooked and ground with animal grease and tied upon the navel.

On Descent of the Womb

[51] If it happens that after birth the womb descends too far down from its
place, let oats, having first been moistened and put into a sack, be heated and
applied.

[52] Sometimes the womb is moved from its place, and sometimes it
descends, and sometimes it goes all the way out through the vagina. And this
happens on account of a weakening of the ligaments and an abundance of
cold humors inside. A weakening and chilling of this kind happens from cold

air entering in from below through the orifices[26] of the womb, and sometimes if uncovered she has exposed herself directly to cold air, or sat upon a cold stone. And sometimes [this happens] from a bath of cold water, for by this [the womb] is weakened and goes out from its place, and sometimes [it happens] from the effort of giving birth.

[53] Treatment. If it descends and does not come all the way out, aromatic substances ought to be applied to the nose, such as balsam, musk, ambergris, spikenard, storax, and similar things. Let her be fumigated from below with fetid substances, such as burnt linen cloth, and similar things. Let the navel be fomented with wool steeped in wine and with oil.

[54] But if the womb has come out, let aromatic substances be mixed with juice of wormwood, and from these things let the belly be anointed with a feather. Then take rue, castoreum, and mugwort, and let them be cooked in wine until two parts have been consumed, then give it in a potion.

[55] Let the belly and the navel be covered with small sacks filled with cooked grain.

[56] Then let the extruded womb be restored manually to the place from which it was shaken. Afterward, let the woman enter water in which there have been cooked pomegranate, roses, rind of pomegranate, oak apples, sumac, bilberries, the fruit and leaves and bark of oak, and juniper nuts, and lentils.

[57] Then let there be made for them a steambath, which works very well. For Dioscorides prescribes that there be made for them a steambath of boxwood placed in a pot upon live coals, and let the woman, covered on top, sit on it, and let her receive the smoke inside [her vagina].

[58] Let her diet be cold and styptic, without cumin and pepper and all pungent things. For fruit, let her eat quinces, medlars, service-berries, quinces,[27] bitter apples, and similar things. Let her drink wine mixed with warm seawater.

[59] A proven remedy for an extruded womb: Let one ounce each of powder of deer heart[28] and laurel leaves, and one scruple of myrrh be ground and mixed with wine, and let them be given to drink. And thus the womb will be returned to its prior place.

On Movement of the Womb from Its Place

[60] Sometimes the womb is moved from its place, but it is not lifted upward toward the organs of respiration, nor does it extrude outside

through the orifice [of the vagina], nor does it descend. The sign of this is that the woman experiences pain in the left side, retention of the menses, contortion of the limbs, difficulty of urinating, [and] twisting and rumbling of the belly.

[61] Treatment. Take wild celery and fenugreek, and having ground them with wine, give them to drink.

[62] In another fashion, take ground agaric, great plantain seed, savory seed, and powder them and give them in a drink with wine or cooked honey.

[63] So that the vagina not be moved from its place and so that it not be afflicted by any hardness, take deer marrow and goose fat, red wax and butter, of each two ounces. Then take fenugreek and linseed, and cook them in water on a slow fire with the above-mentioned substances until they are fully cooked. And let this be inserted by means of a pessary. This is a necessary remedy for many illnesses of the mouth of the womb.

On Excessive Heat of the Womb

[64] It happens sometimes that the womb is distempered in hotness, so that great burning and heat is felt there. Treat it in this way. Take one scruple of juice of opium poppy, one scruple of goose fat, four scruples each of wax and honey, one ounce of oil, the whites of two eggs, and the milk of a woman. Let these be mixed together and inserted by means of a pessary.

On Lesion of the Womb

[65] Sometimes swellings and lesions of a different color[29] are generated in the womb. If the cause of the lesion is yellow bile coming out of the gall bladder, then she has fever and cancer. If the cause is from cold humors, the lesion is rigid and hard. The woman feels heaviness in the hips, buttocks, and thighs, and in the lower legs accompanied by great pain. Sometimes lesions are generated there from windiness or a blow or from other kinds of injuries, or because the menses never cease.[30] If they are generated in the higher or front part of the womb, pain is felt around the vagina and thence strangury[31] is generated. If the lesion is inside in the orifice of the womb, pain is felt around the navel and the loins. If in the posterior part, pain is felt in the back under the ribs, and the belly is constipated. If the lesion is born of blood or

red bile, there will be chronic or acute fever, thirst, and excessive pain.

[66] If, therefore, it comes from a hot cause, it is expedient that the female parts be anointed, and that blood be drawn from the vein which runs under the foot, just as Galen asserts, not from the hand. For it is harmful if it is drawn from the hand in an affliction of the womb because such a bloodletting draws the blood upward and takes away the menses.[32] On this account, let the blood be drawn from the lower part according to the strength of the patient, and if the woman is strong [enough] that she can stand it, let her be bled twice a day. Afterward, let her take in a drink the water of those things which mitigate heat, such as juice of deadly nightshade, great plantain, houseleek, henbane, mandrake, and similar things. Also, let there be made a plaster which mitigates pain and restores strength, such as from the juice of purslane, houseleek, fleawort, great plantain, prickly lettuce, [and] rose oil. Afterward, let maturatives[33] be applied, such as linseed with butter, marsh mallow, fenugreek, all cooked with goose or hen's fat, egg white, and melilot. From these things, either singly or compounded, let there be made a pessary.

[67] Likewise, Galen[34] says that it is beneficial to sit in water in which spikenard has been cooked.

[68] Paul[35] teaches that there should be made a pessary for hardness of the womb and its inversion and swelling, and for expelling windiness from the body. Take veal marrow and fat of a capon, a squirrel, and a badger[36] in the weight of twelve denarii, and three scruples of buckhorn marrow, two drams of goose and hen's fat, two drams of honey, and the weight of seven denarii of a *cerotum* made of hyssop.[37] Let all these things be ground and commingled and mixed with woman's milk and rose oil, and let it be inserted by means of a pessary, and let there also be made a plaster from this.

[69] If the lesion is cold and it has been generated by thick humors, take fenugreek, melilot, linseed, and rue. Cook in water and from the substance let there be made a plaster, and let the juice be applied in a pessary. Let her often use baths and plasters. Let her diet be subtle so that the grossness of the humors is attenuated. And if we wish to bring the lesion to sanies,[38] let maturatives be applied and substances which rupture the skin so that the sanies will flow out, such as linseed, fenugreek, barley flour cooked together with wheat flour, or beans cooked with the dung of wild doves. If, however, the lesion breaks and the sanies flows out inside [the body] into the bladder, let her drink goats' or asses' milk, or let there be made a pessary of a ptisan and honey and let it be inserted into the womb.

On Ulcers of the Womb

[70] Sometimes the womb is ulcerated from the intensity of a medicine or matter, sometimes from miscarriage; this is recognized by the sanies flowing out and by an ache and stabbing pain of the womb. If there are wounds from sanies and from corrosion of the vein, the sanies will turn a little bit blackish with a horrible stench. First, therefore, there ought to be applied things to clean out the sanies and to mitigate the pain, such as juice of deadly nightshade, great plantain with rose oil, and white of egg with woman's milk and with purslane juice and lettuce, which are by nature cold. Let the diet be cold. Let her be bathed in water where roses, sweet gale, fenugreek, skin of pomegranate, lentils, oak apples, pomegranate, and similar things have been cooked. But if the veins have putrefied, let dragon's blood or myrrh or [Armenian] bole or frankincense or birthwort be given. From these uncompounded things, make an enema or a pessary.

[71] No less useful is acacia with honeysuckle, inserted by means of a pessary.

On Itching of the Vagina

[72] If there is itching of the vagina, take camphor, litharge, laurel berry, and egg white, and let a pessary or enema be made.

[73] Galen[39] says that a powder of fenugreek with goose tallow is good for hardness of the womb, just as Hippocrates attests [too].[40]

On Impediment to Conception

[74] There are some women who are useless for conception, either because they are too lean and thin, or because they are too fat and the flesh surrounding the orifice of the womb constricts it, and it does not permit the seed of the man to enter into [the womb]. Some women have a womb so slippery and smooth that the seed, once it has been received, is not able to be retained inside. Sometimes this also happens by fault of the man who has excessively thin seed which, poured into the womb, because of its liquidity slips outside. Some men, indeed, have extremely cold and dry testicles. These men rarely or never generate because their seed is useless for generation.

[75] Treatment. If a woman remains barren by fault of the man or herself, it will be perceived in this manner. Take two pots and in each one place wheat bran and put some of the man's urine in one of them with the bran,

and in the other [put] some urine of the woman [with the rest of the bran], and let the pots sit for nine or ten days. If the infertility is the fault of the woman, you will find many worms in her pot and the bran will stink. [You will find the same thing] in the other [pot] if it is the man's fault. And if you find this in neither, then in neither is there any defect and they are able to be aided by the benefit of medicine so that they might conceive.

[76] If she wishes to conceive a male, let her husband[41] take the womb and the vagina of a hare and let him dry them, and let him mix the powder with wine and drink it. Similarly, let the woman do the same thing with the testicles of a hare, and at the end of her period let her lie with her husband and then she will conceive a male.

[77] In another fashion, let the woman take the liver and testicles of a small pig which is the only one a sow has borne, and let these be dried and reduced to a powder, and let it be given in a potion to a male who is not able to generate and he will generate, or to a woman and she will conceive.

[78] In another fashion, let the woman take damp wool dipped in ass's milk and let her tie it upon her navel and let it stay there until she has intercourse.

On the Regimen of Pregnant Women

[79][42] Note that when a woman is in the beginning of her pregnancy, care ought to be taken that nothing is named in front of her which she is not able to have, because if she sets her mind on it and it is not given to her, this occasions miscarriage. If, however, she desires clay or chalk or coals, let beans cooked with sugar be given to her. When the time of birth comes, let her be bathed often, let her belly be anointed with olive oil or with oil of violets, and let her eat light and readily digestible foods.

[80] If her feet swell up, let them be rubbed with rose oil and vinegar, and after the remaining foods let her eat poultry, quince, and pomegranate.

[81] If her belly is distended from windiness, take three drams each of wild celery, mint, and cowbane, three drams each of mastic, cloves, watercress, and madder root, five drams of sugar, two drams each of castoreum, zedoary, and Florentine iris. Let there be made a very fine powder, and let it be prepared with honey, and let three scruples of it be given to her with wine. This medicine takes away windiness and [danger of] miscarriage if it is taken as it should be needed.

A Proven Procedure for Becoming Pregnant

[82][43] If a woman wishes to become pregnant, take the testicles of an uncastrated male pig or a wild boar and dry them and let a powder be made, and let her drink this with wine after the purgation of the menses. Then let her cohabit with her husband and she will conceive.

[On Women Who Ought Not Have Sexual Relations with Men]

[83] Galen[44] says that women who have narrow vaginas and constricted wombs ought not have sexual relations with men lest they conceive and die. But all such women are not able to abstain, and so they need our assistance.

On Those Who Do Not Wish to Conceive

[84] If a woman does not wish to conceive, let her carry against her nude flesh the womb of a goat which has never had offspring.

[85] Or there is found a certain stone, [called] "jet," which if it is held by the woman or even tasted[45] prohibits conception.

[86] In another fashion, take a male weasel and let its testicles be removed and let it be released alive. Let the woman carry these testicles with her in her bosom and let her tie them in goose skin or in another skin, and she will not conceive.

[87] If she has been badly torn in birth and afterward for fear of death does not wish to conceive any more, let her put into the afterbirth as many grains of caper spurge or barley as the number of years she wishes to remain barren. And if she wishes to remain barren forever, let her put in a handful.

On Preservation of the Fetus

[88] Galen reports that the fetus is attached to the womb just like fruit to a tree, which when it proceeds from the flower is extremely delicate and is destroyed by any sort of accident. But when it has grown and become a little mature and adheres firmly to the tree, it will not be destroyed by any minor accident. And when it is thoroughly mature it will not be destroyed by any mishap at all. So it is when at first the infant is brought out from the conceived seed, for its ligaments, with which it is tied to the womb, are thin and

not solid, and from a slight [accident] it is ejected through miscarriage. Whence a woman on account of coughing and diarrhea or dysentery or excessive motion or anger or bloodletting can loose the fetus. But when the soul is infused into the child, it adheres a little more firmly and does not slip out so quickly. But when the child has matured, it is led out quickly by the function of Nature. Whence Hippocrates[46] says that if a woman needs purging or bloodletting [during pregnancy], she ought not be purged or let blood before the fourth month. But in the fifth or sixth month, she can be purged or let blood, but nevertheless gently and carefully with a medicine that purges bile or a decoction, and only as much as the strength of the patient is able to tolerate. But beyond this [i.e., what her strength can endure] and before this time purgation is dangerous.

[89] When the time of birth has arrived, the child moves itself vehemently and it exerts itself toward its egress when, in its own time, Nature makes the vagina open so that the fetus finds liberty of its exit. And so the fetus is expelled from its bed, that is to say the afterbirth, by the force of Nature.

On Difficulty of Birth

[90] But there are some women who are so afflicted in the function of birth that hardly ever or never do they deliver themselves, which has to come about from several causes. Sometimes extraneous heat supervenes around the inner organs, whence they are excessively constricted in birth. Sometimes the exit of the womb is too small, either because the woman is too fat, or sometimes because the fetus is dead and cannot aid Nature in its movement. And this last condition happens to a young woman giving birth in the winter when naturally she has a tight orifice of the womb, made more so on account of the coldness of the season, for she is more constricted by the coldness of the air. Sometimes from the woman herself all the heat evaporates and she is left without any strength, and she has none left to help herself [in giving birth].

[91] Treatment. It is expedient for a woman giving birth with difficulty that she be bathed in water in which mallow, fenugreek, linseed, and barley have been cooked. Let her sides, belly, hips, and vagina be anointed with oil of violets or rose oil. Let her be rubbed vigorously and let *oxizaccara*[47] be given in a drink and some powder of mint and wormwood, and let one ounce be given. Let sneezing be provoked with powder of frankincense placed in the nostrils. Let the woman be led about at a slow pace through the house.[48]

[92] And those men who assist her ought not look her in the face, because women are accustomed to be shamed by that during and after birth.[49]

[93] If the child does not come out in the manner in which it ought, as when the legs or arms exit first, let a midwife assist with a small and smooth hand moistened in a decoction of linseed and fenugreek, and let her replace the child in its place and let her put it in its correct position.

[94] If the child is dead, take rue, mugwort, wormwood, and black pepper. This whole mixture, having been ground and given in wine, is good [for this condition], or [when it is given] with water in which lupins have been cooked.

[95] Or let summer savory be ground and tied upon the belly, and the fetus will come out whether it is alive or dead.

[96] This does the same thing: vervain drunk with wine or water or vinegar.

[97] Or let salt water or rose water and ass's milk each be taken, and let it be given to drink.

[98] Or let these names be written on cheese or butter: "+ sa. e. op. ab. z. po. c. zy. e pe. pa. pu c. ac. sator arepo tenet os pera rotas,"[50] and let them be given to eat.

[99] Or let butter be taken with honey and wine and let it be given to drink.

[100] But if birth is up to now still delayed or if the fetus is dead inside her and she is not delivered of it, let her drink "a. ii. i. c. r. z. py. di," the milk of another woman and immediately she will be delivered.[51]

[101] Likewise, take rue, mugwort, opoponax, and wormwood. Let them be ground with some oil and a little sugar and place this upon the pubic area or upon the navel, and it works even better.

[102] Likewise, let the woman be girded with a snake's skin from which the snake has emerged.

[103] Or let the root of gourd be tied to her loins, and let it be taken away as soon as the fetus exits, lest the womb come out after the egress of the child.[52]

[104] If the afterbirth remains inside, haste must be made to eject it. Therefore, let sneezing be provoked, and let this be done with the mouth and nose closed.

[105] In another fashion, let lye be made of cinders from an ash tree and let it be mixed with one dram of powder of the seed of marsh mallow, and let it be given to her to drink and immediately she will vomit.

*[106] And if the blood does not come out, let those things be done which have been said to provoke the menses.[53]

[107] Or let the powder of the seed of marsh mallow itself be given with warm water. And if she vomits, this is good.

[108] And let her be suffumigated from below with the eyes of salty fish or with some horse's hoof[54] or with some dung of a cat or lamb. For these things bring down the afterbirth.

[109] Also it helps to cook linseed in hot water and to give it to drink.

[110] This does the same thing: bdellium with wine.

[111] If, however, the blood does not exit after the afterbirth, let those things be done which have been said to provoke the menses.

[112] If after birth the womb aches, take one dram each of storax, frankincense, and the juice of opium poppy, and two drams of the seed of black grapes. Let them be placed upon some coals and let the woman be suffumigated. This aids greatly.

On the Signs of Pregnancy

[113] In order to know whether a woman is carrying a male or a female, take water from a spring and let the woman extract two or three drops of blood or milk from her right side and let these be dropped in the water. And if they fall to the bottom, she is carrying a male; if they float on top, a female.

[114] Whence Hippocrates says: a woman who is carrying a male is well-colored and her right breast is bigger. If she is pale, she is carrying a female, and the left breast is bigger.[55]

On Difficulty of Birth[56]

[115] Against difficulty of birth arising from constriction of the orifice (which cause is sometimes the most severe of all), we append this counsel. Let the woman herself see to it that in the last three months [of pregnancy] her diet consists of light and digestible foods, so that by means of these the organs are dilated. Such foods are the yolks of eggs, the flesh and innards of young fowl and small birds, that is, partridges and pheasants, and scaly fish with good sauces. Let there be made for them a bath of sweet water, and do this often. And if softening herbs are added to the bath, such as marsh mallow and the like, so much the better. Let her avoid open-air baths and steambaths, and when she comes out of the bath, let her be anointed with hot unguents, such as oil of laurel and oil of linseed and goose or duck or hen's grease. And let this anointing be done from the navel down with the above-mentioned hot unguents.

On the Regimen for a Woman Giving Birth

[116] When the time of birth arrives, let the woman prepare herself as is customary, and likewise the midwife should do the same with great care. And let sneezing be induced with the nose and mouth constricted, so that the greatest part of her strength and spirit tends toward the womb. Then let her be given a decoction of fenugreek, spurge laurel, flax and fleawort, or a little *theriac* or *diathessaron*57 with a decoction of mugwort in wine.

[117] Likewise, let troches58 be made from galbanum with asafetida and myrrh or rue, and let a fumigation be made to the nose. Above all, let her beware of the cold, and let there not be any aromatic fumigation to the nose. But this can be applied more safely to the orifice of the womb, because the womb follows sweet-smelling substances and flees foul-smelling ones. For this, odoriferous spices are good, such as musk, ambergris, aloewood, and similar things, and also odoriferous herbs, such as mint, fennel, oregano, and similar things.

[118] Likewise, it should be noted that there are certain physical remedies whose power is obscure to us, which are helpful when done by midwives. Therefore, let the patient hold a magnet in her right hand and it helps.

[119] Let her drink ivory shavings.

[120] Coral suspended from the neck is good.

[121] Likewise, the white stuff which is found in the excrement of the hawk, given in a potion, is good.

[122] In a similar fashion, the water in which the stone of the firstborn found in the belly of a swallow or in its nest is washed is good for the same condition and for many others.

On the Mode of Generation of the Embryo59

*[123] In the first month, there is purgation of the blood. In the second month, there is expression of the blood and the body. In the third month, [the fetus] produces nails and hair. In the fourth month, it begins to move and for that reason women are nauseated. In the fifth month, the fetus takes on the likeness of its father or its mother. In the sixth month, the nerves are constituted.60 In the seventh month, [the fetus] solidifies its bones and nerves. In the eighth month, Nature moves and the infant is made complete in the blessing of [all] its parts. In the ninth month, it proceeds from the darkness into the light.

On the Regimen for the Infant[61]

*[124] The ears of the infant ought to be pressed immediately, and this ought to be done over and over again. Then, attention needs to be paid that the milk does not enter the ears and the nose when [the child] is nursing. And let the umbilical cord be tied at a distance of three fingers from the belly, because according to the retention of the umbilical cord the male member will be greater or smaller. And so that it might talk all the more quickly, anoint the palate with honey and the nose with warm water, and let it always be cleaned with unctions, and let the mucous secretions always be wiped off and cleaned. And so the child ought always to be massaged and every part of its limbs ought to be restrained and joined by bandages, and its features ought to be straightened, that is, its head, forehead, nose. The belly and loins should be tempered, lest much oiliness or humidity exit from them. If either of these appears, for a time try to abstain from the accustomed bandaging and let it sleep for a while. Then let it be bathed in warm water and let it be restored to the accustomed practice [of binding]. A little bit of soporific medicine should be given so that it sleeps. Its skin ought equally to be massaged, which also is customary to be done after taking the breast. Right after birth its eyes ought to be covered, and especially it ought to be protected from strong light. There should be different kinds of pictures, cloths of diverse colors, and pearls placed in front of the child, and one should use nursery songs and simple words; neither rough nor harsh words (such as those of Lombards) should be used in singing in front of the child. After the hour of speech has approached, let the child's nurse anoint its tongue frequently with honey and butter, and this ought to be done especially when speech is delayed. One ought to talk in the child's presence frequently and easy words ought to be said. When the time for the extrusion of its teeth comes, the gums ought always to be rubbed each day with butter and goose grease, and they ought to be smeared with barley water. The throat and the vertebrae ought to be anointed. If its belly becomes lax, let a plaster which is made from cumin and vinegar and mixed with sugar be placed over it; gum arabic, Armenian bole, and similar things ought to be mixed together and given to the child. But if its belly is constricted, let a suppository be made for it from honey and cotton and mouse dung, which should then be inserted. When the time comes when it begins to eat [solid foods], let lozenges be made from sugar and similar things and milk in the amount of an acorn and let them be given to the infant so that it can hold them in its hand and play with them and suck on them and swallow a little bit of them. The meat of the breast of hens and pheasants and partridges ought to be given because after it

begins to take these things well, you will begin to change reliance upon the breasts and you should not permit the child to suck them at night, as was said above.[62] Thus, it ought to be drawn away [from the breast] day by day and in an orderly way, and care should be taken that it not be weaned during a hot season.

*[125] If one limb of any child is larger than another, it can be reduced to its customary size if the affliction is recent. If it is old, there is no way it can be reduced. For a recent affliction, we aid in this manner. First, let the limb be fomented with a decoction of these herbs, that is, bear's breech with root of marsh mallow and with leaves of wild celery, parsley, and fennel, and all diuretic herbs. Boil these in water. And let the limb of the patient be placed above the vessel, and let it be covered with a linen cloth so that it sweats. Then let chamomile and marsh mallow be cooked in water, and in this thick mixture let wax be melted, and let the whole limb then be covered with this. Afterward, let it be tied tightly with linen bandages, and thus let the limb of the patient sweat through one night; in the morning, let it be rubbed so that the spirits are aroused and flow to the painful part. This having been done, let the limb be rubbed with *dialtea*, thus composed: two parts *dialtea* and a third of laurel oil mixed together; and let the limb be anointed in the above-mentioned manner three or four times a day. Now take *diaceraseos*, *ceroneum*, and *oxicroceum*, and let them be powdered in turn.[63] Then let marsh mallow be cooked and let the powder be softened with this viscous liquid until it adheres well, and let the whole limb of the patient be covered and tied with bandages, and thus it will be able to be ameliorated with fomenting and the application of plasters. These things having been done, let rest and leisure be ordered; let the patient have a warm and moist diet, with good quality, moderately red wine, which s/he should drink until s/he is cured. Let the patient use baths of fresh water.

On Choosing a Wet Nurse

*[126] A wet nurse ought to be young, having a clear color, a woman who has redness mixed with white, who is not too close to her last birth nor too far removed from it either, who is not blemished, nor who has breasts that are flabby or too large, a woman who has a large and ample chest, and who is a little bit fat.

*[127] Her diet. She should not eat salty or spicy or pungent things, nor those things in which heat is strong, nor styptic things, nor leeks or onions, nor the rest of those spices which are added to foods for flavoring, such as

pepper, garlic, garden rocket, but above all garlic. Also, let her avoid anxiety and let her beware provoking her own menses. And if her milk is diminished, let porridges made of bean flour and likewise of rice, and wheat bread and milk and sugar be given to her to drink, by which things the milk is augmented, and let a little fennel seed be mixed in. If, on the other hand, her milk becomes thick, let her nutriment be made subtle, and so let her be compelled to work. In addition, vinegary syrup and light wine ought to be given to her. If the milk becomes thin, let her nutriments be thick and strong, and let her get more sleep. If the bowel of the child is loose, let constipating things be given to the nurse.

On Pustules of Children[64]

*[128] Small pustules arise in children, which ought to be dissolved with ground salt and tied with bandages so that they resolve; neither oily nor sweet things ought to be given to them. If a carbuncle appears in the body of the child, let barley water be given to the nurse, and occasionally let her be scarified. Let her eat neither sweet nor salty things. Also, the [quality of] the woman's milk is recognized in this manner: a drop dropped onto the nail ought to be neither too thin nor too runny nor too thick nor too coagulated; it should have a good odor and a pure sweetness. Salty milk, however, or that which smells bad is not suitable nutriment for the infant.

On Impediment of Conception[65]

*[129] Conception is impeded as much by the fault of the man as by the fault of the woman. The fault of the woman is double: either excessive warmth or humidity of the womb. For the womb at times, because of its unnatural slipperiness, is unable to retain the seed injected into it. And sometimes from its excessive humidity it suffocates the seed. And sometimes she is unable to conceive because of the excessive heat of the womb burning the semen. If, therefore, excessive heat and dryness is the cause, the signs will be these: their lips are ulcerated and excoriated as if from the north wind, they have red spots, unremitting thirst, and loss of hair. When, therefore, you see this, and if the woman is thirty years old and has suffered this for a long time, you will judge it to be untreatable. If she is young and the disease is not chronic, you should aid her in this way: take marsh mallow and mugwort, and cook them in water, and with such a decoction you should fumigate the patient three or

four times. Between these fumigations you will make suppositories and also pessaries for the vagina with musk oil and some musk itself, so that the womb might be strengthened. But on the seventh day after her purgation or after the fumigation has been made, take *trifera magna*[66] in the size of an acorn and similarly wrap it in cotton, and from this you will make a suppository for the vagina, so that from the many fumigations the womb receives some strength, smoothness, and softness, and from the benefit of this suppository and these fumigations it will be dried out, and from this medicine she should receive some strength. On the following day, you will make her have sex with her husband, and if necessary you will use the same treatment the following week, making the above-mentioned fumigations and applying the other remedies, as noted. You should do this until the above-mentioned symptoms have subsided, and you should make her have intercourse twice or three times a week, because thus more quickly will she be able to become pregnant.

*[130] If, on the other hand, she is not able to conceive because of excessive humidity of the womb, these will be the signs: she will have teary eyes constantly. For because the womb is tied to the brain by nerves, it is necessary that the brain suffer with the womb. Whence, if the womb has within itself excessive humidity, from this the brain is filled, which [humidity], flowing to the eyes, forces them involuntarily to emit tears. And because the brain suffers together with the womb, the sign of this is mental distress of the woman [when she suffers] from retention of the menses.[67] Therefore, first of all let her be purged with *Theodoricon euporiston*. Afterward we prescribe that you make three or five pills of the same *Theodoricon* or of *Paulinum*,[68] and also that you wrap them in cotton lest they dissolve, and insert however many you can via the genitals. If the womb has not been well purged, on the second day you will make a pessary in the same manner of *trifera* with some musk. You should do this for a long time until you see that she has been evacuated of the superfluous humidity, and afterward take a little bit of musk with oil or another odoriferous substance which again you insert into the vagina. And if she has been well purged, she will sense the odor [of the musk] in her mouth, and if anyone should kiss her, he will think that she is holding musk in her mouth.[69] Likewise, if she becomes thirsty on account of this purgation, you should know that she has been well purged. And thus purged, let her have intercourse frequently so that she might conceive.

On Sterility on the Part of the Man

*[131] If conception is impeded because of the fault of the man, either this comes about from a defect of the spirit impelling the seed, or from a defect of spermatic humidity, or from a defect of heat. If from a defect of heat, he will not desire intercourse. Whence it is necessary in such men to anoint the loins with *arrogon*,[70] or take rocket seed and spurge and reduce them into a fine powder, and you should mix these with musk oil and pennyroyal oil and anoint the loins. If it happens from defect of the spirits, he will have no desire and he will not be able to have an erection. We aid him with an unguent generative of many spirits. If it is because of a defect of the seed, when they have intercourse they emit little or no semen. We help men such as this with substances which augment and generate seed, such as onions, parsnip, and similar things.

[On Treatments for Women]

Treatment[1]

[132] In order that we might make a concise summary of the treatment of women, it ought to be noted that certain women are hot, while some are cold. In order to determine which, one should perform this test. We anoint a piece of lint with oil of pennyroyal or laurel or another hot oil, and we insert a piece of it the size of the little finger into the vagina at night when she goes to bed, and it should be tied around the thighs with a strong string. And if it is drawn inside, this is an indication to us that she labors from frigidity. If, however, it is expelled, we know that she labors from heat. In either case, assistance ought to be given in this manner.

[133] If she labors from a hot cause, there should be set up a fumigation of cold herbs in this manner. Because contraries are cured by contraries, let us place marsh mallows, violets, and roses in water, and we fumigate her with a decoction of these things.

[134] If, however, she labors from frigidity, which is better, we should make for the woman a fumigation and pessary of pennyroyal and laurel leaves and willow-weed, and thus when the excessive abundance of humors has been cleaned out, she will be ready for conceiving. Afterward we make a fumigation for females[2] which in a marvelous manner is effective and strengthens. Take clove, spikenard, calamite storax, and nutmeg, and let them be placed in an eggshell upon a few hot coals. And let there be prepared a perforated chair so that all the fumes go toward the inside.

On Provoking the Menses

[135] There are some women who, when they come to their time of menstruation, have either no or very few menses. For these, we proceed thus. Take root of the red willow with which large wine jars are tied and clean them well of the exterior bark, and, having pulverized them, mix them with wine or water and cook them, and in the morning give them in a potion when it has become lukewarm. If she labors greatly, we give her things to eat such as

these. We grind madder and marsh mallow, and we mix them with barley flour and white of eggs, and then we make from them little wafers. Also good for provoking the menses is a fumigation made from these same herbs.

[On Immoderate Menstruation]

[136] There are also those others who, on the contrary, have excessive menstruation, whom we aid thus. Take old soles of shoes and pennyroyal and laurel leaves and set them to cook. Once cooked, make a fumigation. Let hot ashes be mixed with hot, red wine and let them be mixed in the manner of a dough, and soften it, and then let some be taken in the form of a small cone and, wrapped in a new linen cloth, let it be inserted lukewarm.

[137] Also, this other one restrains [the menses], which is made thus. Take buck's-horn plantain powdered with ashes of white dead nettle, and let it be diluted with rainwater. We give it to drink, but we do not omit the above-mentioned fumigation, which strengthens cold wombs.[3]

[138] They are also strengthened by this. Take some spikenard, clove, nutmeg, and the rest of the purgatives which we said were good for conception.

[On Those Giving Birth with Difficulty]

[139] But to those giving birth with difficulty[4] we give aid in this manner. We should prepare a bath and we put [the woman] in it, and after she leaves [the bath] let there be a fumigation of spikenard and similar aromatic substances. For strengthening and for opening [the birth canal], let there be sternutatives[5] of white hellebore well ground into a powder. For just as Copho says, the organs are shaken and the cotyledons ruptured and thus the fetus is brought out and comes out.[6]

[On Pain of the Womb after Birth]

[140] For pain of the womb after birth, make a remedy like this. The womb, as though it were a wild beast of the forest, because of the sudden evacuation falls this way and that, as if it were wandering. Whence vehement pain is caused. Therefore, take the tops of elder and grind them and, having extracted the juice, mix with barley flour and with the white of an egg, and then

make little wafers with suet for eating. And we give to these women warm wine to drink in which cumin has been boiled.

On the Preservation of Celibate Women and Widows

[141] There are some women to whom carnal intercourse is not permitted, sometimes because they are bound by a vow, sometimes because they are bound by religion, sometimes because they are widows, because to some women it is not permitted to take fruitful vows.[7] These women, when they have desire to copulate and do not do so, incur grave illness. For such women, therefore, let there be made this remedy. Take some cotton and musk or pennyroyal oil and anoint it and put it in the vagina. And if you do not have such an oil, take *trifera magna*[8] and dissolve it in a little warm wine, and with cotton or damp wool place it in the vagina. This both dissipates the desire and dulls the pain. Note that a pessary ought not be made lest the womb be damaged, for the mouth of the womb is joined to the vagina, like the lips to the mouth, unless, of course, conception occurs, for then the womb withdraws.

[For Conception]

[142] There is another treatment with which we render the womb ready for conception. But because some women are fat, as though they had dropsy, and some women thin, both the former and the latter are incapable of conceiving. Each of them we treat in a different manner. If she is phlegmatic and fat,[9] we should make her a bath of seawater, moderately salty, with rainwater.[10] We put in [various herbs], that is, juniper, catmint, pennyroyal, spurge laurel, wormwood, mugwort, hyssop, and hot herbs of this kind. In this bath she should stay until she sweats sufficiently; afterward let her be received in bed carefully and let her be well covered. And if she desires some food, let her at first be given *rosata novella*.[11] Also, let her be given good and wholesome and warm food, and wine of the best quality taken moderately. Thus let there be made for her a bath three or four times that day, and likewise the following day. On the third day, let there be a very good, strong-smelling fumigation, as we described above.[12] We also do this treatment for cold men, and instead of a fumigation we give them warm strengthening medicines.

[143] If, however, the woman is fat and seemingly dropsical, let us mix cow dung with very good wine and with such a mixture we afterward anoint

her. Then let her enter a steambath up to the neck, which steambath should
be very hot from a fire made of elder [wood], and in it, while she is covered,
let her emit a lot of sweat, and as though in a sweat bath let her remain there
until she has purged herself a little through the inferior members, and that
which comes out will be rather greenish. After she has thoroughly sweated,
let her wash herself with the water of the previous bath, and thus let her cau-
tiously enter her bed. And let this be done twice or three times or four times
a week, and she will be found to be sufficiently thin. You will feed her well,
and let her drink good and sweet-smelling wine. We also render fat men thin
with this treatment.

[For Fat Men]

[144] We also treat fat men in another way. We make for them a grave next
to the shore of the sea in the sand, and in the described manner you will
anoint them, and when the heat is very great we place them halfway into the
grave, halfway covered with hot sand poured over. And there we make them
sweat very much. And afterward we wash them very well with the water of
the previous bath.

On Extracting the Dead Fetus

[145] Those who labor excessively in giving birth to a dead fetus we assist
thus. Let us place the patient on a linen sheet and let us have it held by four
strong men at the four corners, the head of the patient a little bit elevated.
We will make the sheet be pulled strongly this way and that at the opposite
corners, and immediately she will give birth.

On Retention of the Afterbirth

[146] There are some women to whom the afterbirth remains inside after
birth, to whom we give aid for its expulsion thus. We extract the juice of a
leek and mix it with pennyroyal oil or musk oil or juice of borage, and let us
give it to drink, and immediately [the afterbirth] will be brought out perhaps
because she will vomit and from the effort of vomiting it will come out. Nevertheless, the juice itself has such a power that it is sufficient for expulsion.

On Excessive Flow of Blood After Birth

[147] There are other women who after birth have an immoderate flow of blood, to whom we give aid thus. Let us extract the juice of mugwort, sage, pennyroyal, willow-weed, and other herbs of this kind, and let us make little wafers and we give them to eat. And let us place them frequently in baths, and in the above-mentioned manner we aid them in order to restrain the blood.

[148] Or otherwise, take clay and mix it with vinegar and make a plaster for the liver on the right side. And if the blood flows through the nose, we place some of this plaster on the forehead and the temples, stretching sideways across the temples and the forehead. And note that this flow from the nose does not happen unless she has borne a son.

On the Dangerous Things Happening to Women Giving Birth

[149] There are some women for whom things go wrong in giving birth, and this is because of the failure of those assisting them: that is to say, this is kept hidden by the women.[13] For there are some women in whom the vagina and the anus become one opening and the same pathway. Whence in these women the womb comes out and hardens. We give aid to such women by repositioning [the womb]. We put on the womb warm wine in which butter has been boiled, and diligently we foment it until the womb has been rendered soft, and then we gently replace it. Afterward we sew the rupture between the anus and the vagina in three or four places with a silk thread. Then we place a linen cloth into the vagina to fill the vagina completely. Then let us smear it with liquid pitch. This makes the womb withdraw because of its stench. And we heal the rupture with a powder made of comfrey, that is, of bruisewort, and daisy[14] and cumin. The powder ought to be sprinkled [on the wound], and the woman should be placed in bed so that her feet are higher [than the rest of her body], and there let her do all her business for eight or nine days. And as much as necessary let her eat; there let her relieve herself and do all customary things. It is necessary that she abstain from baths until she seems to be able to tolerate them. Also, it is fitting that she abstain from all things that cause coughing and from all things that are hard to digest, and this especially ought to be done. In [subsequent] birth we should aid them thus. Let a cloth be prepared in the shape of an oblong ball and place it in the anus, so that in each effort of pushing out the child, it is to be pressed into the anus firmly so that there not be [another] solution of continuity of this kind.[15]

On the Exit of the Womb and Its Treatment

[150] There are also some women to whom it happens that the womb comes out from another cause, such as those who are not able to tolerate the virile member because of its magnitude or length; having been forced all the same, they endure it. But when [the womb] comes out, it hardens. For such women we offer aid in the above-mentioned manner.[16] And if we do not have pitch, we take a cloth and anoint it with warm pennyroyal oil or musk oil, and then we squeeze it and we smear it on or lay it on the vagina, and we tie it on until the womb recedes by itself and becomes warm. For this condition, we suggest that whatever causes coughing not be eaten.

On the Entry of Wind into the Womb

[151] There are some women who take in wind through the vagina, which, having been taken into the right or left part of the womb, generates so much windiness that they seem to be suffering from a rupture or intestinal problem.[17] Whence it happened that Trotula[18] was called in as a master of this operation[19] when a certain young woman was about to be operated on for a windiness of this kind as if she suffered from rupture, and she was thoroughly astonished. Therefore, she made her come to her own house so that in secret she might determine the cause of the disease. Whereupon, she recognized that the pain was not from rupture or inflation of the womb[20] but from windiness. And so she saw to it that there be made for her a bath in which marsh mallow and pellitory-of-the-wall were cooked, and she put her into it. And she massaged her limbs frequently and smoothly, softening them, and for a long time she made her remain in the bath. And after her exit, she made for her a plaster of the juice of wild radish and barley flour, and she applied to her the whole thing somewhat warm in order to consume the windiness. And again she made her sit in the above-mentioned bath, and thus she remained cured.

On Exit of the Anus

[152] Protrusion of the anus is an affliction common to men as well as women, and it causes the blood to flow. In order to restrain the blood and replace the anus, we give aid in this manner. First, we should foment the patient with a decoction of wine in which wormwood has been boiled, and with this decoction we should foment the anus, and we smear it well all over

with ink[21] in order to constrict it. After having made ashes from willow and its root and the spine of any sort of salty fish, we sprinkle them [over the anus] and replace the anus with a linen cloth. Let this be done for three days twice a day and [the patient] will be healed.

[153] There are also others[22] in whom the anus does not come out; rather, they suffer intense pain, and to these we give aid in such a manner. We pulverize aloe and mix it with warm wine. While it is still lukewarm, dip linen or wool or cotton in it and place it in the anus; this diminishes the pain and takes away the swelling of the anus.

On Swelling of the Penis

[154][23] There are some men who suffer swelling of the virile member, having there and under the prepuce many holes, and they suffer lesions. To these we offer aid in this manner. We boil marsh mallow in water and, having boiled it, we squeeze it out so that no water remains. Afterward we grind it up with warm suet or butter without salt, or with oil, and we place it on the fire. Having placed it warm on cabbage leaves and on a linen cloth, we wrap it around the virile member. This makes the swelling go away. Then, with the prepuce turned out, we wash the ulcerous or wounded neck of the prepuce with warm water, and sprinkle on it powder of Greek pitch and dry rot of wood or of worms and rose and root of mullein and bilberry. And if you lack bilberry, these [other] four herbs are sufficient. And let this be done twice or three times each day until he is cured.

On Pain of the Intestine

[155] There happens to some people[24] pain of the intestine. For these we offer aid thus. We cook black nightshade in water with ash and we place it upon the painful spot.

*[156] Or alternately, we cook raw sesame with [its] seed, and we place it upon the pain.

On Strangury

[157] Both men and women suffer strangury.[25] For men we should proceed thus. We place cooked watercress on the pubic area, and we put the patient in a decoction of the same [herb]. Women, indeed, labor from this same

affliction, for whom we make a fumigation of horsemint, catmint, and pennyroyal. For both men and women we should make a steambath, and place them in water in which juniper, catmint, fleabane and horsemint, laurel leaves, pennyroyal, wormwood, [and] mugwort have been boiled, and in the bath we give [to them] uncompounded hemlock.[26] And thus the patient is freed even if s/he has a bladder stone because, so long as it is not yet solidified, patients purge it through their urine as if little grains of sand were coming out.

On the Stone

[158] Likewise for the stone we cook saxifrage in water, which we give in a drink to those suffering from the stone. And if they desire wine, with water of this kind we dilute it. We do this twice a day for four or five days, either twice or three times a day. It should be noted that if they do not urinate, a sign is given to us that the stone has solidified.

[159] Here follow some treatments of Master Ferrarius[27] for breaking up or drawing out the stone if it is in the neck of the bladder. Take marsh mallow, rock samphire, wild cabbage, saxifrage, pellitory-of-the-wall, and *senationes*, that is, watercress, cowbane, [and] nettle seed. Cook these in a liquor of which a third part is wine, a third oil, and a fourth seawater or saltwater; with this decoction we should foment well, drawing those herbs especially around the parts. With this treatment he [Master Ferrarius] freed a certain man[28] having a stone in the bladder, which after a long fomentation he had extracted by sucking through an opening made around the perineum, and he had the penis anointed, and especially the head of the penis, with oil of laurel and *unguentum aureum*.[29]

On Flux from a Lesion

[160] There are some women who suffer, or who seem to suffer, from flux of a lesion or flux of semen[30] in the womb, just as there are some old women who emit a sanious flux. To these, in order to provoke the menses, aid ought to be given thus because they are sterile.[31]

[161] And there are other sterile women who in a similar manner emit a sanies. And this happens at the time when the menses are accustomed to come to them. For when their menses are denied to them, instead of the

menses they emit sanies because of their frigidity, as if a hot flux were descending from the liver. To such women aid ought to be offered thus. We should make for them a fumigation from wine or water in which the above-mentioned hot herbs[32] are cooked. Afterward we mix *trifera magna* in pennyroyal oil or musk oil, and in a linen or woolen or cotton cloth we wrap it up and place it in the vagina.

[162] There are also other young women who labor in the same manner on account of failure of the menses, but these women are freed when the menses are provoked. And it ought to be noted that some hot women are rendered sterile, yet they do not labor from this kind of flux but remain dry as though they were men.

[163] There are some women who have a sanious flux together with the menses. Such women we make to sit upon a mass of wild rocket cooked in wine, a linen cloth having been interposed while it is still warm.

[164] Likewise for the same: take powdered pennyroyal and let it be placed in a small sack which is made as long as it is wide, so that both sides of the private parts can be tied, which sack the patient ought to wear upon her vagina in order to prevent the flux. But before it is tied on, it ought to be warmed by the fire so that the anus as well as the vagina might be strengthened.

On Wind Enclosed Within the Womb

[165] There are some women, as we said,[33] who take in wind through the female members, which, once it has been taken in, causes pain and swelling. These women we foment with a decoction of mustard or turnip.

[On Itching and Excoration of the Pudenda]

[166] In these same women sometimes these parts itch, which they excoriate in trying to scratch them. Sometimes there arise pustules which turn into a very large lesion. Hence, we should anoint these parts with an unguent which is good against burns caused by fire or hot water, and for excoriations of this kind. Take one apple, [Armenian] bole, mastic, frankincense, oil, warm wine, wax, and tallow, and prepare them thus. We should place the apple, cleaned of both the exterior and interior rind and ground, on the fire in a pot with the oil, wax, and tallow; and when they have boiled, we put in

the mastic and the frankincense, both of which have been powdered. Afterward, it should be strained through a cloth. Note that if anyone because of any burn has been anointed with this ointment, on the anointed place there ought to be put a leaf of ivy cooked in wine or vinegar, or a leaf of gladden. This remedy is decent.[34]

[Ointment for Sunburn][35]

[167] An ointment that the Salernitan women make that is very good for sunburn and fissures of any kind, and especially for those caused by wind; and it is good for pustules caused by the air and blemishes and excoriations of the face. Take one ounce of lily root, two ounces of white lead, mastic and frankincense—of each a half dram—, one dram of camphor, one ounce of animal grease, [and] rose water as needed. Let it be prepared thus: let the lily root, having been cleaned, be cooked in water, and once this is extracted we grind it thoroughly. And we pour in the fat, which has been liquefied on the fire and well strained and cleaned of its salt in order to dissolve it. Then we put in the white lead, which has been dissolved in the rose water and somewhat pulverized. And note that this ointment is good both for the treatment of the above-mentioned conditions and for their prevention. And so with this ointment the patient ought to anoint herself in the evening in front of the fire, so that in the morning they might preserve themselves in the daylight hours from the above-mentioned conditions, that is to say from sunburn and fissures and pustules and things of this kind whether caused by the air or the heat of the sun. This [ointment] raises the skin and colors it beautifully. In the morning it need not be removed with washings or by any other [means] from the face, because it does not detract from the color in whatever manner it is spread on or put on. This is the ointment with which the Salernitan women anoint themselves for rivulets and floods [of tears?] made in mourning the dead; also it is good for suppressing pustules in lepers and it is a good cleanser.[36]

On Those Who Wet Their Beds

[168] There are some women who urinate in their beds at night, whether they want to or not, because their urinary passages suffer paralysis. These women we foment with hot herbs.

[On Those Suffering from Dysentery]

[169] There are some women suffering from dysentery whom we do not treat before twenty days.[37] Sometimes the cause is bile, sometimes phlegm. Against dysentery caused by phlegm first we fumigate with thyme, thyme dodder, or Greek tar. Afterward, we foment them with wild rocket. Against dysentery caused by bile, we should boil roses in rainwater and we soak cotton in it and place it in the anus.

On Flesh Growing in the Womb

[170] There are some women in whom pieces of flesh hang from the womb. And note that this happens to them from semen retained inside and congealed, because they do not clean themselves after intercourse. These women we always foment with a decoction of hot herbs.

On Treatment of Lice

[171] For lice which arise in the pubic area and armpits, we mix ashes with oil and anoint.

[172] And for lice which are around the eyes, we should make an ointment suitable for expelling them and for swelling[38] of the eyes and soothing them. Take one ounce of aloe, one ounce each of white lead[39] and frankincense, and bacon as needed. Let it be prepared thus. We grind the bacon very finely and we place [in it] the remaining ingredients which have been powdered.

On Treatment of Scabies[40] in Humans

[173] For scabies of the hips and other parts, a very good ointment. Take elecampane, vinegar, quicksilver, as much oil as you like, and animal grease. Let it be prepared thus. Take root of the elecampane, clean it and cut it very finely, and cook it in the vinegar. After it has been well cooked, grind it in a mortar with the grease. Then put in the quicksilver with the oil and with the vinegar in which the dissolved elecampane has been cooked. This ointment is also good for those who excoriate themselves[41] because of itching. Note that

if anyone[42] should anoint him- or herself with this ointment, let him/her keep cold water in his/her mouth lest the teeth be damaged by the quicksilver, which flows around every which way.

On Whitening the Face

[174] For whitening the face, take root of bistort and clean it, and root of cuckoo-pint. Grind them in a mortar with animal grease and mix them with warm water, and strain through a cloth. And afterward stir [the mixture] well and thus let it sit all night. And in the morning gently remove the water, pouring in fresh water; water made from honeysuckle as well as from roses is the best thing for this. You should do this for five days. This is done to repress [the herbs'] harsh properties lest they cause lesions to the face. On the sixth day, having thrown out the water, expose [the mixture] to the sun and let it dry, and afterward take three parts of white lead and a fourth of camphor, and one dram each of borax and gum arabic. We dissolve the borax in rose water, rubbing it between the hands. All these we mix with rose water. Note that when you wish to whiten the face, take from this [mixture] a quantity the size of a bean and mix it with cold water and, rubbing a little between the hands, with both hands we anoint the face, but first we should wash the face with water and soap. Then we sprinkle [the face] with cold water and we place on it a very delicate cloth; this should be done either in the morning or in the evening. And note that it lasts for three days or four.

On Making the Face Red

[175] For making the face red, take root of red and white bryony and clean it and chop it finely and dry it. Afterward, powder it and mix it with rose water, and with cotton or a very fine linen cloth we anoint the face and it induces redness. For the woman having a naturally white complexion, we make a red color if she lacks redness, so that with a kind of fake or cloaked whiteness a red color will appear as if it were natural.

For Removing Wrinkles

[176] For wrinkled old women, take stinking iris, that is gladden,[43] and extract its juice, and with this juice anoint the face in the evening. And in the

morning the skin will be raised and it will erupt, which rupture we treat with the above-mentioned ointment in which root of lily is employed.[44] And first pulling off the skin,[45] which after the rupture has been washed, it will appear very delicate.

On Freckles of the Face

[177] For freckles of the face which occur by accident, take root of bistort and reduce it to a powder, and cuttlefish bones and frankincense, and from all these things make a powder. And mix with a little water and then smear it, rubbing, on the hands[46] in the morning, rubbing them with rose water or water of bran or with breadcrumbs until you have removed [the freckles].

On Stench of the Mouth

*[178] For stench of the mouth caused by a disorder of the stomach, let the tips of myrtleberry be ground and cooked in wine until reduced by half and, with the stomach having been purged, let the wine be given to drink.

On Removing Redness of the Face

[179] For removing redness from the face, we put on leeches[47] of various colors, which are in reeds, but first we wash with wine the place to which they ought to adhere; they are usually placed around the nose and ears on both sides. Or we place cupping glasses between the shoulder blades.

For Veins in the Face

[180] For veins which appear in the nose or on the face, we apply to the place three parts soap and a fourth part pepper, [all] powdered, and we cure it in the above-mentioned manner.[48]

On Gout of the Mouth

[181] For gout of the mouth, we wash the mouth with warm wine, rubbing the teeth well, and this in the morning and the same thing in the evening.

Later we spread around rose oil[49] during the night and she will be freed in a short time.

For Black Teeth

[182] For black and badly colored teeth, take walnut shells well cleaned of the interior rind, which is green,[50] and we rub the teeth three times a day, and when they have been well rubbed, we wash the mouth with warm wine, and with salt mixed in if desired.

On Treating Cancer

[183] We wash a cancer wherever it is in the body, and we sprinkle over it a powder made of cumin[51] and green copper. And when it has become necrotic, we foment it as befits a dried-out, afflicted place. We anoint it with this ointment: Take frankincense, mastic, wax, oil, Greek pitch, galbanum, aloe, wormwood, mugwort, pellitory-of-the-wall, rue, and sage. Prepare them thus. Let the herbs be ground and let the oil be poured in and mixed upon the fire, and when it is exceedingly hot, strain the oil and place it again upon the fire, and when it begins to boil let the wax be added. Afterward let the other things, which have been powdered and cooked, be strained and added. The sign of thorough cooking is when a drop placed upon marble stays there and hardens. And note that leaves of wild ivy, cooked in wine and laid upon the cancerous place, work very well.

On Fissures of the Lips

[184] There are some women who suffer from fissures of the lips, and this on account of the excessive embraces of their lovers and their kisses with their lips rubbing between them. For in the morning her lips are found to be cracked, dried by the heat. We treat these women with an ointment made of fleawort or with the unguent made from lily.[52]

[185] Likewise there are other women who suffer fissures caused by the air and the wind and similar causes. For these, then, we anoint the lips with honey, and afterward we sprinkle on powdered Greek pitch.

[186] And another way, according to Master Ferrarius:[53] take walnut and cook it under some ashes, and grind the core. And after tartar has been put on, apply [the walnut] to the fissure and it will be healed.

On Loosening of the Teeth

[187] There are some women in whom the teeth are loosened by the cold. These we treat in this manner. We make them take in their mouth wine in which ginger and galangal have been boiled, and after this ablution we sprinkle powder of frankincense around the teeth. And for those who have an excoriated palate, we have the mouth washed with this same wine, and afterward we apply alum with sugar.[54]

On the Fall of the Uvula

[188] For those who suffer from fall of the uvula, we offer aid thus. We cook a powder of ginger, pellitory, and cinnamon in wine and we make them gargle, and we apply a powder of these hot things to the uvula.

On Prolapse of the Vagina of Women

[189] In prolapse of the vagina[55] after birth we place a tampon, pressing it so that it does not come out except when she urinates. On the third day we make her bathe. Also we make the powders mentioned above in later [chapters] be blown through the nostrils lest they become swollen.[56]

A Good Constrictive

[190] A constrictive for the vagina so that they may appear as if they were virgins. Take the whites of eggs[57] and mix them with water in which pennyroyal and hot herbs of this kind have been cooked, and with a new linen cloth dipped in it, place it in the vagina two or three times a day. And if she urinates at night, put it in again. And note that prior to this the vagina ought to be washed well with the same warm water with which these things were mixed.

[191] Take the newly grown bark of a holm oak. Having ground it, dissolve it with rainwater, and with a linen or cotton cloth place it in the vagina in the above-mentioned manner. And remove all these things before the hour of the commencement of intercourse.

*[192] Likewise take powder of natron or blackberry and put it in; it constricts [the vagina] marvelously.[58]

[193] Likewise, there are some dirty and corrupt prostitutes who desire to seem to be more than virgins and they make a constrictive for this purpose, but they are ill counseled, for they render themselves bloody and they wound the penis of the man. They take powdered natron and place it in the vagina.[59]

[194] In another fashion, take oak apples, roses, sumac, great plantain, comfrey, Armenian bole, alum, and fuller's earth, of each one ounce. Let them be cooked in rainwater and with this water let the genitals be fomented.

[195] What is better is if the following is done one night before she is married: let her place leeches in the vagina (but take care that they do not go in too far) so that blood comes out and is converted into a little clot. And thus the man will be deceived by the effusion of blood.

On Swelling of the Vagina

[196] The vagina of women sometimes swells in coitus.[60] Let the woman sit in water where there have been cooked marsh mallows and pennyroyal, and she will be freed.

For Swelling of the Face

[197] For sudden swelling of the face, a fumigation of hot water alone suffices.

*[198] Likewise for swelling of the same and of the eyes, let fresh pork grease be ground with groundsel and let it be applied upon [the swelling].

On Warts

[199] For removing warts, with a needle we lift them up all around. Afterward we apply slaked lime to the place, and so we remove them. Then we heal [the wound] with the ointment made of lily.[61]

On Pain of the Breasts

[200] For pain of the breasts caused by milk, we should mix clay with vinegar and make a plaster; this diminishes the pain and constricts the milk. But first we should foment the place with warm water.

On Lesions of the Breasts

[201] There are some women who have lesions in the breasts. For this we make a maturative from marsh mallow and mayweed, wormwood, mugwort, and animal grease, and when the head [of the lesion] appears, grind together nuts and apply them. And if it does not rupture let it be opened with a lancet, and press out a little in the beginning lest by a sudden evacuation it becomes bad, and each day apply a lint twice or three times smeared with egg yolk.

[202] But if this place has become fistulous, with a probe you will be able to determine this. Put in root of black hellebore cleaned and dipped in oil or honey. Place a powder of burnt burdock upon [the fistula] and sprinkle it on, too. For this cleans every fistula and makes it become necrotic, as long as it is not between any bones. And this ought to be applied there until it has dried and become necrotic. Afterward it will be treated like any other wound.

[203] Note that the pain which occurs in the breasts of young women passes easily, for this distress is healed with the eruption of the menses, because in certain girls laboring from the falling sickness it happens from suffocation of the womb compressing the organs of respiration.[62]

On Cough of Children

[204] For the disease of children which is like a very harsh cough,[63] we give aid thus. Take hyssop and pellitory of Spain, cook them in wine, and we give it to drink. Or we mix grains of juniper with wine and we give it.

On Foul-Smelling Sweat

[205] There are some women who have sweat that stinks beyond measure. For these we prepare a cloth dipped in wine in which there have been boiled leaves of bilberry, or the herb itself or the bilberries themselves.

On Swelling of the Vagina

[206] For swelling of the vagina. Take pennyroyal, fleabane, and four fronds of laurel, and boil them in water, and you should make her sit in this water, and afterward make a fumigation from all these [herbs].

For Antlike Itching and Itch-Mites

[207] For antlike itches and itch-mites wherever they might be in the body, especially in the face and on the forehead, we mix grain with wine, and with a powder of frankincense applied in the manner of a plaster, we place it on the [afflicted] spot.

On Pain of the Eyes

[208] For pain[64] of the eyes, take marsh mallow, the herb of violets, tips of bramble, dried roses, vervain, and sermountain. [With this] foment the eyes in the evening, and make a plaster from the same herbs with white of egg, and apply it.

On Web of the Eye

[209] If there is a web in the eye, take conch and frankincense and burn them. [Also take] cuttlefish bone that has not been burned. Pulverize them and place them on the eyes twice or three times a week.

[210] If this occurs from phlegm, take mountain germander, pennyroyal, laurel leaves, oregano, and caraway, and foment the eyes.

[211] An ointment for the same. Take two parts of aloe, and as much frankincense and plaster of Paris[65] as of the aloe; pulverize them finely and prepare them with fresh animal grease and anoint the place.

On Cancer of the Nose

[212] For cancer of the nose, take lungwort, sage, Greek tar, wild garlic, and "blacking," that is, earth of the countryside,[66] and pulverize them all equally. But before you apply this powder, wash the place with warm wine in which wormwood has been cooked. Afterward, place upon it the above-mentioned powder.

[For Provoking the Menses]

[213] For provoking the menses, take vervain and rue, and pound them heavily, and cook them with bacon, and give them to the patient to eat. Afterward, grind root of delicate willow and root of madder, and give the juice to the patient with wine.

[For Pain of the Womb]

[214] For pain of the womb when it rises due to its hardness, take saxifrage, sea holly, old cabbages, mugwort, marsh mallow, and root of dove's-foot cranesbill. Cook all these herbs in water thoroughly, and make the patient sit in it up to her breasts. And when she exits from the bath, pound marsh mallow, mugwort, and camphor, and warm these pounded things in a pot, and make lozenges with laurel oil or a little pennyroyal oil, and insert them as a suppository.

On Swelling of the Feet

[215] Sometimes it happens that the feet are swollen due to pain of the womb. Then take sea brambles and cook them in sea- or saltwater, and fumigate the feet often. And after the fumigation, when the mixture has become lukewarm, you will wash the feet.

[For Restraining the Menses]

[216] For restraining the menses, take sage and camphor,[67] pound them thoroughly, and make little wafers with wine, and cook them upon a tile, and give them to the patient. Afterward, take nettle seed and buck's-horn plantain, and give a powder made of this to drink with wine.

[On Cutting the Umbilical Cord]

[217] When the umbilical cord of the child is cut, you should say as follows, holding the stump extended: "Jesus Christ is dead, he was pierced by the lance, and he took no thought of any ointment or of his pain or of any unguent."[68] But first tie the umbilical cord, and afterward, having said this charm, wrap it with a string of an instrument that is plucked or bowed or some other musical instrument.[69] And if [the child] feels pain, for nine days give it to drink *trifera magna* in the amount of a chickpea [mixed] with milk or wine or water.

On Itch-Mites of the Hands and Feet

[218] For extracting the worm from the hands and the feet, that is, the itch-mite, which in English is called *degge*,[70] take a heated brick and any kind of

vessel full of water, and afterward let henbane seed be placed upon the burning brick. And let the patient hold her feet above the smoke, and you will see
the worms falling into the water just like hairs.

[219] Likewise take oat chaff and burn it to ashes. Afterward let there be
applied water as warm as the patient is able to stand it, and let her leave her
feet there until they have become cold. Then let it be strained so that none of
the water remains, and let the ashes be squeezed well so that the water goes
out, and let them be separated bit-by-bit, and there will be found worms just
like threads [extracted] by the smoke of the henbane. In a similar fashion
itch-mites of the hand fall out.

[220] Note that if the place is corroded by the worms, take chaff and
incinerate it and afterward let it be placed in warm water. And in water as hot
as she is able to stand it let the limb of the patient be placed, and the worms
will come out; afterward let the place be healed just like any other wound.[71]

For Deafness of the Ears

*[221] For deafness of the ears. Take the fatty residue of fresh eels which
appears after cooking them, and juice of honeysuckle, and houseleek, and a
palmful of ants' eggs; grind them and strain them. And let all these things be
mixed together with oil and cooked. After the cooking, let vinegar be added
to it so that it might be the more penetrating, or wine as suffices. And pour it
into the healthy ear and stop up the afflicted one, and let [the patient] lie
upon the healthy part. And in the morning let him take care that he come
near no draft. And make him for a little while lie on the healthy ear, and again
upon the afflicted one.

For Worm of the Ears

*[222] Likewise for worm of the ears. Take an apple and hollow it out and
place in on the ear, and if there is any worm, it will come out.

For Swelling of the Testicles

[223] A fomentation for swollen testicles. Take marsh mallow, wormwood,
vervain, marsh mallow,[72] henbane, mugwort, and cabbages. Let all these be
cooked in strong or old wine, and you will foment [the testicles] two or three

times a day. And grind these herbs and mix them with honey and boil them; apply this with wine.

[For Tumors]

[224] Mugwort applied warm or ground dissolves tumors. Also, when ground in wine and cooked in honey [and] placed upon tumors of the face,[73] it softens, matures, and attenuates them.

On Pain of the Womb

[225] Pain of the womb happens from miscarriage, [or] sometimes before that time from retention of the menses.[74] This happens often from frigidity, but only rarely from heat. If from frigidity, the sign is ache and a stabbing pain on the left side. Treatment. Take pennyroyal, oregano, catmint, fronds of laurel or its grains, and marsh mallows, make them boil in water and then foment the patient. Afterward, take clove, spikenard, nutmeg, and galangal, and let a fumigation be made, and let her receive the smoke through a funnel. Then apply *trifera magna* or the potion of Saint Paul[75] in the amount of a hazelnut with [a piece of] cotton.

[226] If, however, [the pain] comes from heat, the womb is dried out and made hot from the use of Venus.[76] The sign is that there is excessive warmth around these parts. Treatment. Take marsh mallow, herb of violets, roses, and root of rush, and cook them thoroughly in water, and foment the patient, and put on *trifera saracenica*[77] the whole day.

[For Exit of the Womb after Birth]

[227] For exit of the womb after birth, take juniper, camphor, wormwood, mugwort, and fleabane,[78] and cook them in water, and bathe the patient [in this water] and make her sit in it up to her breasts. And afterward gently put her in bed, so that she lies suspended by the feet so that the womb may be inverted into its proper place. And with the womb having been put back inside, take a powder of these spices, that is, pennyroyal, galangal, spikenard, nutmeg, [and] clove, and combine them and mix them with musk oil or pennyroyal oil. And take an old linen cloth, thin and fine, and tie inside it these powders, and form the cloth with all these powders in the shape of a ball. The womb having been put back in, stuff up the mouth of the vagina with

this ball so that the womb does not come out again, and tie the ball on here with bandages so that it is not able to come out, and you should make [the bandages] go across in the back up to the loins and between the hips and let it be tied there. But before it is tied there, let this plaster be made [to be placed] upon the loins. Take garden cress, laurel berries, frankincense, and cinnamon.[79] When these have been pulverized and warmed on the fire in a pot and mixed with honey and when they are still lukewarm, place them upon the loins and tie them with the bandage with which the ball is tied to the vagina, and let both the plaster and the ball stay there strongly and firmly. Let her lie on top of them for nine days, and more if necessary, and do not let her move herself unless for reason of necessity. And give to her such a diet that for ten days she does not defecate[80] or urinate often.

On Rupture of the Genitals after Birth

[228] For rupture of the lower parts after birth, take root of comfrey, dry it and then pulverize it well, and put [it together with] very fine powder of cumin and also cinnamon in the vagina,[81] and [the rupture] will be solidified.

[For Pain of the Vagina after Birth]

[229] For pain of the vagina after birth, take rue, mugwort, and camphor,[82] grind them well and, having prepared them with musk oil or pennyroyal oil and warmed them in a pot, wrap them in a cloth and insert as a suppository.

For Hemorrhoids

[230] For hemorrhoids brought on by the strain of birth. Take wormwood, southernwood, henbane, and cassia, cook them thoroughly in wine, and you should make her be bathed therein, and when she leaves the bath, take powder of aloe together with musk oil or pennyroyal oil, and dip in some cotton, and insert it as a suppository.

[231] In another fashion, take old sandals and pine herb and cook them in wine, and make her sit in it as long as she is able to stand it. And when she comes out of this fomentation, take powdered white alum and insert it as a suppository. This renders a violated woman more than a virgin.[83]

[For Aiding Birth and Bringing Out the Afterbirth]

[232] For birth of the womb[84] and for bringing out the afterbirth. Take root of parsley, leaves of leek, and borage, and extract the juice, and mix in a little oil, and give to the patient to drink, and put vinegar into the vagina,[85] and she will be freed.

Against Miscarriage

*[233] Against miscarriage [which is] accustomed to happen to certain women in the seventh or ninth month. Take oil, wax, powder of frankincense, and mastic, and mix them, and let the woman be anointed in front and in back two or three times a week. This very much strengthens the womb and the cotyledons.[86]

For Scabies of the Hands

*[234] For healing scabies of the hands. Take red dock and fumitory, prepare them in the manner of an unguent with pork grease and butter made in May, and anoint the hand.

*[235] Likewise in another fashion. Take red dock and place it on the fire so that it burns in front of the woman; she will urinate whether she wants to or not.[87]

For Whitening the Face

*[236] An ointment for whitening the face.[88] Take two ounces of the very best white lead, let them be ground; afterward let them be sifted through a cloth, and that which remains in the cloth, let it be thrown out. Let it be mixed in with rainwater and let it cook until the consumption of the water, which can be recognized when we will see it almost completely dried out. Then let it be cooled. And when it is dried out and cooled, let rose water be added, and again boil it until it becomes hard and thick, so that from it very small pills can be formed. And when you wish to be anointed, take one pill and liquefy it in the hand with water and then rub it well on the face, so that the face will be dried. Then let it be washed with pure water, and this [whitened look] will last for eight days.

For Whitening the Teeth

*[237] For whitening black teeth and strengthening corroded or rotted gums and for a bad-smelling mouth, this works the best. Take some each of cinnamon, clove, spikenard, mastic, frankincense, grain, wormwood, crab foot, date pits, and olives. Grind all of these and reduce them to a powder, then rub the affected places.

    *[238] Likewise in order to make black teeth white, take ten drams of roasted pumice, ten drams of salt, two drams each of cinnamon and cloves, and honey as needed. Mix the pumice and salt with a sufficient amount of honey, and place them on a plain dish upon coals until they burn, and reduce the other spices to a powder. And when there is need, rub the teeth.

[For Pain of the Teeth]

*[239] For pain of the teeth and for strengthening them if they have moved. Take eleven drams of ammonium salt, fourteen drams of costmary, fourteen drams of black pepper, and two drams of clove. Prepare them thus. Put the salt and [some] bran in a pot until they turn to charcoal. And when this has become cold, grind it with the remaining spices and reduce it into a very fine powder, and rub the teeth and the ulcerous places with it.

    *[240] Likewise in another fashion, some juice of scarlet pimpernel whitens the teeth excellently; also the herb [of pimpernel] ground and applied excellently cleans out inflammation of the gums.

For Whitening the Hands

*[241] For whitening and smoothing the hands, let some ramsons be cooked in water until all the water has been consumed. And stirring well, add tartar and afterward two eggs, and with this you will rub the hands.

[On Women's Cosmetics]

On Adorning Women[1]

[242] In order that a woman might become very soft and smooth and without hairs from her head down, first of all let her go to the baths, and if she is not accustomed to do so, let there be made for her a steambath in this manner.[2] Take burning hot tiles and stones and with these placed in the steambath, let the woman sit in it. Or else take hot tiles or hot black stones and place them in the steambath or a pit[3] made in the earth. Then let hot water be poured in so that steam is produced, and let the woman sit upon it well covered with cloths so that she sweats. And when she has well sweated, let her enter hot water and wash herself very well, and thus let her exit from the bath and wipe herself off well with a linen cloth.

[243] Afterward let her also anoint herself all over with this depilatory, which is made from well-sifted quicklime. Place three ounces of it in a potter's vase and cook it in the manner of a porridge. Then take one ounce of orpiment and cook it again, and test it with a feather to see if it is sufficiently cooked. Take care, however, that it is not cooked too much and that it not stay too long on the skin, because it causes intense heat. But if it happens that the skin is burned from this depilatory, take *populeon*[4] with rose or violet oil or with juice of houseleek, and mix them until the heat is sedated. Then anoint [the burned area] with *unguentum album*[5] until the heat is sedated.

[244] Another depilatory. Take quicklime and orpiment. Place these in a small linen sack and put them to boil until they are cooked. You will test this decoction just like [the one described] above. And if the depilatory should be too thick, put in fresh water to thin it.[6] And note that the dried powder of this is good for abrading bad flesh, and also for making hair grow again on the heads of people with tinea. But first [the affected place] ought to be anointed with oil or honey. Then the powder is sprinkled on.

[245] An ointment for noblewomen which removes hairs, refines the skin, and takes away blemishes. Take juice of the leaves of squirting cucumber and almond milk; with these placed in a vessel, gently mix in quicklime and orpiment. Then [add] pounded galbanum mixed with a small amount of wine for a day and a night, and cook with this. Once this has been well cooked, you should remove the substance of the galbanum and put in a little

oil or wine and quicksilver. Having made the decoction, you should remove it from the fire and add a powder of the following herbs. Take an equal amount each of mastic, frankincense, cinnamon, nutmeg, [and] clove. This ointment smells sweetly and it is gentle for softening [the skin]. Salernitan noblewomen are accustomed to use this depilatory.[7]

[246] When the woman has anointed herself all over with this depilatory, let her sit in a very hot steambath, but she should not rub herself because her limbs will be excoriated. But when she has stayed there a little while, try to pull out the hairs from the pubic area. If they do not fall out easily, let her have hot water be poured over her and let her wash herself all over, drawing her palm [over her skin] gently. For if she should rub herself vigorously when the skin is tender, she will quickly be excoriated by this depilatory. Having done this, let her enter lukewarm water and let her be washed well. Then let her exit and then let her take bran mixed with hot water, and afterward let her strain it and pour it over herself. This cleanses the flesh and smooths it. Then let her wash herself with warm water, and let her stand a little while so that the skin can dry a little bit. Then take henna[8] with whites of eggs and let her anoint all her limbs. This smooths the flesh, and if any burn should happen from the depilatory, this removes it and renders [the skin] clear and smooth. And let her remain thus anointed a little while. Then let her rinse herself with warm water, and finally with a very white linen cloth wrapped around her, let her go to bed.

On Various Kinds of Adornments

[247] After leaving the bath, let her adorn her hair, and first of all let her wash it with a cleanser such as this. Take ashes of burnt vine, the chaff of barley nodes, and licorice wood (so that it may the more brightly shine), and sowbread; boil the chaff and the sowbread in water. With the chaff and the ash and the sowbread, let a pot having at its base two or three small openings be filled. Let the water in which the sowbread and the chaff were previously cooked be poured into the pot, so that it is strained by the small openings. With this cleanser let the woman wash her head. After the washing, let her leave it to dry by itself, and her hair will be golden and shimmering.

[248] But when she combs her hair, let her have this powder. Take some dried roses, clove, nutmeg, watercress, and galangal. Let all these, powdered, be mixed with rose water. With this water let her sprinkle her hair and comb it with a comb dipped in this same water so that [her hair] will

smell better. And let her make furrows in her hair and sprinkle on the above-mentioned powder, and it will smell marvelously.⁹

[249] Also, noblewomen should wear musk in their hair, or clove, or both, but take care that it not be seen by anyone. Also the veil with which the head is tied should be put on with cloves and musk, nutmeg, and other sweet-smelling substances.

[250] If the woman wishes to have long and black hair, take a green lizard and, having removed its head and tail, cook it in common oil. Anoint the head with this oil. It makes the hair long and black.

[251] A proven Saracen preparation. Take the rind of an extremely sweet pomegranate and grind it, and let it boil in vinegar or water, and strain it, and to this strained substance let there be added powder of oak apples and alum in a large quantity, so that it might be thick as a poultice. Wrap the hair with this, as though it were a kind of dough. Afterward, let bran be mixed with oil and let it be placed in any kind of vessel upon the fire until the bran is completely ignited. Let her sprinkle this on the head down to the roots. Then she should wet it thoroughly and again let her wrap her head (prepared thus in the above-mentioned little sack)¹⁰ in the same above-mentioned strained liquid, and let her leave it throughout the night so that she might be the better anointed. Afterward, let her hair be washed and it will be completely black.

[252] If, indeed, you wish to have thick, black hair, take colocynth and, having thrown away the insides, let it be filled with oil of laurel to which have been added henbane seed and a bit of orpiment. And let the hair be anointed with this often.

[253] If, indeed, you wish to have hair soft and smooth and fine, wash it often with hot water in which there is powder of natron and vetch.

[254] For coloring the hair so that it is golden. Take the exterior shell of a walnut and the bark of the tree itself and cook them in water, and with this water mix alum and oak apples, and with these mixed things you will smear the head (having first washed it), placing upon the hair leaves and tying them with a bandage for two days; you will be able to color [the hair].¹¹ And comb the head so that whatever adheres to the hair as excess comes off. Then place a coloring which is made from oriental crocus, dragon's blood,¹² and henna (whose larger part has been mixed with a decoction of brazilwood), and thus let the woman remain for three days, and on the fourth day let her be washed with hot water, and never will [this coloring] be removed easily.

*[255] Likewise, cook down dregs of white wine with honey to the consistency of a *cerotum*¹³ and anoint the hair, if you wish to have it golden.

[256] For blackening the hair. First the hair is prepared in the above-mentioned manner so that it will be ready for coloring. Then let oak apples be placed with oil in a dish and let them be burned. Then let them be pulverized and placed in vinegar in which there has been placed blacking made in Gaul,[14] and let them be mixed.

[257] Likewise for the same. Mix powder of galangal with juice of a walnut and make it boil and anoint [the hair].

[258] For coloring the hair, cook flower of myrtleberry and clary in vinegar and let the head be anointed, and let her stay away from strong wine and strong cleansers because these corrode or corrupt the hair.

[259] A powder for spots in the eyes which remain after redness. Take two ounces of meerschaum[15] and one-half ounce each of frankincense and cuttlefish bones. Reduce the meerschaum and the frankincense to a powder and, finely scraping the cuttlefish bone, put this on the eyes. If it is a child, let it be mixed with rose water and place it on the eyes.

*[260] For making the hair golden. Take the middle bark of boxwood, flower of broom, crocus, and egg yolks, and cook them in water. Collect whatever floats on top, and [with this] anoint the hair.

[261] For whitening the hair.[16] Catch as many bees as possible in a new pot and set it to burn, and grind with oil, and then anoint the head.

[262] For the same, agrimony ground with goat's milk is good.

[263] So that hair might grow wherever you wish. Take barley bread with the crust, and grind it with salt and bear fat. But first burn the barley bread. With this mixture anoint the place and the hair will grow.

[264] In order permanently to remove hair. Take ants' eggs, red orpiment, and gum of ivy, mix with vinegar, and rub the areas.

[265] In order that the hair might be made blond, cook greater celandine and root of agrimony and shaving of boxwood, and tie on oat straw. Then [take] ashes of oat or vine and make a cleanser, and wash the head.

[266] Likewise for the same. Take root of greater celandine and madder, grind each and with oil in which cumin and boxwood shavings and greater celandine and a little bit of crocus have been carefully cooked, anoint the head. And let it stay anointed day and night, and wash it with a cleanser of cabbage ash and barley chaff.

[267] For making the hair curly. Grind root of danewort with oil and anoint the head, and tie it on the head with leaves.

[268] In order to make the hair thick. Take agrimony and elm bark, root of vervain, root of willow, southernwood, burnt and pulverized linseed, [and] root of reed. Cook all these things with goat milk or water, and wash the area (having first shaved it). Let cabbage stalks and roots be pulverized,

and let pulverized shavings of boxwood or ivory be mixed with them, and it should be pure yellow. And from these powders let there be made a cleanser which makes the hair golden.[17]

[269] For making hair long. Grind root of marsh mallow[18] with pork grease, and you should make it boil for a long time in wine. Afterward put in well-ground cumin and mastic and well-cooked egg yolks, and mix them together a little. After they have been cooked, strain [this mixture] through a linen cloth and set it aside until it becomes cold. Then take the fatty residue which floats on the top and, having washed the head well, you should anoint it with it.

[270] For itch-mites eating away at the hair. Take myrtleberry, broom, [and] clary, and cook them in vinegar until the vinegar has been consumed, and with this rub the ends of the hair vigorously. This same thing removes fissures of the head if the head is washed well with it.

[271] Likewise, pulverize bitter lupins and you should boil them in vinegar, and then rub the hair between the hands. This expels itch-mites and kills them.

On Adornment of Women's Faces

[272] After beautifying the hair, the face ought to be adorned, [because] if its adornment is done beautifully, it embellishes even ugly women. The woman will adorn herself in this manner. First of all, let her wash her face very well with French soap and with warm water, and with a straining of bran let her wash herself in the bath. Afterward take oil of tartar and, having first dried her face, let her anoint it.

[273] Oil of tartar is made thus. Take tartar and [break] it into little bits, and wrap it in a new piece [of cloth] and dip it in strong vinegar so that it becomes thoroughly soaked, and then let it be placed on the fire until it turns to coals. Then let it be placed in an iron bowl and let it be mixed together between the fingers with oil. And thus for three or four nights leave it exposed to the air, and let it stay in an inclined spot so that the oil is able to flow out. Having collected this oil in a jug, let the woman anoint her face for seven nights and as many days, and even for fifteen days if she has an abscessed and freckled complexion. And if she is embarrassed to anoint her face during the day, let her anoint it at night, and in the morning let her wash it with warm water in which fatty residue of starch is dissolved in order to soften it.

*[274] Starch is made in this way. Take grain or fresh barley while it is

still in milk, and grind it vigorously in a mortar, and pound it, and put in three parts water, and let it stay there until it putrefies. Then press out the whole thing and expose it to the sun until the water is thoroughly evaporated and reserve this for [later] use.

[275] Having done this, let [the woman] go to the baths and enter a steambath and there she will anoint her face with the above-mentioned oil of tartar, and thus anointed let her sweat very well. Afterward, let her wash her face, just as we previously prescribed the whole body should be washed. After the anointing with the depilatory, let her go to the baths again and, having dried it well with a cloth, let her smear her face with this depilatory, which is made as follows.

[276] Take Greek pitch and wax, and dissolve them in a clay vessel. And these things having been dissolved, let a small drop of galbanum be added, [and] let them cook for a long time, stirring with a spatula. Likewise, take mastic, frankincense, and gum arabic, and let them be mixed with the rest. Having done this, let it be removed from the fire, and when it is lukewarm let her smear her face; but let her take care [not to touch] the eyebrows. Let her leave it on for an hour until it becomes cold. Then let her remove it. This refines the skin and makes the face beautiful, and it removes hairs and renders every blemish well colored and clear.

*[277] Likewise for removing abscesses after birth, you should smear the face with onion or squill and then the skin will be raised. Having raised the skin, place on the face fresh goat tallow and then you should remove the raised skin.

[278] A *cerotum* with which the face can be anointed every day in order to whiten it is made thus. Let oil of violets or rose oil with hen's grease be placed in a clay vessel so that it boils. Let very white wax be dissolved, then let egg white be added and let powder of well-powdered and sifted white lead be mixed in, and again let it be cooked a little. Then let it be strained through a cloth, and to this strained cold mixture let camphor, nutmeg, and three or four cloves be added. Wrap this whole thing in parchment. We do not apply this in any fashion until the *cerotum* smells good. From this let the woman anoint her face, and afterward let her redden it thus. Take shaving of brazilwood and let it be placed in an eggshell containing a little rose water, and let there be placed in the same place a little alum, and with this let her anoint some cotton and press it on her face and it should make her red.

[279] Note that every wax that ought to be put in a *cerotum* is whitened thus. Let the wax be dissolved in a clay vessel and take a jug full of cold water. Or let this be done with another method. And having done this many times over, let the whole of the wax be extracted pulling it out leaf by

leaf.[19] And when the whole of it has been extracted, take the wax made into leaves and let it be exposed to the sun upon a tile and sprinkle on cold water. And when it has dried, let it be sprinkled again. And let this be done for one day, and it will become white just like a linen cloth.

[280] Likewise, the face is whitened in another manner. Reduce to a powder sowbread cleaned of the exterior and dried in the sun, or in a hot oven. With this powder the woman whitens her face. But first she should prepare her face, and she should make red a whitened face, as we said.

[281] An ointment with which you can anoint the face at any time. Take crystals, varnish, eglantine, borax, gum tragacanth, and camphor with a little bit of white lead. Pulverize these with almonds, and let it be mixed with hen's grease.

[282] For whitening the face, take juice of sowbread, red and white bryony, bistort, and cuckoo-pint, together with skimmed honey. Mix these powders,[20] and put in the juice of each [substance] in the amount of a goose egg or a half. Then take a little white lead cleaned in the sun with water, and add heated rose water to the above-mentioned things, and make it boil a little on a slow fire, and after it is half-boiled add ground ginger, frankincense, white or wild mustard, [and] cumin in equal amounts. [Mix] all these with wax and honey, and when she goes to bed, let her anoint her face vigorously with this ointment, first having dried her face with the steam coming out of a pot full of warm water. And in the morning let her wash herself vigorously with breadcrumbs, or with a powder made from beans or with flour of lupins. And if she cannot have this, let her simply wash herself well.

[283] For roughness of the face caused by the sun or the wind, or for whitening and brightening the face, let deer tallow boil in water. Then strain it into another water and, once it is strained, stir it for a long time with the hands, and then let her add powder of crystal and varnish.

[284] For whitening the face, let whole eggs be placed in very strong vinegar and let them remain there until the exterior shell is like the interior skin [of the egg], and then let white mustard be mixed in and four ounces of ginger, and let them be ground together. Then let the face often be anointed.

*[285] Or, what is even better, let lily root be ground vigorously, but first let it be washed and cleaned and ground until it is white. Then, when the woman goes to the baths, let her mix one or two of the eggs with the ground-up root and leave it. Then let her anoint the face, and when she wishes to leave the bath, let her wash herself well.

[286] For refining the skin on the face. Grind bistort or marsh mallow, or pound red or white bryony vigorously, and then mix it with white honey,

and make it boil for two hours. And at the end of the cooking, add powder of camphor, borax, and rock salt, stirring a long while with a spatula, and save for [later] use. With the face having been washed in warm water and with bran three times during the week, on Sunday anoint with this ointment. Take camphor, lily root boiled in water, and fresh pork grease. Prepare all these with rose water and use it.

[287] For eliminating worms of the face, which cause some people to lose their hair. Take some each of red dock, frankincense, bistort, and cuttlefish bone; make a powder, rub [it on] three times during the week, first having washed the face well in water of bran. And on Saturday wash the face well with egg white and starch, and let it remain for one hour, but first wash it with fresh water and smear it on.

[288] For intense scabies[21] on the face. Take a little bit of red dock and pound it vigorously, and rub the afflicted area for a long time. Afterward, take bran and pour in boiling water, and wash the afflicted area with this, and then let it be dried. And make this ointment: take some well-chopped elecampane and cook it for a long time in vinegar. Afterward, pound it vigorously and mix in powder of three ounces each of frankincense, mastic, litharge, aloe, orpiment, cumin, and quicksilver extinguished with saliva, plus cuttlefish bone, soap, and grease. Prepare these with vinegar in which root of spurge has been cooked.[22]

*[289] The Salernitan women put root of red and white bryony in honey, and with this honey they anoint their faces and it reddens them marvelously.[23]

[290] Against sunburn. Take root of domesticated lily, cleaned and cooked in water; pound it vigorously. Then take one ounce each of mastic powder and frankincense, two scruples each of camphor and white lead, pork grease with which it should be prepared, and let it be prepared likewise with rose water, and keep it for [later] use.[24] It is prepared thus. We clean the lily root and we cook it with water. Having cooked it, we pound it vigorously, and we pour on fat liquefied on the fire and cleaned of salt and mixed. Then we place the above-mentioned powder in rose water. And it ought to be noted that this is good against sunburn and fissures of the lips and any kind of pustules in the face, and for excoriations and for preventing them. In the evening the woman ought to anoint herself in front of the fire, so that in the morning she is freed from all the above-mentioned afflictions. This elevates the skin and embellishes it beautifully, nor need it be removed in the morning with either washings or by any other means, for it does not detract from the color. With this ointment women only[25] anoint the face for floods [of

tears?][26] made [in mourning] for the dead. It covers up well the pustules of lepers.

*[291] A proven remedy for fistula. Take leaf of red cabbage and seed of madder root, let each of these be pounded and let them be cooked in very good wine until reduced to a third. Let it be strained and, having added some honey, let it be cooked until thick. Let two spoonfuls be given to the patient daily morning and evening.

*[292] Note that if the fistula should be in any place where the channel penetrates to the eyes, such as near the nose, it is not treatable, for we are able neither to make an incision nor [to apply] any medicine there on account of the tender substance of the eyes. Nevertheless, certain people[27] claim that such things can be cured from agrimony alone when used habitually, either in a potion or in a powder.[28]

*[293] Wood avens and dropwort are good for the same, and the grains found at the end of a radish.[29]

On the Same

[294] Women adorn their faces thus, and thus the lips can be adorned. They have skimmed honey, to which they add a little white bryony, red bryony, squirting cucumber, and a little bit of rose water. They boil all these things until [it is reduced] by half. With this ointment, women anoint their lips. They wash them with hot water at night and in the morning; it solidifies the skin of the lips, refines it, and renders it extremely soft, and preserves it from every ulceration, and if ulcerations should arise there, it heals them.

[295] If, however, a woman needs to color herself, let her rub the lips very well with the bark of the root of the nut tree. Let her put cotton upon the teeth and gums and let her dip it in composite color, and with this cotton let her anoint the lips and the gums inside.

[296] Composite color is to be made thus. Take the marine herb with which the Saracens dye leather hides green.[30] Let this boil in a new clay vessel with egg white until it is reduced to a third. To the substance strained [from this] add brazilwood finely chopped, and let it boil again. And again leave it to cool. And when it is lukewarm, let there be added powder of alum, and then let it be placed in a golden or glass jug. Reserve for [later] use. The women of the Saracens dye their faces in this manner: their faces having been anointed and dried, they put on any of the above-mentioned substances

for whitening the face, such as a *cerotum* or anything else, and a most beautiful color appears, combining red and white.

On Fissures of the Lips

*[297] Fissures of the lips are removed by anointing them thoroughly with rose oil or linseed cooked in a hollowed-out sowbread. And also they should be smeared with saxifrage seed pounded with juice of common centaury or with round birthwort.

*[298] Juice of wormwood is good for the same.

*[299] Thickness of the lips is attenuated with an unction of honey or water in which root of bistort, Florentine iris, or figwort has been boiled, or even starch dissolved in honey water, and let powder of marble and powder of roasted pumice, and cuttlefish bone be mixed in, and let the area be anointed with a mixed powder of agaric with dried mastic.

*[300]31 Once these things have been well dried, let a powder be made and let it be placed upon cancerous and even putrid gums. These, then, having been well washed with warm vinegar in which mullein root has been boiled, once the putridity has been consumed, let her have a powder of cinnamon and roses and let her sprinkle it on.

[301] If there is stench of the mouth caused by the stomach or the intestines, let it be treated thus. Let there be a powder made from the best aloe that can be found, and let it be mixed in the manner of a syrup with juice of wormwood. Let her take four spoonfuls from this each day at sunrise and, having taken them, let her take just as much honey, and she will be healed.

On Whitening the Teeth

[302] The teeth are whitened thus. Take burnt white marble and burnt date pits, and white natron, a red tile, salt, and pumice. From all of these make a powder in which damp wool has been wrapped in a fine linen cloth.32 Rub the teeth inside and out.

[303] The same thing cleans the teeth and renders them very white.33 The woman should wash her mouth after dinner with very good wine. Then she ought to dry [her teeth] well and wipe [them] with a new white cloth. Finally, let her chew each day fennel or lovage or parsley, which is better to chew because it gives off a good smell and cleans good gums and makes the teeth very white.

[304] If a woman has a stinking mouth because of putridity of the gums, [her condition] ought to be aided thus. Take quicklime, natural sulfur,[34] and orpiment, as much lime as sulfur, and some powder of burnt gourd and some pepper, and let her have one piece of scarlet cloth or any other red cloth, and let her cut it as finely as she is able, and add it to the above-mentioned things. Then let her take the strongest vinegar possible and let her place it in another clay vessel, and leave it to boil a little while. And afterward add the orpiment, then the sulfur, then the powder of the gourd and pepper alternately. Finally, let her put in the piece of cloth and let her remove [the mixture] from the fire, and then let it be extracted from the pot and placed upon a table divided into small tablets in the sun, and let them be left there to dry. From all these dried [tablets] let there be made a powder, and let it be placed upon cancerous and putrid gums, these having first been washed with warm vinegar in which mullein root has been boiled. Once the putridity has been consumed, let her have a powder of cinnamon and roses and let her sprinkle it on.[35]

[305] I saw a certain Saracen woman liberate many people with this medicine. Take a little bit of laurel leaves and a little bit of musk, and let her hold it under the tongue before bad breath is perceived in her.[36] Whence I recommend that day and night and especially when she has to have sexual intercourse with anyone that she hold these things under her tongue.

*[306] For removing an abscess of the face, wrap in tow tartar boiled with the strongest white wine and with the urine of a child, and with a linen cloth leave it through the night under hot ashes. In the morning you should throw away the cloth and grind the tartar and mix it with honey, and anoint the face as we said above.

*[307] So that a woman who has been corrupted might be thought to be a virgin. Take one or two ounces each of dragon's blood, [Armenian] bole, cinnamon, pomegranate rind, alum, mastic, and oak apples, or however much of each you want singly, [and] reduce them into a powder. All these things, having been heated a little in water, let them be prepared together. Put some of this confection in the opening which leads into the womb.

*[308] In another fashion, so that the vagina might be constricted. Take hematite, oak apples, [Armenian] bole, and dragon's blood, grind each one very finely so that the powder is able to pass through a cloth, and mix the powder with juice of plantain and dry it in the sun. And when you wish to use it, take some powder with the above-mentioned juice and insert it by means of a pessary, and let her lie for a little while with her thighs and hips tightly together. This powder is good for bloodflow from the nose and for [excessive] menses.

*[309] Another. Take oak apples and place them in water, and with this decoction let her wash the vagina, and sprinkle on a powder of Armenian bole and oak apples, and it will constrict.

*[310] For whitening the face and clarifying it. Take the juice of pignut and mix steer or cow marrow with it, and let them be ground, and in these ground things add powder of aloe, cuttlefish bone, white natron, and dove dung. Let all these be ground, and let there be made an ointment. With this ointment the woman should anoint her face.

*[311] Another. Take some lovage and cook it well and wash the face with it.

*[312] For the same and for removing hairs. Take quicklime, leaving it for a month in the sun in water; let it be strained and dried in the manner of white lead, and let it be mixed with *dialtea*[37] and butter. And let her be anointed with this at night, but let her take care not to get it in the eyes. And in the morning let her wash with warm water. Amen.

Here ends Trotula. But thou, O Lord, have mercy upon us.[38]

Appendix: Compound Medicines Employed in the *Trotula* Ensemble

The following compound medicines are employed in one or more of the *Trotula* texts. The exact ingredients and methods of preparation undoubtedly varied from one practitioner to the next. I present here translations of the descriptions from the *Antidotarium Nicholai* (The book of compound medicines of Nicholaus), which was composed in Salerno in the mid-twelfth century and came to be one of the chief pharmaceutical authorities throughout medieval Europe.[1]

Arrogon (¶131): *Unguentum aragon*. *Aragon* means "aid." It is good for the pain of cold in both men and women when anointed in this manner: first, warm it on the fire in an eggshell. Then [the patient] should be anointed, and then the warm shell should be placed upon the afflicted spot. It is good for spasm and tetanus,[2] and for pain of the intestine and kidneys [when administered] in the manner we just described. It is very good for those suffering from arthritis and sciatica. For those suffering from quartan fever, if the back is anointed before the hour of crisis, as has been said, it works marvelously. A fourth part is six pounds.[3] Take three and a half drams each of rosemary, marjoram, root of cuckoo-pint, pellitory of Spain, rue, and succulent radish; three ounces each of bay leaf, sage, and savin; nine ounces of greater and lesser fleabane; three ounces of white or red bryony; nine ounces of spurge laurel; half a pound of catmint; seven drams each of mastic gum and frankincense; one ounce each of pellitory, spurge, ginger, and pepper; half an ounce of musk oil; one ounce of petroleum; three ounces each of bear fat and laurel oil; four ounces butter; five pounds common oil; and one pound wax. The roots of all these herbs should be collected at the above-mentioned hour over the course of one or two days, as was said above. Having been crushed thoroughly, let them be placed in the oil for seven days. On the eighth day, [this mixture] should be placed on the fire and cooked until the herbs have completely disintegrated. Then they should be strained thoroughly through a sack. Then they should be put back on the fire. And when they begin to boil, the laurel oil, butter, bear fat, and wax should be added. Once all this has liquefied, add the petroleum and the musk oil. Then add the mastic gum, frankincense, ginger, pepper, pellitory, and spurge. Now it should be taken off the fire and stored away.

Benedicta (¶157): *Benedicta* is so called because from all things from which it is comprised it is blessed [*benedicta*] if it is given to those having the infirmities against which it was invented. It is good for arthritic gout and podagric conditions arising from coldness. It purges the kidneys and the bladder. The average amount made is two pounds. Take ten drams each of vegetable turpeth, spurge, and sugar; five drams each of scammony, wild garlic, and roses; one dram each of cloves, spikenard, ginger, saffron, saxifrage, long pepper, poppy, watercress, parsley, gromwell, rock salt, galangal, mace, caraway, fennel, dove's-foot cranesbill, butcher's broom, and gromwell;[4] and honey as needed. This is given in the evening in the amount of a chestnut with warm wine.

Diaciminum (¶48): *Diaciminum* is so called because there is more of cumin [*ciminum*] in it than any other spice. It is good especially for coldness of the chest and stomach and head. It dissolves flatulence of the intestines. It works marvelously for those suffering quartan fevers. A twelfth part is one pound. Take eight drams and one scruple of cumin which has been steeped in vinegar and dried on the previous day; two and a half drams each of cinnamon and cloves; two drams and five grains each of ginger and black pepper; one dram and two scruples each of galangal, summer savory, and calamint; one dram and eighteen grains each of cowbane and lovage; one dram of long pepper; two and a half scruples each of spikenard, caraway, and mastic; and honey as needed. It is given with wine in doses of three drams after meals.

Dialtea (¶¶125, 312): *Unguentum dialtea malasticon et calausticon*. It is called *dialtea* from the root of marsh mallow [*altea*], *malasticon* because it is softening, and *calausticon* because it produces heat. The average amount is four pounds. Take two pounds of marsh mallow root; one pound each of linseed and fenugreek; half a pound of squill; four pounds of oil; one pound of wax; two ounces each of turpentine, ivy gum, and galbanum; half a pound each of Greek tar and resin. Note that if these are included,[5] that is to say elder and sowbread, this works well for consolidating wounds. And some people add butter. All these herbs and roots should be washed well. And the linseed, fenugreek, and squill should be ground together, and when they are well ground they should be put in seven pounds of water for three days. On the fourth day, they should be put on the fire and they should boil until they thicken. Then, little by little they should be placed in a sack, and when you wish to squeeze it out, a little boiling water should be added in order to extract its viscous juice. Two pounds of this juice should be taken and placed in four pounds of oil. And they should boil until the juice has been consumed, which will be when none of the juice floats on top. Afterward, one pound of wax should be added, and when it has liquefied, the turpentine should be added. Then the ivy gum, crushed galbanum, and finally the powder of Greek tar and resin should be added. And when it is cooked (which will be when a drop that has been placed on marble thickens), let it be taken off the fire. And when it has been strained and chilled, gently put it away. It is good particularly for pain of the chest from coldness. For pleurisy, it cures [if] it is first heated on the fire in an eggshell and then anointed on the chest. It heats, softens, and moistens all chilled and desiccated places.

Diathessaron (¶¶10, 11, 116): *Tyriaca diatesereon.* It is called *theriac* because it is the mistress of all medicines.[6] It is called *diathessaron* because it is made from four things, from which it used to be made in ancient times.[7] But later other philosophers added other things. It is particularly good for people who have been poisoned and for bites from rabid dogs or other poisonous animals. It is given to drink with the juice of mint; and [the person who has been bitten] should be anointed with it directly upon the wound itself, and it should be anointed on venomous conditions, that is *bonum malanum*, which the Salernitans call *scagia*. For those suffering from quartan fever and for true quotidian fever, [if] given with a decoction of meadow rue or felwort, it helps. A tenth part is two pounds. Take one ounce plus two scruples less eleven grains each of myrrh, round aristolochia, felwort, and husked laurel berries; one dram and two scruples each of fenugreek, black cumin, and zedoary; one dram, two scruples, and seven grains each of dittany of Crete, wall germander, and meadow rue; one dram each of ivy gum and burnt vitriol; one dram of *Esdra magna*;[8] one dram each of deer heart bone, mummy,[9] and columbine; three drams of burnt deer horn; and honey as needed. This is given in the amount of a hazelnut.

Hieralogodion (¶11): *Yeralogodion memphytum.* *Yera* [i.e., *hiera*] means "sacred," *logos* means "speech," and *memphytum* means an obstruction. For it cures impeded speech no matter what the cause. Given simply or as a laxative with warm water it marvelously purges both black bile and phlegm. It is given to epileptics with warm water, salt, and a mixture of honey and water. It cures those with stomach ailments and vertiginous epileptics who foam at the mouth and bite their tongues. [It is also good] for those suffering from headaches or migraines and who are so vexed by excitements of the head that they seem to be possessed by a demon. Given each month, as we have said, as a purgative, it heals paralytics suffering from trembling. It helps those suffering from pleurisy, liver conditions, and spleen conditions. It also brings on the menses. It relieves nephritic, sciatic, and arthritic conditions. It improves leprous lesions, hernias, and various blemishes. A tenth part is a pound. Take two ounces each of colocynth and the insides of polypody; one and a half drams plus six grains each of spurge, wall germander, and laurel fruit; one ounce and twelve grains each of wormwood and myrrh; one dram each of common centaury, agaric, ammoniacum incense, clove, spikenard, squill, and scammony; one scruple and fourteen grains each of aloe, thyme, madder tips, cassia tree bark, wall germander, bdellium, and white horehound; half a dram each of cinnamon, opoponax, castoreum, long aristolochia, white and black and long pepper, saffron, *serapinum* gum, and parsley; six grains each of white and black hellebore; and honey as needed. It is given morning and evening in the amount of a chestnut with warm water.

Hierapigra (¶11): *Yerapigra Galyeni*. It is called *yera* [i.e., *hiera*] because it is sacred, *picra* because it is bitter. It is made for various diseases of the head, or diseases of the ears or distemper of the eyes. It also purges the stomach very well. It relieves disorders of the liver, and it removes and thins out hardness and density[10] of the spleen. It is good for the kidneys and the bladder, and it cleanses distemper of the womb. A tenth part is one pound. Take two scruples each of cinnamon, spikenard, saffron, camel grass, hazelwort, cassia tree bark, balsam wood, balsam fruit, violet, wormwood, agaric, roses, vegetable turpeth, colocynth, and mastic; aloe in the weight of all the spices, i.e., ten drams and two scruples; and honey as needed. Its dose is three drams, [to be given] with warm water in the morning while fasting. If, however, you make pills, give fifteen or seventeen of them with a sufficient amount of scammony.

Oleum rosaceum (¶¶66, 68, 70, 80, 91, 181, 243, 278, 297): *Oleum rosatum* has a cold and styptic power and thus is the best thing for head pains from fever or from the heat of the sun. Moreover, it takes away burning and heat when the stomach is full of bile [and when] its windiness fills the whole head or just part of it. It is good for those pains which happen sometimes in the whole head or part of it if the head is anointed with this. It also is good for pains arising in the stomach or intestines from sharpness of the humors if it is mixed with two drams of mastic and enough wax dissolved in it and then anointed on the affected parts. It is useful against erysipelas that does not appear on the surface [of the skin] and for many other conditions of this kind. This oil is made in the following manner. One and a half pounds of slightly crushed fresh roses should be placed in two pounds of common (and in our opinion, cleaned) oil; these should be placed in a full pot suspended in a cauldron full of water. And let these boil for a while until they are reduced to a third of their original quantity. Only then should this be put into a white linen cloth and squeezed through a press. The liquid should be saved. In the same manner oil of elder, violet, and sweet gale is made, that is, those oils which are good in acute diseases; anointed on the liver, pulse points, temples, and palms of the hands and soles of the feet, they extinguish heat completely.

Oxizaccara (¶91): *Oxizaccare* is so called from *oxi*, which is vinegar, and *zucharo*, "sugar." It is good for acute tertian fevers and pseudo-quartan fevers. It purges bile from the stomach. Take one pound of sugar, eight ounces of pomegranate juice, and four ounces of vinegar, and place in a tin[11] vessel on the fire. And let it boil for a while, stirring constantly with a spatula, until it is reduced back to the quantity of the sugar; it should become so thick that it can be carried. Let one and a half ounces of this be given in the morning with warm water.

Paulinum (¶130): *Paulinum antidotum*. It is called *Paulinum* because it is large, *antidotum* because it is given as an antidote, for it has great power and efficacy. Properly, it is given for chronic and acute coughing, which arises from a flowing out of rheum from the head. It is good for disorders of the chest caused by cold [when given] in the evening with warm wine. But if [the patient] is not able to take it diluted, make from it nine or eleven pills made with the juice of opium poppy. But if it has been made without the juice of opium poppy and you wish to make a laxative, give two drams with two scruples of Levant scammony made into pills. It purges the head and stomach of phlegm and foulness, and it takes away heaviness of the eyes. The fourth part is one pound because in each dose they put a pound and half of skimmed honey. Take eleven drams and fifteen grains of aloe; four and a half drams each of saffron, costmary, marking nut, agaric, coral, myrrh, ammoniacum, turpentine, galbanum, *serapinum* gum, opoponax, confected cleavers, calamite storax, and Florentine iris; two drams and fifteen grains each of juice of opium poppy, frankincense, mastic gum, bdellium, and *cozumbrum*; one dram and a half each of balsam and cloves; [and] two drams of balm. Mix them together in the following fashion. Take the gums—galbanum, *serapinum* gum, ammoniacum, and opoponax—and grind them a little bit, and let them be placed in white and moderately sweet-smelling wine for one night. In the morning, let them be placed on the fire, and let them boil. Afterward, add four ounces of skimmed honey and let them continue to boil until they begin to thicken. Then, having ground thoroughly the calamite storax, confected cleavers, and *cozumbrum* with a hot pestle, let them be placed in a cauldron, stirring constantly with a spatula until they liquefy. Then let the turpentine be added. And if you wish to test whether it is cooked, place a little bit on some marble, and if it immediately congeals into the consistency of honey, [then it is cooked]. A little later, the cauldron having been placed on the ground, let the myrrh, together with the bdellium, be added. Then the mastic and the frankincense. Then the costmary, marking nut, agaric, coral, Florentine iris, juice of opium poppy, cloves, and balm. Having ground all these together and pulverized them, let them be placed in the cauldron. Then spread this whole mixture onto a slab of marble that has first been covered with oil of laurel. And let this be softened with the powder of aloe, while the saffron is ground with the spices. Finally, let lozenges be formed with oriental crocus. Let this be given in the amount of a hazelnut with warm wine.

Populeon (¶243): *Unguentum populeon* is so called because it is made from poplar buds [*oculus populi*]. It is good against the heat of an acute fever and for those who are unable to sleep if it is anointed on the temples and the pulse points and the palms of the hands and soles of the feet. This same unguent, when mixed with oil of roses or violets and anointed above the kidney, takes the heat away marvelously; when anointed on the abdomen, it provokes sweating. An average quantity is two pounds. Take one and a half pounds of poplar buds; three ounces each of red poppy, leaves of mandrake, the tips of the most delicate leaves of bramble, henbane, black nightshade, common stonecrop, lettuce, houseleek, burdock, violet, and *scantuncelus* (i.e., pennywort); [and] two pounds of new unsalted pork fat. Let the poplar buds be pounded well by themselves, and then again with the fat. Let them be formed into little lozenges. Leave them alone for two days. On the third day, gather all the above-mentioned herbs and let them be ground well by themselves. Then let them be ground again and mixed with the lozenges. And having formed lozenges from this mixture, let them sit for nine days. Afterward, let the lozenges be put piece by piece in a cauldron with one pound of excellent, odoriferous wine. Let them boil until the wine evaporates, stirring constantly with a spatula. Afterward, having squeezed it all out in a sack, drain [the mixture] well. Set the drained mixture aside to cool and store in a vase.

Potio Sancti Pauli (¶225): *Potio Sancti Pauli* is called *potio* from *potando* [drinking], *sancti Pauli* because Saint Paul created it. This is the same potion which the Romans called *potio maior*, because Paul the Great modified it.

Properly it is given to epileptics, cataleptics, analeptics, and those suffering in the stomach; it is given with wine in which incense or mixed peony has been cooked. This potion is given with *Esdra*[12] in the wintertime and in the springtime to those suffering from quartan fever. It cures when given before the hour of crisis with wine in which felwort or golden gorse and castoreum have been cooked. It likewise heals those suffering from diseases of the windpipe and paralytics when given with wine in which sage or castoreum has been cooked. A fifteenth part is one pound. Take three drams and one scruple of natron; one dram and one scruple each of castoreum, antimony, houseleek, cloves, laurel berry, willow, wild celery, parsley, fennel, wild carrot, and stavesacre; three scruples each of sweet flag, myrobalans, licorice, vitriol, peony, and pellitory; one scruple and eighteen grains of costmary, colocynth, agaric, mastic, both long and round aristolochia, roses, juice of wild cabbage, hazelwort, wood sage, cuckoopint, dittany, basil, bear's breech, horsemint, oregano, pennyroyal, wall germander or hyssop, savory, white pepper and black pepper and long pepper, and rue seed; one scruple and four grains each of watercress and frankincense; one scruple each of balsam, spikenard, saffron, camel grass, Chinese cinnamon, myrrh, opoponax, sulfur, mandrake, felwort, malt, spurge, poppy, and cormorant blood; one scruple minus four grains each of cinnamon, cloves, ginger, marking nut, bark of the balsam tree, rhubarb, hog's fennel, fruit of the balsam tree, calamite storax, *serapinum* gum, hazelwort, dragon's blood, hare's rennet, sheep's and goat's and veal rennet, bear's gall, goose blood, and petroleum; seven drams and four grains of cowslip; and honey as needed. This is given in the evening, in the amount of a hazelnut, or with the above-mentioned decoctions, to those suffering from diseases of the head.

Rosata novella (¶¶32, 142): *Rosata novella*. It is called *rosata* from roses; *novella* [new] in contrast to the old *rosata*, which had *tibar*, that is, mercury. It gets rid of vomiting and upset stomach. It represses weakness and thirst. It takes away defects from a long sickness marvelously. It suppresses *diaphoretic* sweats. The twentieth part is two pounds. Take one ounce and one dram and two and a half scruples each of rose, sugar, and licorice; two drams, two scruples, and two grains of cinnamon; one scruple and eight grains each of cloves, spikenard, ginger, galangal, nutmeg, zedoary, storax, watercress, and wild celery; and honey as needed. This is given morning, noon, and night with cold water.

Theodoricon euporiston (¶130): *Theodoriton yperiston*. It is called *Theodoriton* from *deo datum* [given by God]. *Yperiston* is to be interpreted as "well proven." This is made for migrainous pain and dizziness of the head, and for phlegmatic flux which flows in the jaws and the throat, which sometimes causes loss of the voice. It is good also for feverless conditions of the spleen. It makes good color if it is given by itself. But if you wish to use it as a purgative, you should employ two scruples of Levant scammony and it will work more forcefully. A twelfth part is two pounds. Take three drams, three grains, plus a third of one grain of aloe; three drams each of cinnamon, wall germander, and sweet flag; two drams and sixteen grains each of saffron, cassia tree bark, and rhubarb; two and a half drams of agaric; one and half drams of spikenard, costmary, mastic, hazelwort, silphium,[13] squill, asafetida, ammoniacum, bdellium, Indian electuary, St.-John's-wort, dodder, polypody, wild cabbage juice, and white and long pepper; two scruples each of camel grass, Smyrnian ginger, myrobalans, colocynth, Smyrnian *serapinum* gum, opoponax, castoreum, wormwood, long aristolochia, parsley, felwort, and poppy; one scruple each of scammony and black pepper; and honey as needed. It is given morning and evening [in the amount of] three drams with warm wine.

Theriac (§§116, 299n): *Tyriaca magna Galeni*. It is called *theriac* because it is the mistress of all medicines. *Galeni* [of Galen] because it was created by him. It is made against the most serious diseases of the whole human body: for epileptic conditions, cataleptic, apoplectic, cephalargic, stomach-related, and migrainous. It is good for hoarseness of the voice and tightness of the chest. It is best for respiratory, asthmatic, blood-spitting,[14] jaundiced, dropsical, peripneumonic, and intestinal conditions, and for those having wounds in the intestines. It treats nephritic, calculous,[15] and choleric conditions. It brings forth the menses and expels the dead fetus. It improves leprous lesions and variolas and periodic chills and other diseases of long standing. It is especially good against all kinds of poisons and the bites of serpents and reptiles. But the quantity and quality of the doses for each disease are different, and they are written at the end. It relieves every deficiency of the senses. It strengthens the heart, brain, liver, and stomach. It makes the whole body sound and keeps it that way. The ninth part is two pounds. Take two drams and two scruples of troches made from squill; two drams of long pepper; one dram and one scruple each of troches of Tyre and *diacorallum*;[16] one scruple and seven grains of balsam wood; one scruple and fourteen grains each of juice of opium poppy, agaric, Florentine iris, rose, crow garlic, wild turnip seed, cinnamon, and juice of the balsam tree; one scruple and seven grains each of rhubarb, wax, spikenard, costmary, camel grass, ginger, cassia tree bark, calamite storax, myrrh, turpentine, frankincense, calamint, dittany,

French lavender, wall germander, roots of creeping cinquefoil, parsley, and white pepper; one scruple each of cloves, gum arabic, sweet flag, burnt vitriol, *serapinum* gum, sealed earth or Armenian bole, juice of dodder, Celtic nard, germander, felwort, hog's fennel, balsam fruit, poppy, wild celery, fennel, wild caraway, sermountain, garden cress, garden cress seed, anise, and St.-John's-wort; one scruple each of mummy, castoreum, opoponax, pitch, galbanum, lesser centaury, long aristolochia, and wild carrot; and skimmed honey as needed. Grind those things that need to be ground, and having melted the gums in wine, mix with the powder and with sufficient honey or grind with the spices. It is given in the amount of a hazelnut with lukewarm water to those suffering from apoplexy, scotomia, cephalargia, migraines, hoarseness of the voice, and chest pains; for these, it should be given with honey or gum tragacanth so that it can be tolerated by the mouth. For asthmatics, give it with a decoction of wood sage. For those with blood-spitting conditions of the chest and disease of the lung, give it in a ptisan. For long-standing diseases, give it with a decoction of hyssop. For those suffering jaundiced conditions, give it with a decoction of hazelwort. For those suffering from dropsy, give it with *oximel* or *oxizaccara*. For those with peripneumonia, give it with the juice or a decoction of white horehound. For those with an intestinal complaint, give it with a decoction of wild celery. For those having wounds in the intestines, give it with a decoction of sumac. For nephritics, those suffering from stones, and cholerics, give it with a decoction of gromwell, and wild or domestic celery. For those suffering from conditions of the windpipe, give it with the juice or a decoction of meadow rue. For poisons and for bringing on the menses or the fetus, give it with warm wine, or with *mulsa* made with water in which mint or sweet basil has been cooked. And for those suffering from a periodic chill and all other diseases, give it with lukewarm water.

Trifera magna (¶¶129, 130?, 141, 161, 217, 225): It is called *trifera magna* because it confers great utility to women and makes them fruitful. It is given for pain of the stomach in men and women with water in which fennel seeds, anise, and mastic have been cooked. It is [also] given for disorder of the womb caused by frigidity if it is drunk mixed with wine in which mugwort has been cooked. It also provokes the menses if it is made with well-ground mugwort and mixed with musk oil. A pessary made from cotton, if it has been anointed with [the *trifera*] and inserted into the vagina of the woman, provokes the menses in a woman who is not conceiving. If it is given with wine in which mandrake or dwarf elder has been cooked, it works in a wonderful way for children who are not able to sleep. And in the night when they chatter excessively, it works when an amount the size of a chickpea is mixed with woman's milk and drunk. An eighth part is one pound. Take two drams of juice of opium poppy; one dram each of cinnamon, cloves, galangal, spikenard, zedoary, ginger, costmary, calamite storax, sweet flag, galingale, Florentine iris, hog's fennel, yellow flag, mandrake, Celtic nard, dog rose, pepper, anise, wild celery, parsley, alexanders, wild carrot, henbane, fennel, sweet basil, and cumin; and honey as needed. This is given in the amount of a chestnut, as we explained above.

Trifera saracenica (¶¶32, 226): *Trifera saracenica* (otherwise known as "juvenile") renders a person young again. It is called *saracenica* because it was invented by the Saracens [i.e., Muslims]. It is given particularly for those suffering from jaundice and liver problems, and to those suffering from head pain on account of a fumosity of red bile. It is given against double-tertian fever. And it restores sight lost from [excessive] heat, and it brings back lost color to its original state. It is given in the morning with warm water. An eighth part is one pound. Take three ounces of sugar; one ounce and a half each of the bark of citrine myrobalans, and the fleshy innards of cassia tree bark and tamarinds; six drams, two scruples, and five grains each of cleaned chebulic myrobalans and manna; one-half ounce each of Indian [myrobalan] and fresh violets if they can be found; two drams and fifteen grains each of anise and fennel; one dram and seven and a half grains each of mastic and mace; one-half ounce and four grains each of belleric and emblic. Prepare thus: in two pounds of water let there be placed three ounces of fresh violets if they can be found.[17] If not, used dried ones and boil them until the water becomes a purple color and the violets are dissolved. Then, having lightly squeezed out [the substance], let it be strained. Take part of the strained water, and let the cassia tree bark and the tamarinds be washed through a colander, and let them be strained through it as well. In another [container of] water, there should be put one pound and eight ounces of sugar, and let them be placed on the fire and boil until it becomes thick: and when it begins to thicken, let the strained water of cassia tree bark and tamarinds be added, and then the manna. When you wish to know whether it is cooked, let a drop be placed on marble. If it congeals like honey, then it is cooked. Then let it be taken off the fire, and when it has chilled, let a powder of the above-mentioned spices be added, all the while stirring with a spatula until it is incorporated. Finally, put in the above-mentioned sugar, which has been well pulverized. This is given in the amount of a chestnut; if [the disease] comes from a distemperance of heat, it is given with cold water; if it comes from an abundance of a cold humor, it is given with hot water.

Unguentum album (¶243): *Unguentum album* [white unguent] [is good for] salty phlegm. [To make] one pound: Take two ounces of white lead; one ounce of litharge; three drams of frankincense; and two drams of mastic gum. Each ingredient should be ground separately in the following manner. The powder of white lead should be mixed with a little oil, and then added to the litharge. Then the mastic gum and the frankincense should be added. While stirring constantly with a pestle, rose water should be added a little at a time. And when it begins to thicken, [more] oil and rose water should be added. This should be continued until everything is thoroughly incorporated. Then it should be stored away and it should not be allowed to get too thick or too thin.

Unguentum aureum (¶159): *Unguentum aureum* [golden unguent] is good against all acute, cold gouts, and especially against kidney stones and dropsical conditions. Take two pounds each of marsh mallow root, valerian, and hog's fennel; one pound each of both aristolochias [i.e., the long and the round], elecampane, hyssop, pennyroyal, mugwort, creeping cinquefoil, rue, bay leaves, sweet flag, greater knapweed, rosemary, honeysuckle, saxifrage, galingale, wall germander, asparagus, butcher's broom, fennel, and anise; one-half pound each of wild celery, Florentine iris, lovage, gromwell, parsley, sermountain, poppy, watercress, dill, laurel berries, juniper, and lynx stone; four ounces each of snakeroot, nettle seed, citron seed, mustard seed, and spurge; three ounces each of bear fat and fox fat, laurel oil, and petroleum; two ounces each of camel's hay, costmary, pellitory, incense, mastic, and myrrh; one ounce of musk oil; and oil and wax as needed. The herbs should be collected in the month of May and, having been thoroughly ground, should be put in oil or white wine for twenty days. Afterward, let oil be added as needed and let the herbs boil until they begin to dissolve and let them be strained through a sack. And let there be placed there twelve pounds of wax. These should boil until the wax is thoroughly mixed in. Then let the fats, having been well dissolved and strained, be put on top, and leave them to boil a little. Afterward let the laurel oil be poured over and, having taken [the pot] off the fire, let the other oils be added, then the powders of costmary, pellitory, and camel's hay; then the frankincense; then the myrrh. Let all this be done with a brief interval between each addition. Then add the wax and, having taken it from the fire, the spurge. Finally, the petroleum should be added.

Materia Medica Employed in the *Trotula*

The following list of *materia medica* includes all substances employed as medicinal agents in the text of the *Trotula*; I have also included those used in the compound medicines described in the Appendix.

The list is in alphabetical order according to the common English names, which are listed in the first column. In the second column, I have listed the medieval Latin term from my edition of the Latin text. In some cases, there will be multiple entries for a single English name; this is because different Latin words are sometimes identified in English by a single plant or name (e.g., both *aaron* and *yarus* are identified as cuckoo-pint). In the third column, I have listed the modern scientific designation for plants; this column is left blank for substances of animal or mineral origin, except for a few instances where I offer a brief description. I must stress again (cf. the Introduction) that these identifications should not be construed as definitive or exhaustive of all possibilities. Finally, in the fourth column, I list all places in the text (including the Appendix) where this substance is employed.

I have used the following sources to identify items of *materia medica*. Simple ingredients are translated according to the common name provided in Tony Hunt, *Plant Names of Medieval England* (Cambridge: D. S. Brewer, 1989). In cases where several alternatives are offered, I have chosen in the translation the one that seemed to have greater currency; a complete list of Hunt's identifications can be found in the Index Verborum to the Latin edition. For forms not found in Hunt, I have used the following sources to identify the modern Linnaean classification: J. André, *Lexique des termes de botanique en latin* (Paris: Klincksieck, 1956), and *Les Noms de plantes dans la Rome antique* (Paris: Belles Lettres, 1985); Willem F. Daems, *Nomina simplicium medicinarum ex synonymariis Medii Aevi collecta: Semantische Untersuchungen zum Fachwortschatz hoch- und spätmittelalterlicher Drogenkunde*, Studies in Ancient Medicine, 6 (Leiden: E. J. Brill, 1993); and Jerry Stannard, "Identification of the Plants Described by Albertus Magnus, *De vegetabilibus*, lib. VI," *Res Publica Litterarum* 2 (1979); 281–318, reprint *Pristina Medicamenta: Ancient and Medieval Medical Botany* (Aldershot: Ashgate, 1999), Essay 15. I have also employed D. J. Mabberley, *The Plant-Book: A Portable Dictionary of the Vascular Plants*, 2d ed. (Cambridge: Cambridge University Press, 1997), to confirm the currently accepted scientific names and the common English names. For more obscure items of *materia medica*, I have consulted the *Circa instans* attributed to Mattheus Platearius, a twelfth-century herbal from Salerno, from the edition of Hans Wölfel, *Das Arzneidrogenbuch "Circa instans" in einer Fassung des XIII. Jahrhunderts aus der Universitätsbibliothek Erlangen. Text und Kommentar als Beitrag zur Pflanzen- und Drogenkunde des Mittelalters* (Berlin: A. Preilipper, 1939).

acacia	*accatia*	*Acacia arabica* L.	¶71
agaric	*agaricus*	*Polyporus officinalis* L.	¶¶62, 299, *Hieralogodion, Hierapigra, Paulinum, Potio sancti Pauli, Theodoriton euperiston, Theriac*
agrimony	*agrimonia*	*Agrimonia eupatoria* L.	¶¶33, 262, 265, 268, 292
alexanders	*macedonicum*	*Smyrnium olusatrum* L.	*Trifera magna*
almond	*amigdala*	*Prunus amygdalus* Batsch	¶¶245, 281
aloe	*aloes/aloes epatici*	*Aloë* L. ssp., esp. *succotrina* Lam.	¶¶117, 153, 172, 183, 211, 230, 288, 301, 310, *Hieralogodion, Hierapigra, Paulinum, Theodoriton euperiston*
aloewood	*lignum aloes*	*Aquilaria agallocha* Roxb.	¶117
alum	*alumen*		¶¶187, 194, 231, 251, 254, 278, 296, 307
ambergris	*ambra*	a morbid secretion of the sperm whale	¶¶53, 117
ammoniacum	*armoniac/ ammoniacum thimiatis*	*Dorema ammoniacum* D.	*Hieralogodion, Paulinum, Theodoriton euperiston*
anise	*anisum*	*Pimpinella anisum* L.	¶14, *Theriac, Trifera magna, Trifera saracenica, Unguentum aureum*
antimony	*antimonium*		*Potio sancti Pauli*
apple	*pomum*		¶¶166, 222, 252

aristolochia.
  See birthwort

Armenian bole	*bolus/bolus armenicus*	a kind of medicinal earth	¶¶33, 70, 124, 166, 194,307, 308, 309, *Theriac*
asafetida	*usa fetida*	var. umbelliferae, esp. *Ferula foetida* Regel and *F. assafoetida* L.	¶117, *Theodoriton euperiston*
ash(tree)	*fraxinus*	*Fraxinus excelsior* L.	¶105
ashes	*cineres*		¶¶105, 136, 137, 152, 155, 171, 219, 247, 265, 266
asparagus	*asparagus*	*Asparagus officinalis* L.	*Benedicta, Unguentum aureum*
bacon	*lardum*		¶¶40, 172, 213
badger. *See* fat			
balm	*mellissa*	*Melissa officinalis* L.	¶14, *Paulinum*
balsam tree (gum of)	*balsamus*	*Commiphora opobalsamum* (L.) Engl.	¶53, *Paulinum, Potio sancti Pauli*
balsam tree, fruit of	*carpobalsamus*		*Hierapigra, Potio sancti Pauli, Theriac*
balsam tree, juice of	*opobalsamus*		*Theriac*
balsam tree, bark of	*xilobalsamus*		*Hierapigra, Potio sancti Pauli, Theriac*
barley. *See also* bread; flour	*ordeum*	*Hordeum* L. ssp.	¶¶34, 69, 87, 91, 124, 128, 135, 140, 151, 247, 266, 274
bdellium	*bdellium*	a bitter, aromatic gum found in India and Africa (*Commiphora africana* Engl.)	¶110 *Hieralogodion, Paulinum, Theodoriton euperiston*
bean. *See also* flour, bean	*faba*		¶¶69, 79 127, 174, 282
bear. *See* fat; gall			

brazilwood	*brasilium*	*Caesalpinia sappan* L.	¶¶254, 278, 296
bread	*panis*		¶¶34, 177, 282
barley bread	*panis ordeaceus*		¶¶34, 263
wheat bread	*panis simule*		¶127
broom	*genesta*	*Sarothamnus scoparius* (L.) Wimmer ex Koch	¶¶260, 270
bryony; red and white bryony	*uiticella*	*Bryonia dioica* Jacq.	¶¶175, 282, 289, 294
bryony, white or red	*brionia*	*Bryonia dioica* Jacq.	¶¶286, 294, *Arrogon*
buck's-horn plantain	*cornu cerui*	*Plantago coronopus* L.	¶¶33, 59n, 137, 216, *Diathesseron*
bull. *See* gall			
burdock	*bardana*	*Arctium lappa* L.	*Populeon*
burdock	*lapa*	*Arctium lappa* L.	¶202
butcher's broom	*bruscus/bruxum*	*Ruscus aculeatus* L.	*Benedicta, Unguentum aureum*
butter	*butirum/butyrum*		¶¶24, 63, 66, 98, 99, 124, 149, 154, 234, 312, *Arrogon, Dialtea*
cabbage	*caulis*	*Brassica oleracea* L.	¶¶154, 214, 223, 266, 268
cabbage, red	*caulis rubea*		¶¶21, 291
cabbage, wild	*brasica*	*Brassica oleracea* L.	*Theodoriton euperiston*
cabbage, wild	*cauliculus agrestis*	*Brassica oleracea* L.	¶159
calamint	*calamentum*	*Calamintha* L. ssp.	¶¶10, 26, 48, *Diaciminum, Theriac*
camel grass	*squinantum*	*Cymbopogon schoenanthus* (L.) Spreng.	*Hierapigra, Potio sancti Pauli, Theriac, Theodoriton euporiston*
camel's hay	*schoenanthus*	*Cymopogon schoenanthus*	*Unguentum aureum*
camphor	*camphora*	a laureaceous plant and/or its juice (esp. *Camphora laurus* L./ *Dryobalanops camphora* L.)	¶¶72, 167, 174, 214, 216, 227, 229, 278, 281, 286, 290
caper spurge	*cathapucia*	*Euphorbia lathyrus* L.	¶87
capon. *See* fat			
caraway	*carui*	*Carum carvi* L.	¶¶12, 210, *Benedicta, Diaciminum, Theriac*

carrot. *See*
  deadly carrot;
  wild carrot

cassia, fruit of	*cassia fistula*	*Cinnomomum aromaticum* Nees	¶230, *Trifera saracenica*
cassia, bark of	*cassia lignea*		*Hieralogodion, Hierapigra, Potio sancti Pauli, Theodoriton euperiston, Theriac*
castoreum	*castoreum*	an odorous secretion of the beaver	¶¶16, 48, 54, 81, *Hieralogodion, Potio sancti Pauli, Theodoriton euperiston, Theriac*
cat	*catus*		¶¶43, 108
catmint	*nepita*	*Nepeta cataria* L.	¶¶10, 13, 22, 23, 48, 142, 157, 225, *Arrogon*
celery, wild	*apium*	*Apium graveolens* L.	¶¶12, 17, 23, 48, 61, 81, 125, *Potio sancti Pauli, Rosata novella, Theriac, Trifera magna, Unguentum aureum*
Celtic nard	*celtica*	*Valeriana celtica* L.	*Theriac, Trifera magna*
ceroneum	*ceroneum*	a compound medicine made with wax?	¶125
chalk	*creta*		¶¶4, 79
chaff	*palea*		¶220
chamomile	*camomilla*	*Chamaemelum nobile* (L.) All.	¶¶48, 125
cheese	*caseum*		¶98
chickpea	*cicer*	*Cicer arietinum* L.	¶217
chickweed	*morsus galline*	*Stellaria media* (L.) Vill.	¶15
cinnabar	*minium*	sulfide of mercury	¶183n
cinnamon	*cinamonum/cynamomum*	*Cinnamomum zeylanicum* Blume	¶¶188, 227, 228, 237, 238, 245, 300, 304, 307, *Diaciminum, Hieralogodion, Hier-*

			apigra, Potio sancti Pauli, Rosata novella, Theodoriton euperiston, Theriac
citron	*citrus*	*Citrus medica* L.	*Unguentum aureum*
clary	*gallitricum*	*Salvia sclarea* L.	¶¶258, 270
clay	*argilla*		¶¶79, 148, 200
cleavers	*rubea*	?rubea minor (*Galium aparine* L.)	*Paulinum*
clove	*antifolium*	*Eugenia caryophillata* Thunb.	¶238
clove	*folium*	*Syzygium aromaticum* (L.) Merr. et Perr.	¶239, *Hieralogodion, Potio sancti Pauli, Theriac*
clove	*gariofilus*	*Syzygium aromaticum* (L.) Merr. et Perr.	¶¶81, 134, 138, 225, 227, 237, 245, 248, 249, 278, *Benedicta, Diaciminum, Potio sancti Pauli, Rosata novella, Trifera magna*
clover	*trifolium*	*Trifolium* L. ssp.	¶24
colocynth	*coloquintida*	*Citrullus colocynthis* (L.) Schrad.	¶¶22, 252, *Hieralogodion, Hierapigra, Potio sancti Pauli, Theodoriton euperiston*
columbine	*antefarmacum*	*Aquilegia vulgaris* L. or *Geranium* L. ssp. esp. *G. columbinum* L.	*Diathesseron*
comfrey	*anagallus*	*Symphytum officinale* L.	¶149n
comfrey	*consolida maior*	*Symphytum officinale* L.	¶¶149, 194, 228
comfrey	*simphitum*	*Symphytum officinale* L.	¶149
common centaury	*centaurea*	*Centaurium erythraea* Rafn	¶¶16, 297, *Hieralogodion*
common germander	*germandrea*	*Teucrium chamaedrys* L.	¶50
common stonecrop	*uermicularis*	*Sedum acre* L.	*Populeon*
conch	*concha marina*		¶209
copper	*es*		¶183
coral	*corallus*		¶¶33, 120, *Paulinum*

coriander	*coriandrum*	*Coriandrum sativum* L.	¶40
cormorant. *See* blood, cormorant			
costmary	*costus*	*Chrysanthemum balsamita* L.	¶¶48, 239, *Paulinum, Potio sancti Pauli, Theodoriton euperiston, Theriac, Trifera magna, Unguentum aureum*
cotton	*bombax*		¶¶124, 129, 130, 141, 153, 161, 169, 175, 191, 225, 230, 278, 295
cowbane	*ameos*	*Cicuta virosa* L.	¶¶12, 14, 81, 159, *Diaciminum*
cowslip	*herba peralisis*	*Primula veris* L.	*Potio sancti Pauli*
cozumbrum	*cozumbrum*	a kind of aromatic gum, ?storax	*Paulinum*
crab	*cancer*		¶237
creeping cinquefoil	*pentafilon*	*Potentilla reptans* L.	*Theriac, Unguentum aureum*
crocus. *See* oriental crocus; saffron			
crow garlic	*scordeon*	*Allium vineale* L.	*Theriac*
cuckoo-pint	*aaron*	*Arum maculatum* L.	*Potio sancti Pauli*
cuckoo-pint	*yarus*	*Arum maculatum* L.	¶¶174, 282, *Arrogon*
cumin	*ciminum/ cuminum*	*Cuminum cyminum* L.	¶¶12, 14, 26, 28, 49, 58, 124, 140, 149, 183, 228, 266, 269, 282, 288, *Diaciminum, Trifera magna*
cuttlefish, bones of	*os sepie*		¶¶177, 209, 259, 287, 288, 299, 310
daisy	*consolida minor*	*Bellis perennis* L.	¶149
danewort	*ebulus*	*Sambucus ebulus* L.	¶¶50, 267
date pit	*os dactilorum*		¶¶237, 302
deadly carrot	*tapsia*	*Thapsia garganica* L.	¶14
deadly nightshade	*morella*	*Atropa bella-donna* L.	¶¶66, 70
deer. *See*			

heart; horn;
marrow;
tallow

dill	*anetum*	*Anethum graveolens* L.	¶¶14, 26, *Unguentum aureum*
dittany, dittany of Crete	*diptamus*	*Origanum dictamnus* L. or *Dictamnus albus* L.	*Diathesseron, Potio sancti Pauli, Theriac*
dodder, thyme dodder	*epithimum*	*Cuscuta epithymum* (L.) Murr.	¶169, *Theodoriton euperiston*
dodder	*ypoquistidos*	*Cytinus hypocistus*	*Theriac*
dove. *See* dung			
dove's-foot cranesbill	*sparagus*	*Geranium molle* L.	¶214, *Benedicta, Unguentum aureum*
dragon's blood	*sanguis draconis*	a kind of red gum or resin from a variety of species, esp. *Daemomorops draco* Blume or *Dracaena draco* L.	¶¶33, 70, 254, 307, 308, *Potio sancti Pauli*
dropwort	*philipendula*	*Filipendula vulgaris* Moench	¶293
dry rot	*caries*		¶154
duck. *See* blood; grease			
dung	*stercus*		¶¶43, 108, 121, 124, 143
dove's dung	*fimus columbarum/ columbinus*		¶¶69, 310
eel	*anguilla*		¶221
egg	*ouum*		¶¶44, 64, 66, 70, 72, 115, 134, 135, 140, 190, 201, 208, 246, 260, 269, 278, 285, 287, 296
ant's egg	*ouum formice*		¶221
egg white	*albugo*		¶70
egg white	*albumen*		¶¶64, 66, 72, 135, 140, 190, 208, 246, 278, 287, 296
egg yolk	*uitellum*		¶¶115, 201, 260, 269
goose egg	*ouum anseris*		¶282
eglantine	*bedegar*	*Rosa rubiginosa* L.	¶¶33, 281

elder	*actis*	*Sambucus nigra* L.	*Dialtea*
elder	*sambucus*	*Sambucus nigra* L.	¶¶140, 143
elecampane	*enula/enula campana*	*Inula helenium* L.	¶¶173, 288
elecampane	*helenium*	*Inula helenium* L.	*Unguentum aureum*
elephant bones, burnt	*spodium*		¶33
elm	*ulmus*	*Ulmus* L. ssp.	¶¶42, 268
emblic	*emblicus*	*Emblica officinalis*	*Trifera saracenica*
fat			
badger fat	*adeps taxonis*		¶68
bear fat	*adeps ursini*		¶263, *Arrogon, Unguentum aureum*
capon fat	*adeps caponis*		¶68
fox fat	*adeps uulpini*		*Unguentum aureum*
goose fat	*adeps anserina/anseris*		¶¶63, 64, 66, 68
hen's fat	*adeps galline*		¶¶66, 68
squirrel fat	*adeps melote*		¶68
felwort	*gentiana*	*Gentiana amarella* (L.) Börner	¶11, *Diathesseron, Potio sancti Pauli, Theodoriton euperiston, Theriac*
fennel	*feniculus*	*Foeniculum vulgare* Mill.	¶¶12, 22, 23, 26, 117, 127, 303, *Benedicta, Trifera magna, Unguentum aureum*
fennel	*maratrum*	*Foeniculum vulgare* Mill.	¶125, *Potio sancti Pauli, Theriac, Trifera saracenica*
fenugreek	*fenugrecum*	*Trigonella foenum-graecum* L.	¶¶50, 61, 63, 66, 69, 70, 73, 91, 93, 116, *Dialtea, Diathesseron*
figwort	*scrophularia*	*Scrophularia nodosa* L.	¶299
fish	*piscis*		¶34
salted fish	*piscis salsus*		¶¶108, 152
scaly fish	*piscis squamosus*		¶¶28, 115
flax	*linum*	*Linum usitatissimum* L.	¶¶116, 153, 190, 279
linen cloth	*pannus lineus/lini*		¶¶48, 53, 125, 136, 149, 152, 154, 161, 163, 175, 190, 191, 227, 242, 246, 269, 279, 302, 306
linseed	*semen lini*		¶¶50, 63, 66, 69, 91,

			93, 109, 115, 268, 297, *Dialtea*
fleabane	*policaria*	*Pulicaria dysenterica* (L.) Bernh.	¶¶157, 206, 227, *Arrogon*
fleawort	*psillium*	*Plantago indica* L.	¶¶66, 116, 184
Florentine iris	*yreos*	*Iris florentina* L.	¶¶22, 299, *Paulinum, Unguentum aureum*
oil of iris	*yreleon*		¶48
Florentine iris	*yris*	*Iris florentina* L.	¶81, *Theriac, Trifera magna*
flour, meal	*farina*		
barley flour	*farina ordei*		¶¶69, 135, 140, 151
bean flour	*farina fabarum*		¶127
lupin flour	*farina lupinorum*		¶282
rice flour	*farina rizi*		¶127
wheat flour	*farina tritici*		¶69
fox. *See* fat			
frankincense	*olibanum*	*Boswellia sacra* Flueck.	¶¶166, 167, 172, 177, 183, 187, 207, 209, 211, 245, 259, 276, 282, 287, 288, 290, *Arrogon, Paulinum, Unguentum album*
frankincense	*thus*	*Boswellia sacra* Flueck.	¶¶70, 91, 112, 227, 233, 237, *Hieralogodion, Potio sancti Pauli, Unguentum aureum*
male frankincense	*tus masculum*		*Theriac*
French lavender	*sticados*	*Lavendula dentata*	*Theriac*
fuller's earth	*chimolea*		¶194
fumitory	*fumus terre*	*Fumaria officinalis* L.	¶¶19, 234
galangal	*galanga*	*Alpinia officinarum* Hance or *Alpinia galanga* (L.) Willd.	¶¶187, 225, 227, 248, 257, *Benedicta, Diaciminum, Rosata novella, Trifera magna*
galbanum	*galbanum*	*Ferula galbaniflua* Boiss. et Buhse	¶¶48, 117, 183, 245, 276, *Dialtea, Paulinum, Theriac*
galingale	*ciperus*	*Cyperus longus* L.	*Trifera magna, Unguentum aureum*
gall	*fel*		¶¶17, 29, 32, 65

bear's gall	*fel ursini*		*Potio sancti Pauli*
bull's gall	*fel tauri*		¶17
garden cress	*nasturcium*	*Lepidium sativum* L.	¶227, *Theriac*
garlic	*allium*	*Allium sativum* L.	¶¶28, 127
ginger	*zinziber*	*Zingiber officinale* Rosc.	¶¶25, 187, 188, 282, 284, *Arrogon, Benedicta, Diaciminum, Potio sancti Pauli, Rosata novella, Theodoriton euperiston, Theriac, Trifera magna*
gladden. *See also* stinking iris	*gladiolus*	*Iris pseudacorus* L.	¶¶166, 176
goat. *See* milk; tallow; uterus			
goose. *See* egg; fat; grease; suet			
gourd	*cucurbita*	*Citrullus colocynthis* (L.) Schrad.	¶¶103, 304
grapes	*racemus*		¶112
grease (animal)	*anxungia/auxungia*		¶¶41, 43, 50, 167, 173, 174, 201, 211, 288
duck grease	*anxungia anatis*		¶115
goose grease	*anxungia anseris*		¶115
hen's grease	*anxungia galline*		¶¶115, 124, 278, 281
pork grease, lard	*anxungia porci/porcina*		¶¶198, 234, 269, 286, 290, *Populeon*
great plantain	*plantago*	*Plantago major* L.	¶¶33, 34, 36, 62, 66, 70, 194, 308
greater celandine	*celidonia*	*Chelidonium majus* L.	¶¶265, 266
greater knapweed	*herba uenti*	*Centaurea scabiosa* L.	*Unguentum aureum*
Greek tar	*colofonia*		¶¶169, 212, 276, *Dialtea*
gromwell	*granum solis*	any one of a number of plants belonging to the family *Boraginaceae* of the genus *Lithospermum*	*Benedicta, Theriac, Unguentum aureum*

gromwell	*litosperma*	*Lithospermon officinale* L.	*Benedicta*
groundsel	*senectio*	*Senecio vulgaris* L.	¶198
gum	*gummi*	perhaps gum arabic?	¶33
gum arabic	*gumi/gummi arabicum*	*Acacia senegal* (L.) Willd.	¶¶124, 174, 276, *Theriac*
gum, ivy	*gumi/gummi hedere*		¶264, *Dialtea, Diathesseron*
gum tragacanth	*dragagantum album*	*Astralagus gummifer* Labill., a kind of tree resin	¶281
hare. *See also* rennet	*lepus*		¶76
hawk	*anceps*		¶121
hazelwort	*asarum*	*Asarum europeum* L.	*Hierapigra, Potio sancti Pauli, Theodoriton euperiston*
heart, deer	*cor cerui*		¶59
hellebore, black	*elleborus nigrus*	*Helleborus niger* L.	¶202, *Hieralogodion*
hellebore, white	*elleborus albus*	*Veratrum album* L.	¶139, *Hieralogodion*
hematite	*lapis emathicis*		¶¶33, 308
hemlock	*benedicta*	*Conium maculatum* L.	¶157
hemlock	*cicuta*	*Conium maculatum* L.	¶16
hen. *See also* fat; grease	*gallina*		¶¶34, 66, 68, 115, 124, 278, 281
henbane	*cassil(l)ago*	*Hyoscyamus niger* L.	¶¶66, 223, 230
henbane	*iusquiamus*	*Hyoscyamus niger* L.	¶¶48, 218, 219, 252, *Populeon, Trifera magna*
henna	*alcanna*	*Lawsonia inermis* L.	¶¶246, 254
hog's fennel	*meu*	*Peucedanum officinale* L.	*Theriac, Unguentum aureum*
hog's fennel	*peucedanum*	*Peucedanum officinale* L.	*Potio sancti Pauli, Trifera magna*
holm oak	*ylex*		¶191
honey	*mel*		¶¶10, 11, 12, 62, 64, 68, 69, 81, 99, 124, 185, 202, 223, 224, 227, 238, 244, 255, 289, 291, 299, 301, 306, *Benedicta,*

			227, 305, *Arrogon,* *Diathesseron,* *Unguentum aureum*
laurel berry	*dampnocrum*	*Laurus nobilis* L.	*Potio sancti Pauli*
laurel, fruit of	*coconidium*	*Daphne gnidium* L. /*laureola* L.	*Hieralogodion*
leech	*sanguissuga*		¶¶179, 195
leek	*porrum*	*Allium porrum* L.	¶¶21, 28, 127, 146, 232
lentil	*lenticulum*	*Lens esculenta* Moench	¶¶56, 70
lesser centaury	*centaurea minor*	*Centaurium minus* Moench	*Theriac*
lettuce	*lactuca*	*Lactuca virosa* L.	¶70, *Populeon*
Levant scammony	*scamonea*	*Convulsus scammonia* L.	*Paulinum, Theodoriton euperiston*
licorice	*liquiricia*	*Glycyrrhiza glabra* L.	*Potio sancti Pauli, Rosata novella*
licorice wood	*lignum liquirum*		¶247
lily	*lilium*	*Lilium* L. ssp.	¶¶167, 176, 184, 199, 285, 286, 290
lime, slaked. *See also* quicklime	*calx extincta*	calcium hydroxide	¶199
linen. *See* flax			
lint	*licinium*		¶¶132, 201
litharge	*litargirum*	"spume of silver or gold"	¶¶72, 288, *Unguentum album*
lizard	*lacerta*		¶250
lovage	*leuisticum*	*Levisticum officinale* Koch	¶¶14, 22, 23, 50, 303, 311, *Diaciminum, Unguentum aureum*
lungwort	*palla marina*	*Pulmonaria officinalis* L.	¶212
lupin bitter lupin	*lupinus* *lupinus amarus*	*Lupinus* L. ssp.	¶¶94, 282 ¶271
lye, cleanser	*lexiuia*		¶¶105, 247, 258, 265, 266, 268
lynx stone	*lapis lyncis*		*Unguentum aureum*
mace	*macis*	the fleshy outer covering of the nutmeg (*Myristica fragrans* Houtt.)	*Benedicta, Trifera saracenica*

madder	*rubea maior*	*Rubia tinctorum* L.	¶¶81, 213, 266, 291
malt	*bracceum*		*Potio sancti Pauli*
mandrake	*mandragora*	*Mandragora officinarum* L.	¶66, *Populeon, Potio sancti Pauli, Trifera magna*
manna	*manna*	gum from the flowering ash tree? (*Fraxinus ornus* L.)	*Trifera saracenica*
marjoram	*maiorana*	*Origanum vulgare* L.	*Arrogon*
marking nut	*anacardum*	*Semecarpus anacardium* L.	*Paulinum, Potio sancti Pauli*
marrow			
cow or steer marrow	*medulla bouina uel uaccina*		¶310
deer marrow	*medulla cerui*		¶63
veal marrow	*medulla uituli*		¶68
marsh mallow	*altea*	*Althaea officinalis* L.	¶¶125, 269
marsh mallow	*bismalua*	*Althaea officinalis* L.	¶223
marsh mallow	*euiscus*	*Althaea officinalis* L.	*Dialtea, Unguentum aureum*
marsh mallow	*malua*	*Althaea officinalis* L.	¶¶66, 91, 105, 107, 115, 129, 133, 135, 151, 154, 159, 196, 201, 208, 214, 223, 225, 226, 286
mastic gum	*mastix*	*Pistacia lentiscus* L.	¶¶81, 166, 167, 183, 233, 237, 245, 269, 276, 288, 290, 299, *Arrogon, Diaciminum, Hierapigra, Oleum rosaceum, Paulinum, Potio sancti Pauli, Theodoriton euperiston, Trifera saracenica, Unguentum album, Unguentum aureum*
mayweed	*maluauiscus*	*Anthemis cotula* L.	¶¶201, 223n
meadow rue	*pigamus*	*Thalictrum flavum* L.	*Diathesseron, Theriac*

			Paulinum, Potio sancti Pauli, Theriac
myrrh	*smirna*		*Theodoriton euperiston*
myrtleberry	*mirta/mirtus*	*Myrtus communis* L.	¶¶11, 33, 70, 178, 258, 270
natron	*nitrum*	soda, hydrated sodium carbonate	¶¶17, 192, 193, 253, 302, 310, *Potio sancti Pauli*
nettle	*urtica*	*Lamium* L./*Urtica* L. ssp.	¶¶26, 159, 216, *Unguentum aureum*
nutmeg	*nux muscata*	*Myristica fragrans* Houtt.	¶¶33, 134, 138, 225, 227, 245, 248, 249, 278, *Rosata novella*
oak	*quercus*	*Quercus* L.	¶¶33, 56
oak apple	*galla*	an excrescence from oaktrees (*Quercus* L.) caused when certain insects lay their eggs in the bark	¶¶33, 56, 70, 194, 251, 254, 256, 307, 308, 309
oat	*auena*	*Avena fatua* L.	¶¶51, 219, 265
oil	*oleum*		¶¶48, 53, 101, 130, 154, 159, 166, 171, 173, 183, 202, 221, 232, 233, 244, 245, 251, 256, 261, 266, 267, 273, *Unguentum album*
common oil	*oleum commune*		¶250, *Arrogon, Oleum rosaceum*
laurel oil	*oleum laurinum/lauri*		¶¶48, 115, 125, 132, 159, 214, 252, *Arrogon, Unguentum aureum*
linseed oil	*oleum seminis lini*		¶¶115, 297
musk oil	*musceleon*		¶48, *Unguentum aureum*
musk oil	*oleum muscelinum/ musceleum*		¶¶129, 131, 141, 146, 150, 161, 227, 229, 230, *Arrogon*
olive oil	*oleum oliuarum*		¶79

pennyroyal oil	*oleum puleginum*		¶¶131, 132, 141, 146, 150, 161, 214, 227, 229, 230
rose oil	*oleum rosaceum/rosatum*	*See* Appendix	¶¶66, 68, 70, 80, 91, 181, 243, 278, 297, *Populeon*
tartar oil	*oleum de tartar /tartari*		¶¶272, 273, 275
violets, oil of	*oleum uiolaceum/ uiolarum*		¶¶79, 91, 243, 278, *Populeon*
olive. *See also* oil, olive	*oliua*		¶¶79, 237
onion	*cepa*	*Allium cepa* L.	¶¶28, 127, 131, 277
opium poppy, juice of	*opium*	*Papaver somniferum* L.	¶¶64, 112, *Paulinum, Theodoriton euperiston, Trifera magna*
opoponax	*oppoponax*	*Opoponax chironium* Koch, a kind of gum resin	¶¶48, 101, *Hieralogodion, Paulinum, Potio sancti Pauli, Theodoriton euperiston, Theriac*
oregano	*origanum*	*Origanum vulgare* L.	¶¶14, 117, 210, 225, *Potio sancti Pauli*
oriental crocus	*crocus orientalis*	*Crocus sativus* L.	¶254, *Paulinum*
orpiment	*auripigmentum*	trisulfide of arsenic	¶¶243, 244, 245, 252, 264, 288, 304
parsley	*petrosellinum/ petroselinum*	*Petroselinum crispum* (Mill.) Nyman	¶¶12, 23, 125, 232, 303, *Benedicta, Hieralogodion, Potio sancti Pauli, Theodoriton euperiston, Theriac, Unguentum aureum*
parsnip	*pastinaca domestica*	*Pastinaca sativa* L.	¶131
partridge	*perdix*		¶¶115, 124
pearl	*margarita*		¶124
pellitory	*piretrum*	*Anacyclus pyrethrum* DC	¶188, *Arrogon, Potio sancti Pauli, Unguentum aureum*

pellitory of Spain	*serpillum*	*Anacyclus pyrethrum* DC	¶204, *Arrogon*
pellitory-of-the-wall	*paritaria/ peritaria*	*Parietaria diffusa* Mert. & Koch	¶¶38, 151, 159, 183
pennyroyal. *See also* oil, pennyroyal	*pulegium*	*Mentha pulegium* L.	¶¶14, 19, 21, 134, 136, 142, 147, 157, 164, 190, 196, 206, 210, 225, 227, *Potio sancti Pauli, Unguentum aureum*
pennywort	*umbellicus ueneris*	*Umbilicus rupestris* (Salisb.) Dandy	*Populeon*
peony	*pionia*	*Paeonia* L. ssp.	*Potio sancti Pauli*
pepper	*piper*	*Piper nigrum* L.; *Piper officinarum* DC	¶¶20, 28, 58, 127, 180, 304, *Arrogon, Trifera magna*
black pepper	*melanopiper*	*Piper nigrum* L.	¶239, *Diaciminum*
black pepper	*piper nigrum*		¶94, *Hieralogodion, Potio sancti Pauli, Theodoriton euperiston*
long pepper	*macropiper*	*Piper longum* L.	*Benedicta, Diaciminum*
long pepper	*piper longum*		*Hieralogodion, Theodoriton euperiston, Theriac*
white pepper	*piper album*		¶48, *Hieralogodion, Potio sancti Pauli, Theodoriton euperiston, Theriac*
petroleum	*petroleum*		*Arrogon, Potio sancti Pauli, Unguentum aureum*
pheasant	*fasianus*		¶¶115, 124
pig. *See also* bacon; grease, pork	*porcus*		¶77
uncastrated male pig	*uerris*		¶82
pignut	*malum terre*	*Conopodium majus* (Gouan) Loret	¶310
pine	*pinea herba*	*Pinus pinea*	¶231
pitch	*aspaltus*		*Theriac*
pitch	*pix*		¶¶48, 149, 150

Greek pitch. *See also* Greek tar	*pix greca*		¶¶154, 183, 185
plaster of Paris	*gipsum*		¶211
polypody	*polipodium*	*Polypodium vulgare* L.	*Hieralogodion, Theodoriton euperiston*
pomegranate	*balaustia*	*Punica granatum* L.	¶¶33, 56, 70
pomegranate	*malum granatum*	*Punica granatum* L.	¶¶33, 56, 80, 251, 307, *Oxizaccara*
skin of pomegranate	*psidia*	*Punica granatum* L.	¶¶33, 70
poplar bud	*oculus populi*	*Populus* L. ssp.	*Populeon*
poppy. *See* also opium poppy, juice of	*amomum*	*Papaver* L. ssp.	*Benedicta, Potio sancti Pauli, Theodoriton euperiston, Theriac, Unguentum aureum*
poppy	*papaueris*	*Papaver* L. ssp.	*Populeon*
prickly lettuce	*scariola*	*Lactuca serriola* L.	¶¶32, 66
pumice	*pumex*		¶¶238, 299, 302
purslane	*portulaca*	*Portulaca oleracea* L.	¶¶33, 66, 70
Queen Anne's lace. *See* wild carrot			
quicklime. *See also* lime, slaked	*calx uiua*	calcium oxide	¶¶243, 244, 245, 304, 312
quicksilver	*argentum uiuum*		¶¶173, 245, 288
quince	*citonium*	*Cydonia oblonga* Mill.	¶¶33, 58, 80
quince	*coctanum*	*Cydonia oblonga* Mill.	¶58
radish	*radix*	*Raphanus sativus* L.	*Arrogon*
ramsons	*affrodilus*	*Allium ursinum* L.	¶241
red dock	*lapacium acutum*	*Rumex aquaticus* L.	¶¶234, 235, 287, 288
reed	*canna*	*Arundo* L./*Calamus* L. ssp.	¶268
rennet	*coagulum*		
calf rennet	*coagulum uituli*		*Potio sancti Pauli*
hare rennet	*coagulum leporis*		*Potio sancti Pauli*
roebuck rennet	*coagulum caprioli*		*Potio sancti Pauli*
sheep rennet	*coagulum agni*		*Potio sancti Pauli*
resin	*resina*		*Dialtea*

rhubarb	*reubarbarum*	*Rheum rhaponticum* L.	*Theriac*
rhubarb	*reuponticum*	*Rheum rhaponticum* L.	¶20, *Potio sancti Pauli, Theodoriton euporiston*
rice	*rizus*	*Oryza sativa* L.	¶127
rock crystal	*cristallum*		¶¶281, 283
rock samphire	*cretanus*	*Crithmum maritinum* L.	¶159
rocket	*eruca*	*Eruca vesicaria* (L.) Cav.	¶¶127, 131, 163, 169
roebuck. See also rennet	*capreolus*		¶49
rose. See also oil, rose; water, rose	*rosa*	*Rosa canina* L.	¶¶33, 56, 70, 133, 154, 169, 174, 194, 208, 226, 248, 300, 304, *Benedicta, Hierapigra, Oleum rosaceum, Potio sancti Pauli, Rosata novella, Theriac, Trifera magna*
rosemary	*ros marinus*	*Rosmarinus officinalis* L.	*Arrogon, Unguentum aureum*
rue	*ruta*	*Ruta graveolens* L.	¶¶21, 22, 54, 69, 94, 101, 117, 183, 213, 229, *Arrogon, Potio sancti Pauli, Unguentum aureum*
rush	*iuncus*	*Juncus* L. ssp.	¶226
saffron, crocus	*crocus*	*Crocus sativus* L.	¶¶68n, 260, 266, *Benedicta, Hieralogodion, Hierapigra, Paulinum, Potio sancti Pauli, Theodoriton euperiston*
sage	*saluia*	*Salvia officinalis* L.	¶¶14, 16, 147, 183, 212, 216, *Arrogon, Potio sancti Pauli*
St.-John's-wort	*ypericon*	*Hypericum perforatum* L.	*Theodoriton euperiston, Theriac*
sal	*sal*		¶¶40, 128, 154, 167, 182, 238, 263, 290, 302
ammonium salt	*sal armoniaca*	ammonium chloride	¶239
rock salt	*sal gemma*		¶¶21, 286, *Benedicta*
savin	*sauina*	*Juniperus sabina* L.	¶¶14, 16, 23, 25, *Arrogon*

saxifrage	*saxifraga*	*Saxifraga* L. ssp.	¶¶158, 159, 214, 297, *Benedicta, Unguentum aureum*
scammony	*diagridium*	*Convulvulus scammonia*	*Benedicta, Hieralogodion, Theodoriton euperiston*
scarlet pimpernel	*pimpinella*	*Anagallis arvensis* L.	¶240
sea bramble	*tribulus marinus*		¶215
sea holly	*creta marina*	*Eryngium maritimum* L.	¶214
sea wormwood	*centonica*	*Artemisia maritima* L.	¶¶16, 19
sealed earth. *See also* Armenian bole	*terra sigillata*	small stamped rounds of a special kind of clay	*Theriac*
serapinum	*serapinum*	gum of an unidentified tree (perhaps of the species *Ferulae*?)	*Hierapigra, Hieralogodion, Paulinum, Potio sancti Pauli*
Smyrnian serapinum	*serapinum smyrne*		*Theodoriton euperiston*
sermountain	*siler*	?	*Potio sancti Pauli, Unguentum aureum*
sermountain	*siler montanum*	*Siler montanum* Crantz	¶208, *Unguentum aureum*
sermountain	*siseleos*	*Laserpitium siler* L.; *Siler montanum* Crantz; or *Seseli montanum* L.	¶14, *Theriac*
service-berry	*sorbum*	*Sorbus domestica*	¶58
sesame	*sisamum*	*Sesamum indicum* L.	¶156
sheep. *See* rennet			
silphium	*silfium*	since true silphium (giant fennel, genus *Ferula*) was extinct by this period, it is not clear what the referent is	*Theodoriton euperiston*
snakeroot	*basilica/basilicon*	*Polygonum bistorta* L.	*Potio sancti Pauli, Unguentum aureum*
soap	*sapo*		¶¶174, 180, 258
French soap	*sapo Gallicus*		¶272
southernwood	*abrotanum*	*Artemisia abrotanum* L.	¶¶230, 268
southernwood	*camphorata*	*Artemisia abrotanum* L.	¶¶216n, 229n

sowbread	*ciclamen*	*Cyclamen hederifolium* Ait.	¶¶282, 297, *Dialtea*
sowbread	*panis porcinus*	*Cyclamen hederifolium* Ait.	¶¶247, 280
spikenard	*spica*	*Nardostachys jatamansi* (Wall.) DC	¶¶12, 53, 67, 134, 138, 139, 225, 227, 237, *Benedicta, Hieralogodion, Hierapigra, Theriac, Trifera magna*
spikenard	*nardus*		*Diaciminum, Potio sancti Pauli, Rosata novella, Theodoriton euperiston*
spikenard oil	*nardileon*		¶48
spurge	*esula*	*Euphorbia* L. ssp.	¶288, *Benedicta*
spurge	*euforbium*	*Euphorbia* L.	¶131, *Arrogon, Hieralogodion, Potio sancti Pauli, Unguentum aureum*
spurge laurel	*laureola*	*Daphne laureola* L.	¶142, *Arrogon*
spurge laurel?	*muscillago*		¶116
squill	*squilla*	*Scilla* L.	¶277, *Dialtea Hieralogodion, Theodoriton euperiston, Theriac*
squirting cucumber	*cucumeris agrestis*	*Ecballium elaterium* A. Rich.	¶¶245, 294
starch	*amidum*		¶¶273, 274, 287, 299
stavesacre	*stafisagria*	*Delphinium staphisagria* L.	*Potio sancti Pauli*
stinking iris	*spatula (fetida)*	*Iris feotidissima* L.	¶176
storax	*storax*	*Styrax officinalis* L.	¶¶53, 112, *Potio sancti Pauli, Rosata novella, Theriac, Trifera magna*
calamite storax	*storax calamita*	"the first and best gum that drips out of the (storax) tree"	¶¶134, *Paulinum, Potio sancti Pauli, Theriac, Trifera magna*
suet, tallow	*sagimen*		¶¶140, 154
goose tallow	*sagimen anseris*		¶73

sugar	zuccara/zuccarus/ zucchara/succara	Saccharum officinarum L.	¶¶79, 81, 101, 124, 127, 187, Benedicta, Oxizaccara, Rosata novella, Trifera saracenica
sulfur	sulfur/sulphur		Potio sancti Pauli
natural sulfur	sulphur uiuum		¶304
sumac	sumac	Rhus coriaria L.	¶¶56, 194, Theriac
summer savory	satureia/saturegia	Satureia hortensis L.	¶¶14, 62, 95, Potio sancti Pauli
summer savory	timbra	Satureia hortensis L.	Diaciminum
swallow	yrundo		¶122
sweet basil	ozimum	Ocimum basilicum L.	Theriac, Trifera magna
sweet flag	acorus	Acorus calamus L.	Theodoriton euperiston, Theriac, Trifera magna, Unguentum aureum
sweet flag	calamus aromaticus	Acorus calamus L.	Potio sancti Pauli, Trifera magna
tallow	sepum	the hard fat of an animal, suet	¶166
deer tallow	sepum ceruinum		¶283
goat tallow	sepum hyrcinum		¶277
tamarind	tamarindus	Tamarindus indica	Trifera saracenica
tansy	tanacetum	Chrysanthemum vulgare L.	¶24
tartar. See also oil of tartar	tartarum	potassium bitartrate	¶¶186, 241, 272, 273, 275, 306
thyme	thimus	Thymus vulgaris L.	¶169, Hieralogodion
thyme dodder. See dodder			
tow	stupa	the coarse and broken part of flax	¶306
turnip	rapa	Brassica rapa L.	¶165, Theriac
turpentine	terbentina	the oleoresin from the terebinth tree (Pistacia terebinthus L.)	Dialtea, Paulinum, Theriac
uterus, goat	matrix capre		¶84
valerian	phu	Valeriana officinalis L.	Unguentum aureum
varnish	uernix		¶¶281, 283

veal. *See* marrow; rennet			
vegetable turpeth	*turbit*	*Ipomoea turpethum*	Benedicta, Hierapigra
vervain	*uerbena*	*Verbena officinalis* L.	¶¶96, 208, 213, 223, 268
vetch	*orobus*	*Lathyrus* L. & *Vicia* L. ssp.	¶253
vine	*uitis*		¶¶247, 265
vinegar	*acetum*		¶¶34, 80, 96, 124, 148, 166, 173, 200, 221, 232, 251, 256, 258, 264, 270, 271, 273, 284, 288, 300, 304, Oxizaccara
violet. *See also* oil of violet	*uiola*	*Viola* L. ssp.	¶¶32, 133, 208, 226, Hierapigra, Populeon, Trifera saracenica
vitriol	*calcantus*		Diathesseron, Theriac
vitriol	*dragantum*		Potio sancti Pauli
wall germander	*camedreos*	*Teucrium chamaedrys* L.	Diathesseron, Hieralogodion, Potio sancti Pauli, Theodoriton euperiston, Theriac, Unguentum aureum
wall germander	*polium*	*Teucrium chamaedrys* L.	Hieralogodion, Theriac
walnut	*nux magna/maior*	*Juglans regia* L.	¶¶182, 186
water bran water	*aqua furfuris*		¶¶177, 287
rainwater	*aqua pluuiali*		¶¶33, 137, 142, 169, 191, 194, 236
rose water	*aqua rosacea/rosata*		¶¶97, 167, 174, 175, 177, 236, 248, 259, 278, 282, 286, 290, 294, Unguentum album
salt or salted water	*aqua salsa*		¶¶97, 142, 159, 215
seawater	*aqua marina/maris*		¶¶34, 43, 58, 142, 159, 215
"sweet" water, fresh water	*aqua dulcis*		¶125
watercress	*cardamomum*	*Rorippa nasturtium-*	¶¶81, 248, Benedicta,

			217, 221, 223, 224, 230, 231, 245, 258, 269, *Theodoriton euperiston*
fine wine	*uinum subtile*		¶127
high-quality wine	*uinum optimum*		¶¶142, 143, 291, 303
red wine	*uinum rubeum*		¶¶34, 125, 136
sweet wine	*uinum dulce*		¶48
white wine	*uinum album*		¶¶37, 48, 255, 306, *Unguentum aureum*
wood avens	*auancia*	*Geum urbanum* L.	¶293
wood sage	*lilifagus*	*Teucrium scorodonia* L.	*Potio sancti Pauli, Theriac*
wool	*lana*		¶¶14, 17, 46, 48, 53, 78, 141, 153, 161, 302
wormwood	*absinthium*	*Artemisia absinthium* L.	¶¶40, 41, 54, 91, 94, 101, 142, 152, 157, 183, 201, 212, 223, 227, 230, 237, 298, 301, *Hieralogodion, Hierapigra, Theodoriton euperiston*
yellow flag	*flammula*	*Iris pseudacorus* L.	¶16
zedoary	*zedoarium*	*Curcuma zedoaria* (Berg.) Roxb.	¶81, *Diathesseron, Rosata novella, Trifera magna*

Notes

Preface

1. I have thus far identified translations into Dutch (three versions), English (five), French (seven), German (three), Hebrew (one), Irish (one), Italian (two), plus one Latin prose and one Latin verse rendition; only a few of these have been edited. For full details on all the Latin and vernacular manuscripts, see Monica H. Green, "A Handlist of Latin and Vernacular Manuscripts of the So-Called *Trotula* Texts. Part 1: The Latin Manuscripts," *Scriptorium* 50 (1996): 137-75, and "Part 2: The Vernacular Translations and Latin Re-Writings," *Scriptorium* 51 (1997): 80-104; and the appendix to *Women's Healthcare in the Medieval West: Texts and Contexts* (Aldershot: Ashgate, 2000).

2. *The Trotula: A Medieval Compendium of Women's Medicine*, ed. and trans. Monica H. Green (Philadelphia: University of Pennsylvania Press, 2001). An edition of one version of the Latin *Liber de sinthomatibus mulierum* only, together with a thirteenth-century verse Anglo-Norman translation, can be found in Tony Hunt, ed., *Anglo-Norman Medicine*, 2 vols. (Cambridge: D. S. Brewer, 1994–1997), vol. 2, pp. 76–128. A Middle English gynecological text commonly referred to as an "English Trotula" (Beryl Rowland, ed., *Medieval Woman's Guide to Health: The First English Gynecological Handbook* [Kent, Ohio: Kent State University Press, 1981]) is not the *Trotula*, but a modified translation of the gynecological chapters of Gilbertus Anglicus's *Compendium of Medicine*. See Monica H. Green, "Obstetrical and Gynecological Texts in Middle English," *Studies in the Age of Chaucer* 14 (1992): 53–88; reprinted in Green, *Women's Healthcare*, essay 4. An edition of an authentic Middle English translation of one of the *Trotula* texts can now be found in Alexandra Barratt, ed., *Knowing of Woman's Kind in Childing*, Medieval Women: Texts and Contexts, 4 (Turnhout: Brepols, 2001).

3. *Trotulae curandarum Aegritudinum Muliebrium, ante, in & post partum liber unicus, nusquam antea editus*, ed. Georg Kraut, published in a collection entitled *Experimentarius medicinae* (Strasbourg: Joannes Schottus, 1544). All twelve subsequent editions (the last in 1778) reprint Kraut's edition with only minor changes.

4. Elizabeth Mason-Hohl, trans., *The Diseases of Women by Trotula of Salerno: A Translation of "Passionibus mulierum curandorum"* (Hollywood, Calif.: Ward Ritchie Press, 1940), an English translation based on the 1547 Aldine (Venice) edition; Clodomiro Mancini, trans., *Il De mulierum passionibus di Trocta salernitana*, Scientia Veterum 31 (Genoa: n.p., 1962), an Italian translation lacking the preface (Mancini does not specify which edition he used, except to say that it is a copy from the Biblioteca Canevari); Pina Cavallo Boggi, ed., Matilde Nubié and Adriana Tocco, trans., *Trotula de Ruggiero: Sulle malattie delle donne* (Turin: La Rose, 1979), an Italian translation based on the 1547 Aldine (Venice) edition; and most recently, Pina Boggi Cavallo, ed., Piero Cantalupo, trans., *Trotula de Ruggiero: Sulle malattie delle donne* (Palermo: La Luna, 1994), a revised Italian translation again based on the 1547

Venice edition though here with a small sampling of variants from two manuscripts, neither of which has the full text of the ensemble.

5. The most famous medieval reference to the author "Trotula" is that of Geoffrey Chaucer, who includes her among the authorities in the clerk Jankyn's notorious antifeminist collection, the "book of wikked wyves"; *Canterbury Tales, Wife of Bath's Prologue*, 3 (D), 669-85, in *The Riverside Chaucer*, ed. Larry D. Benson, 3d ed. (Boston: Houghton Mifflin, 1987), p. 114.

6. In a number of manuscripts, scribes still distinguished between the first text, now dubbed the *Trotula major* ("The Greater Trotula" = ¶¶1–131), and the latter two, which were often seen as a unit called the *Trotula minor* ("The Lesser Trotula" = ¶¶132–312).

7. In his 1566 reprint of Kraut's 1544 edition, Hans Kaspar Wolf claimed that the text was the work of a male physician named Eros, a freed slave of the Roman empress Julia (first century C.E.); see Wolf, *Gynaeciorum, hoc est de Mulierum tum aliis, tum gravidarum, parientium et puerperarum affectibus et morbis libri veterum ac recentiorem aliquot, partim nunc primum editi, partim multo quam ante castigatiores* (Basel: Thomas Guarinus, 1566), coll. 215–16: "Erotis medici liberti Iuliae, quem aliqui Trotulam inepte nominant, muliebrium liber, longè quàm ante hac emendatior." On the history of the "Trotula question," see Susan Mosher Stuard, "Dame Trot," *Signs: Journal of Women in Culture and Society* 1 (1975): 537–42; John F. Benton, "Trotula, Women's Problems, and the Professionalization of Medicine in the Middle Ages," *Bulletin of the History of Medicine* 59 (1985): 30–53; and Monica H. Green, "In Search of an 'Authentic' Women's Medicine: The Strange Fates of Trota of Salerno and Hildegard of Bingen," *Dynamis: Acta Hispanica ad Medicinae Scientiarumque Historiam Illustrandam* 19 (1999): 25–54.

8. This is not to say that medieval editors and scribes never realized how protean the texts were; on the contrary, scribes frequently compared different versions of the texts in order to correct the errors of faulty exemplars. In two fifteenth-century cases, they even attempted to "reconstruct" the ensemble from original versions of the three independent texts. See also the Introduction for some medieval reattributions of the *Trotula*.

9. I have differentiated four versions of *Conditions of Women*, two of *Treatments for Women*, three of *Women's Cosmetics*, and six of the ensemble. The total number of extant Latin manuscripts currently known is 126, comprising 146 copies of the texts. For full details, see Monica H. Green, "The Development of the *Trotula*," *Revue d'Histoire des Textes* 26 (1996): 119–203, reprinted in Green, *Women's Healthcare*, essay 5; "Handlist"; and the appendix to *Women's Healthcare*, s.v. *Trotula*.

10. Adaptations and manipulations of the texts were made long after the mid-thirteenth century, but aside from the vernacular translations (which have a tremendous importance in their own right), most of these later adaptations were isolated revisions that are never found in more than one or two manuscripts.

11. See the Introduction on the difficulties of identifying botanicals. Notably, of the 152 substances recommended for gynecological or obstetrical conditions in the *PDR for Herbal Medicines* (Montvale, N.J.: Medical Economics Company, 1998)—which is itself based in large part on the authoritative German "Commission E" Reports—44 are employed in the *Trotula* (including the compound medicines). The actual overlap is significantly lower, however, since in only some of these cases are the

herbs currently recommended for approximately the same conditions as cited in the *Trotula*. Thus, for example, only 5 of the 27 substances recommended in the *PDR* herbal for "dysmenorrhea" appear in the *Trotula*, and of these, only 3 are actually recommended for conditions connected with difficult menstruation or uterine pain (*ameos, balsamitum,* and *origanum*). In contrast, of the 40 substances recommended in the *PDR* for "menstrual disorders" (admittedly a broad and vague category), fully 17 are found in the *Trotula*, of which 13 are recommended at least once for some kind of menstrual condition or uterine pain.

12. Green, "Handlist."

13. Green, "Development."

14. My arguments about authorial gender will be laid out fully in *Women and Literate Medicine in Medieval Europe: Trota and the "Trotula"* (forthcoming).

15. Benton, "Trotula."

16. Monica H. Green, "The Transmission of Ancient Theories of Female Physiology and Disease Through the Early Middle Ages" (Ph.D. diss., Princeton University, 1985).

Introduction

1. What would have differed are the rates at which these diseases manifested themselves in medieval populations. For excellent examples of the new data and interpretations from scientific paleopathological researches, see Joël Blondiaux, "La femme et son corps au haut moyen-âge vus par l'anthropologue et le paleopathologiste," in *La Femme au moyen âge*, ed. Michel Rouche and Jean Heuclin (Maubeuge: Publication de la Ville de Maubeuge, Diffusion Jean Touzot, 1990), pp. 115–37; Sylvia A. Jiménez Brobeil, "A Contribution to Medieval Pathological Gynaecology," *Journal of Paleopathology* 4 (1992): 155–61; and Anne L. Grauer, "Life Patterns of Women from Medieval York," in *The Archaeology of Gender: Proceedings of the Twenty-Second Annual Conference of the Archaeological Association of the University of Calgary*, ed. Dale Walde and Noreen D. Willows (Calgary: University of Calgary Archaeological Association, 1991), pp. 407–13.

2. Robert L. Benson and Giles Constable, with Carol D. Lanham, eds., *Renaissance and Renewal in the Twelfth Century* (Cambridge: Harvard University Press, 1982).

3. In referring to "Arabic medicine," I refer to its language of composition. Writers of "Arabic medicine" were in some cases non-Arabs; Christians, or Jews, as well as Muslims.

4. In some manuscripts, the rubric *Trotula minor* encompassed both the *Treatments for Women* and *Women's Cosmetics*. See Preface, n. 6, above.

5. *Treatments for Women* cites the Salernitan masters Copho, Trota, Mattheus Ferrarius, and either Johannes Furias or Johannes Ferrarius. Copho is likely to have been active in the second quarter of the twelfth century, while Mattheus Ferrarius flourished in the middle decades of the century. On Trota, see below.

6. The Roman poet Ovid wrote a facetious poem on cosmetics in the first century; see P. Ovidi Nasonis, *Amores, Medicamina faciei femineae, Ars amatoris, Remedia*

amoris, ed. E. J. Kenney (Oxford: Clarendon Press, 1961). A first-century Greek text, *On Cosmetics*, is attributed to Cleopatra; all that remains is a fragment on weights and measures. See Friedrich Hultsch, *Metrologicorum scriptorum reliquiae*, vol. 1, *Scriptores Graeci* (Leipzig: Teubner, 1864), pp. 108–29 and 233–36. There is no evidence that the full text of this pseudo-Cleopatran *Cosmetics* was ever available in Latin, though a reference to it may be behind the attribution of the strictly gynecological (and equally pseudonymous) *Gynecology of Cleopatra* (*Gynaecia Cleopatrae*) and *Pessaries of Cleopatra* (*De pessis Cleopatrae*).

7. Arcangelo R. Amarotta, "Pourquoi Salerne?" in *From Epidaurus to Salerno: Symposium Held at the European University Centre for Cultural Heritage, Ravello, April 1990*, ed. Antje Krug, *PACT* 34 (1992): 11–18; Luis García-Ballester, "Introduction: Practical Medicine from Salerno to the Black Death," in *Practical Medicine from Salerno to the Black Death*, ed. Luis García-Ballester et al. (Cambridge: Cambridge University Press, 1994), pp. 1–29. A controversial book by Piero Morpurgo, *Filosofia della natura nella Schola salernitana del secolo XII*, pref. Enrique Montero Cartelle (Bologna: CLUEB, 1990), argues that the most distinctive aspects of the new Salernitan natural philosophy had their origin not in Salerno itself but within the circle of scholars at the Petit Pont in Paris, several of whom then migrated to Salerno bringing their novel perspectives with them. Patricia Skinner, *Health and Medicine in Early Medieval Southern Italy*, The Medieval Mediterranean, 11 (Leiden: Brill, 1997), follows Morpurgo in expressing skepticism about Salerno's uniqueness. My work with the *Trotula* texts, even though it shows (in the case of the *Treatments for Women*) English influence, offers nothing to suggest a Parisian connection. And there is more than ample evidence — codicological, documentary, and textual — to confirm the vibrant *local* intellectual activity in southern Italy (and Salerno in particular) in the early twelfth century.

8. Salernitan physicians figure in tales by, for example, Marie de France, Chrétien de Troyes, and Hartman von Aue.

9. Benjamin of Tudela, *The Itinerary*, introductions by Michael A. Signer, Marcus Nathan Adler, and A. Asher (Malibu, California: Joseph Simon/Pangloss Press, 1983), p. 66.

10. al-Idrisi, *L'Italia descritta nel "Libro del Re Ruggero" compilato da Edrisi*, trans. (into Italian) Michele Amari and Celestino Schiaparelli, in *Atti della Reale Accademia dei Lincei* 274 [2d ser., vol. 8, 1876–77] (Rome: Salviucci, 1883), p. 96.

11. William of Apulia, *De rebus gestis Roberti Wiscardi*, ed. and trans. (into French) Marguerite Mathieu, *La Geste de Robert Guiscard*, Istituto Siciliano di Studi Bizantini e Neoellenici, Testi e Monumenti, 4 (Palermo: Istituto Siciliano di Studi Bizantini e Neoellenici, 1961), bk. 3, ll. 470–75, p. 190.

12. Philip Grierson, "The Salernitan Coinage of Gisulf II (1052–1077) and Robert Guiscard (1077–1085)," *Papers of the British School of Rome* 24, n.s. 2 (1956): 40–46.

13. S. D. Goitein, *A Mediterranean Society: The Jewish Communities of the Arab World as Portrayed in the Documents of the Cairo Geniza*, 6 vols., vol. 6 with Paula Sanders (Berkeley: University of California Press, 1967–93), 1: 40, 211.

14. Moshe Gil, "Sicily, 827–1072, in Light of the Geniza Documents and Parallel Sources," in *Italia Judaica: Gli ebrei in Sicilia sino all'espulsione del 1492. Atti del V convegno internazionale Palermo, 15–19 giugno 1992*, Pubblicazioni degli Archivi di Stato, Saggi 32 (Palermo: Ministero per i Beni Culturali e Ambientali, 1995), pp. 96–171, esp.

pp. 131–39. On the total integration of Sicily into the much larger world of Muslim and Jewish Mediterranean culture, see also Abraham Udovitch, "New Materials for the History of Islamic Sicily," in *Giornata di Studio: Del Nuovo sulla Sicilia musulmana (Roma, 3 maggio 1993)* (Rome: Accademia Nazionale dei Lincei, 1995), pp. 183–210.

15. The three female houses were S. Giorgio, SS. Michele Archangelo e Stefano, and S. Maria delle Donne. Two further male houses, S. Clementis and S. Trinitatis (Cava), were located outside the city.

16. L. Cassese, *Pergamene del monastero benedettino di S. Giorgio (1038–1698)* (Salerno: Archivio di Stato, 1950); the document regarding the infirmary dates from 1038 (pp. 3–6). Additional documents can be found in Maria Galante, *Nuove pergamene del monastero femminile di S. Giorgio di Salerno*, vol. 1 (993–1256), Edizioni Studi Storici Meridionali, 7 (Salerno: Edizioni Studi Storici Meridionali, 1984).

17. Arcangelo R. Amarotta, *Salerno romana e medievale: Dinamica di un insediamento*, Società Salernitana di Storia Patria, Collana di Studi Storici Salernitani, 2 (Salerno: Pietro Laveglia, 1989). On the tendency for water rights to shift from public control (as had been the case in antiquity) to private control, see Paolo Squatriti, *Water and Society in Early Medieval Italy, AD 400–1000* (Cambridge: Cambridge University Press, 1998).

18. Squatriti, *Water and Society*, pp. 32, 45.

19. Amarotta, *Salerno*, pp. 242–43; A. Garufi, "Di un stabilimento balneare in Salerno nel secolo XII," *Studi medievali* 1 (1904–5): 276–80. Among those granted permission to use the baths at Santa Sofia were the nuns of the neighboring house of S. Maria delle Donne. The monastery of Santa Sofia became a female house in the thirteenth century; see Galante, *Nuove pergamene*, p. 40.

20. See the index under "baths" for pertinent references.

21. Patricia Skinner, "Urban Communities in Naples, 900–1050," *Papers of the British School at Rome* 49, n.s. 62 (1994): 279–99, at p. 281.

22. Skinner, *Health and Medicine*.

23. Armand O. Citarella, "Amalfi and Salerno in the Ninth Century," in *Istituzioni civili e organizzazione ecclesiastica nello Stato medievale amalfitano: Atti del Congresso internazionale di studi Amalfitani, Amalfi, 3–5 luglio 1981* (Amalfi: Centro di Cultura e Storia Amalfitana, 1986), pp. 129–45; and "Merchants, Markets, and Merchandise in Southern Italy in the High Middle Ages," in *Mercati e mercanti nell'alto medioevo: L'area euroasiatica e l'area mediterranea, 23–29 aprile 1992*, Settimane di Studio del Centro Italiano di Studi sull'Alto Medioevo, 40 (Spoleto: Centro Italiano di Studi sull'Alto Medioevo, 1993), pp. 239–84.

24. For the eleventh century, see Huguette Taviani-Carozzi, *La principauté lombarde de Salerne (IX–XI siècle). Pouvoir et société en Italie lombarde méridionale*, 2 vols., Collection de l'École française de Rome, 152 (Rome: École Française, 1991); Kenneth Baxter Wolf, *Making History: The Normans and Their Historians in Eleventh-Century Italy* (Philadelphia: University of Pennsylvania Press, 1995); and Valerie Ramseyer, "Ecclesiastical Power and the Restructuring of Society in Eleventh-Century Salerno" (Ph.D. diss., University of Chicago, 1996). For the twelfth century, see Donald Matthew, *The Norman Kingdom of Sicily* (Cambridge: Cambridge University Press, 1992).

25. Herbert Bloch, *Monte Cassino in the Middle Ages*, 3 vols. (Cambridge: Harvard University Press, 1986), 1: 93–94.

26. Graham A. Loud, "How 'Norman' Was the Norman Conquest of Southern

Italy?" *Nottingham Medieval Studies* 25 (1981): 13–34; Joanna H. Drell, "Family Structure in the Principality of Salerno During the Norman Period, 1077–1154," *Anglo-Norman Studies: Proceedings of the Battle Conference* 18 (1995): 70–103; and "Marriage, Kinship, and Power: Family Structure in the Principality of Salerno Under Norman Rule, 1077–1154" (Ph.D. diss., Brown University, 1996).

27. For their part, however, men could not alienate their female relatives' property without the woman's permission.

28. *The Lombard Laws*, trans. Katherine Fischer Drew (Philadelphia: University of Pennsylvania Press, 1973), esp. p. 92. Evidence concerning the general legal and social history of women in southern Italy in the central Middle Ages has only recently begun to be collected. See in particular the essays of Patricia Skinner, "Women, Wills and Wealth in Medieval Southern Italy," *Early Medieval Europe* 2 (1993): 133–52; "The Possessions of Lombard Women in Italy," *Medieval Life* 2 (spring 1995): 8–11; "Disputes and Disparity: Women at Court in Medieval Southern Italy," *Reading Medieval Studies* 22 (1996): 85–105; "Women, Literacy and Invisibility in Southern Italy, 900–1200," in *Women, the Book and the Godly: Selected Proceedings of the St Hilda's Conference, 1993*, ed. Lesley Smith and Jane H. M. Taylor (Cambridge: D. S. Brewer, 1995), pp. 1–11; and "'And Her Name Was . . .?' Gender and Naming in Medieval Southern Italy," *Medieval Prosopography* 20 (1999): 23–49.

29. Drell, "Marriage, Kinship, and Power," pp. 191–94. Drell notes some shifts in the role of *mundoalds* (men who held a woman's *mundium*) over the course of the twelfth century (pp. 197–212), though she emphasizes that this was more out of concern for limiting the dispersal of family patrimony than granting women power for their own sake.

30. Skinner, "Women, Wills," pp. 144–45; and "Women, Literacy."

31. Drell, "Marriage, Kinship, and Power," p. 15.

32. Copho, for example, distinguishes special remedies for noble people at least six times. See Copho, *Practica*, in Rudolf Creutz, "Der Magister Copho und seine Stellung im Hochsalerno: Aus M. p. med. Q 2 (saec. XIII), fol. 85ᵃ–103ᵃ Würzburg," *Sudhoffs Archiv für Geschichte der Medizin und der Naturwissenschaften* 31 (1938): 51–60, and 33, nos. 5 and 6 (July 1941): 249–338, at pp. 259, 272–73, 318, 325. In one case (p. 323), he identifies a specific remedy for rich people (*divites*).

33. Undoubtedly there were women who fell into none of these categories. See the discussion of prostitutes below. The essays collected by Judith Bennett and Amy Froide in *Singlewomen in the European Past, 1250–1800* (Philadelphia: University of Pennsylvania Press, 1999) have laid out many new avenues for research.

34. Skinner, "Women, Wills," p. 138.

35. Matthew, *Norman Kingdom*, pp. 160–61.

36. Muhammad ibn Ahmad ibn Jubayr, *The Travels of Ibn Jubayr, being the chronicle of a mediaeval Spanish Moor concerning his journey to the Egypt of Saladin, [etc.]*, trans. R. J. C. Broadhurst (London: J. Cape, 1952), pp. 349–50.

37. See the note to ¶245 in the text. It is not clear whether the reference to noblewomen in ¶249, which was added later in the development of the *Trotula* ensemble, comes out of a Salernitan context.

38. David Nirenberg, *Communities of Violence: Persecution of Minorities in the Middle Ages* (Princeton: Princeton University Press, 1996), pp. 8–9.

39. Alfanus, *Ad Guidonem*, as translated by Bloch, *Monte Cassino*, 1: 97. For

Alfanus's career, see pp. 93–98; and Francis Newton, *The Scriptorium and Library at Monte Cassino, 1058–1109*, Cambridge Studies in Palaeography and Codicology, 7 (Cambridge: Cambridge University Press, 1999), pp. 12–13, 246–47.

40. Skinner, *Health and Medicine*, pp. 84–87.

41. Amarotta, "Pourquoi Salerne?" offers a thorough summary of evidence for the thriving economy and presence of physicians in tenth-century Salerno.

42. For example, the polymath Adelard of Bath and several English or Anglo-Norman physicians are known to have studied in Salerno; some Salernitan physicians also emigrated to England. Moreover, some of the earliest extant manuscripts of Constantinian and Salernitan writings come from England. See Charles S. F. Burnett, *The Introduction of Arabic Learning into England*, Panizzi Lectures, 1996 (London: British Library, 1997), pp. 16–29; Morpurgo, *Filosofia della natura*, pp. 112–13; and Florence Eliza Glaze, "The Perforated Wall: The Ownership and Circulation of Medical Books in Medieval Europe, ca. 800–1200" (Ph.D. diss., Duke University, 1999), pp. 286–96. On the specific significance of this English connection to *Treatments of Women*, see below.

43. The definitive study of the institutional history of the school remains Paul Oskar Kristeller, "The School of Salerno: Its Development and Its Contribution to the History of Learning," *Bulletin of the History of Medicine* 17 (1945): 138–94; reprinted in Italian translation with further revisions as *Studi sulla Scuola medica Salernitana* (Naples: Istituto Italiano per gli Studi Filosofici, 1986). See also Vivian Nutton, "Velia and the School of Salerno," *Medical History* 15 (1971): 1–11; and "Continuity or Rediscovery: The City Physician in Classical Antiquity and Mediaeval Italy," in *The Town and State Physician in Europe from the Middle Ages to the Enlightenment*, ed. A. W. Russell (Wolfenbüttel: Herzog August Bibliothek, 1981). For a comprehensive bibliography through 1990, see Andrea Cuna, *Per una bibliografia della Scuola medica Salernitana (secoli XI–XIII)* (Milan: Guerini e Associati, 1993).

44. Glaze, "Perforated Wall," chap. 4. Glaze also demonstrates (pp. 50–51) that a second figure usually associated with eleventh-century Salerno, "Petrocellus," reflects the nineteenth-century scholar Salvatore De Renzi's mistaken identification of a composite late antique text, *Tereoperica*, as the work of a later-twelfth-century Salernitan writer named Petrus Musandinus (or Petruncellus).

45. My thanks to Francis Newton for informing me of his findings on the early date of Alfanus's translation of Nemesius (personal communication, June 2000).

46. There is debate among scholars whether he was Muslim or Christian. His religion of birth is of less import for this story than his native language.

47. On Constantine and his *oeuvre*, see Bloch, *Monte Cassino*, 1: 99–110, 127–34, and 2: 1100–1; and most recently the essays in *Constantine the African and 'Alī ibn al-'Abbās al-Maǧusī: The "Pantegni" and Related Texts*, ed. Charles Burnett and Danielle Jacquart (Leiden: E. J. Brill, 1994). On the intellectual culture of Monte Cassino, see Newton, *Scriptorium and Library*.

48. On the *Viaticum*, see Monica H. Green, "Constantinus Africanus and the Conflict Between Religion and Science," in *The Human Embryo: Aristotle and the Arabic and European Traditions*, ed. G. R. Dunstan (Exeter: Exeter University Press, 1990), pp. 47–69; Mary F. Wack, *Lovesickness in the Middle Ages: The "Viaticum" and Its Commentaries* (Philadelphia: University of Pennsylvania Press, 1990); Gerrit Bos, "Ibn al-Jazzār on Women's Diseases and Their Treatment," *Medical History* 37 (1993):

296–312; and idem, *Ibn al-Jazzār on Sexual Diseases and Their Treatment*, Sir Henry Wellcome Asian Series (London: Kegan Paul, 1997).

49. Mark D. Jordan, "Medicine as Science in the Early Commentaries on 'Johannitius,'" *Traditio* 43 (1987): 121–45; idem, "The Construction of a Philosophical Medicine: Exegesis and Argument in Salernitan Teaching on the Soul," *Osiris*, 2d ser. 6 (1990): 42–61; García-Ballester, "Introduction."

50. By the third quarter of the twelfth century, Galen's *Ars medendi* was added to the collection as well.

51. Brian Lawn, *The Salernitan Questions: An Introduction to the History of Medieval and Renaissance Problem Literature* (Oxford: Clarendon Press, 1963); *The Prose Salernitan Questions* (London: British Academy/Oxford University Press, 1979).

52. Glaze, "Perforated Wall"; Kristeller, *Studi*; Jordan, "Philosophical Medicine."

53. See George Washington Corner, *Anatomical Texts of the Earlier Middle Ages* (Washington, D.C.: Carnegie Institute of Washington, 1927); Karl Sudhoff, "Die erste Tieranatomie von Salerno und ein neuer salernitanischer Anatomietext," *Archiv für Geschichte der Mathematik, der Naturwissenschaften, und der Technik* 10 (1927): 136–47; idem, "Die vierte Salernitaner Anatomie," *Archiv für Geschichte der Medizin* 20 (1928): 33–50; and Ynez Violé O'Neill, "Another Look at the 'Anatomia Porci,'" *Viator* 1 (1970): 115–24.

54. Tips on practitioner-patient relations did not always conform to the spirit of the Hippocratic Oath. In discussing sanious flux from the womb, Master Salernus brutally observes, "Sometimes it happens that after their cure patients remain ungrateful toward the physician. Therefore, let them be given cut alum with any kind of cooked food so that they are afflicted once again. For if alum is taken, a lesion will necessarily be generated in some part of the body and they will fall sick again" (*Catholica Magistri Salerni*, in *Magistri Salernitani nondum editi*, ed. Piero Giacosa [Turin: Fratelli Bocca, 1901], p. 145).

55. Dietlinde Goltz, *Mittelalterliche Pharmazie und Medizin* (Stuttgart: Wissenschaftliche Verlagsgesellschaft, 1976), pp. 43–45. On earlier uses of alphabetization, see Augusto Beccaria, *I codici di medicina del periodo presalernitano (secoli IX, X, e XI)* (Rome: Edizioni di Storia e Letteratura, 1956), regarding the pseudo-Galenic *Alphabetum ad Paternum*.

56. Besides the gynecological sections of the works just mentioned, the only other gynecological materials of Salernitan origin that I have discovered are what seems to be an excerpt from an unidentified *Practica*, a brief tract on infertility, and a collection of recipes drawn from a variety of sources. See the appendix to Monica H. Green, *Women's Healthcare in the Medieval West: Texts and Contexts* (Aldershot: Ashgate, 2000), pp. 11, 15, and 30–31.

57. All these anatomical descriptions derive largely from Constantine's *Pantegni* and the pseudo-Galenic *De spermate*; see Corner, *Anatomical Texts*, pp. 52–53, 64–65, 84, 86, and 103–7. For further discussion of female anatomy, see Danielle Jacquart and Claude Thomasset, *Sexuality and Medicine in the Middle Ages*, trans. Matthew Adamson (Cambridge: Polity Press; Princeton: Princeton University Press, 1988); and Joan Cadden, *Meanings of Sex Difference in the Middle Ages: Medicine, Science, and Culture* (Cambridge: Cambridge University Press, 1993).

58. Cited from the Latin text in W. S. van den Berg, *Eene Middelnederlandsche Vertaling van het Antidotarium Nicolai (MS 15624–15641, Kon. Bibl. te Brussel)* (Leiden:

E. J. Brill, 1917), p. 193. See also the prologue to *Women's Cosmetics*, described below.

59. The only references to physicians in traditional Lombard laws were stipulations that perpetrators of violent crimes were responsible for finding, and paying for, physicians for their victims. See Skinner, *Health and Medicine*, p. 79.

60. Skinner, *Health and Medicine*, p. 83.

61. Monica H. Green, "The *De genecia* Attributed to Constantine the African," *Speculum* 62 (1987): 299–323.

62. The following section summarizes arguments made in Monica H. Green, "The Transmission of Ancient Theories of Female Physiology and Disease Through the Early Middle Ages" (Ph.D. diss., Princeton University, 1985). Annotations here are limited to points that correct or revise that discussion. For a comprehensive list of medieval gynecological texts, see the appendix to Green, *Women's Healthcare*.

63. Literature on Hippocratic gynecology has in recent years become vast. See, for example, Ann Ellis Hanson, "The Medical Writers' Woman," in *Before Sexuality: The Construction of Erotic Experience in the Ancient Greek World*, ed. David Halperin et al. (Princeton: Princeton University Press, 1990), pp. 309–37; and Helen King, *Hippocrates' Woman: Reading the Female Body in Ancient Greece* (London: Routledge, 1998).

64. The Latin translation of *Diseases of Women 1* has been edited twice, most recently and definitively by Manuel Enrique Vázquez Bujan, *El "de mulierum affectibus" del Corpus Hippocraticum: Estudio y edición crítica de la antigua traducción latina*, Monografías de la Universidad de Santiago de Compostela, 124 (Santiago de Compostela, 1986).

65. Vatican, Biblioteca Apostolica Vaticana, cod. Barberiano lat. 160, f. 182v: "Menstruis deficientibus sanguinem ex naribus fluere bonum est"; "Mulieri in utero habenti si subito mamilla siccauerit, abortat."

66. The attribution of the *Gynecology of Cleopatra* to the Egyptian queen is clearly spurious; the work was probably a late antique Latin composition. See Green, "Transmission," pp. 156–60, and n. 6, above. On the *Diseases of Women (De passionibus mulierum*, which is apparently a translation of a Greek text attributed to a female writer named Metrodora), see Green, "*De genecia*"; Ann Ellis Hanson and Monica H. Green, "Soranus of Ephesus: *Methodicorum princeps*," in *Aufstieg und Niedergang der römischen Welt*, gen. ed., Wolfgang Haase and Hildegard Temporini, Teilband 2, Band 37.2 (Berlin: Walter de Gruyter, 1994), pp. 968–1075; and Green, appendix to *Women's Healthcare*, pp. 24–25.

67. For the fate of Soranus's *Gynecology* in the West, see sect. 5 of Hanson and Green, "Soranus of Ephesus."

68. For example, ancient or late antique texts like those of Celsus, Cassius Felix, Oribasius, and Paul of Aegina.

69. The will of Eckhard, count of Auton and Mâcon, written in 876, records the gift of an amazing number of books, among which are two books on prognostics and an unspecified "book of medicine" (*medicinalis liber*). He gave the latter to Theutberga, wife of Lothar II of Lotharingia. See Maurice Prou and Alexandre Vidier, eds., *Recueil des chartes de l'Abbaye de Saint-Benoit-sur-Loire*, 2 vols., Documents publiés par la Société historique et archéologique du Gatinais, 5 (Paris: 1900–1907), 1:66. I have found no evidence of lay ownership of specifically gynecological texts in this early period.

70. See Green, "Transmission," chap. 4; and "*De genecia*."

71. For material derived from the *Book on Womanly Matters* (*Liber de muliebria*), see table 1 in Monica H. Green, "The Development of the *Trotula*," *Revue d'Histoire des Textes* 26 (1996): 119–203; reprinted in Green, *Women's Healthcare*, essay 5. For this title and all other early medieval texts, I cite the Latin form in which they are best known and have not standardized them according to normative Latin grammatical rules.

72. See edition, ¶¶92 and 93.

73. On the topoi of shame and secrecy in gynecological prefaces, see my essay "From 'Diseases of Women' to 'Secrets of Women': The Transformation of Gynecological Literature in the Later Middle Ages," *Journal of Medieval and Early Modern Studies* 30 (2000): 5–39.

74. In the following discussion of the *Trotula* texts, I am describing the texts in their original form (though see below regarding the "rough draft" of *Conditions of Women*, to which I do not allot extended attention here). Where readings differ significantly between the original texts and the standardized ensemble edited below, I quote the original text in the notes. Where the material has been deleted altogether, I note these alterations below and in the notes to the edition.

75. On the distinctions between *Treatise on the Diseases of Women* and *Conditions of Women*, see Green, "Development," pp. 127–32.

76. On the possible reference to a Norman queen, see the note to ¶25 in the edition.

77. *Conditions of Women* is, nonetheless, decidedly uninterested in female anatomy. Bits of its understanding of the structure of the female reproductive system can be gleaned intermittently (e.g., ¶¶47 and 60), but in general it shows its similarity to early medieval texts in ignoring the matter. One striking anatomical feature of material later added to the text (¶130) is the notion that since "the womb is tied to the brain by nerves, the brain must necessarily suffer when the womb does." For contemporary views of female anatomy, some of which were quite detailed, see Constantine the African, *De genitalibus membris*, as edited in Green, "*De Genecia*," pp. 312–23; and the anatomical texts printed by Corner, *Anatomical Texts*.

78. Only four of Galen's works are known to have been translated into Latin in the late antique period.

79. Galen's general views on female physiology are summarized in Green, "Transmission," chap. 1. On bloodletting, see Galen, *On Venesection Against Erasistratus* and *On Venesection Against the Erasistrateans in Rome*, in Peter Brain, *Galen on Bloodletting: A Study of the Origins, Development, and Validity of His Opinions, with a Translation of the Three Works* (Cambridge: Cambridge University Press, 1986), pp. 25–27 and 38–40.

80. On the "Galenization" of Arabic gynecology, see Green, "Transmission," chap. 2 and 5. On Ibn al-Jazzār, see ibid., and the works by Bos (n. 48, above).

81. In these discussions of the concepts of "hot" and "cold," Galen and Galenic physicians were not referring to any measurable differences in heat (for no instruments of thermal measurement then existed) but to general principles of warmth or its absence.

82. The above discussion represents only a schematic summary of Galenic medicine. One amazing feature of medieval Latin medicine (whether it had precedents in Arabic or Greek medicine I do not yet know) was the likening of hemorrhoids in men

to menstruation in women, with the assumption that both are salubrious. A late-twelfth-century author, Roger de Baron, describes the equivalence as follows: "This flux [i.e., hemorrhoidal bleeding] is sometimes natural, sometimes unnatural [i.e., pathological], just as the menstrual flux is in women. Hence, just as women menstruate each month, so some men suffer from the hemorrhoidal flux each month, some four times a year, some once a year. This flux ought not be restrained, because it cleans the body of many superfluities." Roger de Baron, *Practica maior*, in *Cyrurgia Guidonis de Cauliaco, et Cyrurgia Bruni, Teodorici, Rolandi, Lanfranci, Rogerii, Bertapalie* (Venice, 1519), f. 216va. For a curious twist in the later fate of this notion, see Willis Johnson, "The Myth of Jewish Male Menses," *Journal of Medieval History* 24 (1998): 273–95; and Irven Resnick, "On the Roots of the Myth of Jewish Male Menses in Jacques de Vitry's *History of Jerusalem*," *International Rennert Guest Lecture Series* 3 (Ramat Gan: Bar-Ilan University, 1998).

83. It is also for this reason that I disagree with John M. Riddle's suggestions in *Contraception and Abortion from the Ancient World to the Renaissance* (Cambridge: Harvard University Press, 1992), and in *Eve's Herbs: A History of Contraception and Abortion in the West* (Cambridge, Mass.: Harvard University Press, 1997) that the label "to provoke menstruation" is invariably a "code–word" to signal an abortifacient. Provoking menstruation, whether to maintain health or to promote fertility (see below), was in and of itself a vital concern.

84. *LSM 1*, ¶4: "Contingit autem hec purgatio mulieribus circa .xiiii. annum, aut paulo citius aut paulo tardius, secundum quod magis uel minus habundat calor in ipsa." In the standardized ensemble, the average age of menarche has dropped to thirteen.

85. It should be noted that these ages of menarche and menopause are formulaic and cannot be assumed to be historically reliable, as assumed by J. B. Post, "Ages of Menarche and Menopause: Some Medieval Authorities," *Population Studies* 25 (1971): 83–87; and Darrel W. Amundsen and Carol Jean Diers, "The Age of Menarche in Medieval Europe" and "The Age of Menopause in Medieval Europe," *Human Biology* 45 (1973): 363–69 and 605–12. The ages found here replicate exactly those found in the *Conditions of Women*'s source, the *Viaticum*, and can be traced back through the Arabic writers to late antique Byzantine texts. These, in turn, derive from ancient Greek sources, which probably reflect ancient numerological beliefs rather than empirical observation. See Helen King, "Medical Texts as a Source for Women's History," in *The Greek World*, ed. A. Powell (London: Routledge, 1995), pp. 199–218. The ages of menopause especially smack of rigid theoretical speculation. Nevertheless, the numbers varied slightly in different versions of *Conditions of Women* and the ensemble (see note to ¶4 in the edition) and in a few of the vernacular translations. A fifteenth-century Dutch translation, for example, says, "And it comes to some at their 16th year and to some at their 9th year; and if it comes sooner, that is very early, and if it comes after, then it is very late, and if it does not come, that is a too great defect of nature. And some women lose it at their 30th year and that is by nature, but the bad humor depletes her. And otherwise she loses it at her 34th year, that is by nature, and some at their 40th year or 45th. And some have it until they are 50 years old or 56" (Anna Delva, *Vrouwengeneeskunde in Vlaanderen tijdens de late middeleeuwen* [Brugge: Vlaamse Historische Studies, 1983], p. 162; my thanks to Luke Demaitre for this translation). While it is doubtful that all these variations can be attributed to deliber-

ate editorial "contemporizing" to reflect current demographic observations rather than to sheer textual corruption, it is interesting that the Latin manuscript that lists the latest date of menarche also comes from the Low Countries: in London, Wellcome Institute for the History of Medicine, MS 517 (s. XV ex., probably Flanders), which is a collection of excerpts from the proto-ensemble, the scribe had first written "eleven" (*vndecim*) as the age of menarche, then corrected it to "eighteen" (*decem et octo*)!

86. See the concordance in table 1 of Green, "Development," for a breakdown of sources.

87. The *Viaticum* had drawn an analogy between the menses and the resin that often exudes from trees: *Viaticum* 6: 9 (as printed in *Opera omnia Ysaac*, Lyons, 1515, pars 2, fol. 164vb): "multos humores . . . cum menstruis exeunt sicut in arboribus sepe videmus quarum humores cum gummis egrediuntur." The rough draft of the *Conditions of Women*, the *Treatise on the Diseases of Women*, had used *flos* (flower) consistently throughout the text to refer to the menses. The author of the *Conditions of Women* replaced all the references to *flos* with *menses*, but the flower analogy remained intact in ¶3.

88. Other terms used in vernacular translations of the *Trotula* are the Dutch *stonden* (periods), German *dy suberunge* (i.e., *Säuberung*, purgation), and Italian *ragione* (the rule).

89. Hildegard of Bingen, *Causae et curae*, bk. 2, ed. Paul Kaiser (Leipzig: Teubner, 1903; reprint Basel: Basler Hildegard-Gesellschaft, 1980), p. 105. Hildegard extends this metaphor even further to discuss the various stages of sexual maturity in adolescent women. The concept of greenness (*viriditas*) is found throughout Hildegard's writings; see, for example, Constant Mews, "Religious Thinker: 'A Frail Human Being' on Fiery Life," in *Voice of the Living Light: Hildegard of Bingen and Her World*, ed. Barbara Newman (Berkeley: University of California Press, 1998), pp. 52–69.

90. As cited in Alma Gottlieb, "Menstrual Cosmology Among the Beng of Ivory Coast," in *Blood Magic: The Anthropology of Menstruation*, ed. Thomas Buckley and Alma Gottlieb (Berkeley: University of California Press, 1988), pp. 55–74, at p. 58. The usage is also found among the Native American Yurok in northern California. See Thomas Buckley, "Menstruation and the Power of Yurok Women," in ibid., pp. 187–209, at p. 194. See also the popular account of Janice Delaney, Mary Jane Lupton and Emily Toth, *The Curse: A Cultural History of Menstruation*, rev. ed. (Urbana: University of Illinois Press, 1988), esp. pp. 190–93. Note that the "biblical" uses of the term "flowers" that they cite derive from the King James (i.e., seventeenth-century) translation; the term is not used in Jerome's fourth-century Latin Vulgate.

91. Pliny, *Historia naturalis* 7, xv, in *Natural History*, 10 vols., ed. and trans., W. H. S. Jones (Cambridge: Harvard University Press, 1963), 5: 64–66; C. Julius Solinus, *Collectanea rerum memorabilium*, ed. Theodor Mommsen (Berlin: Weidmann, 1864), p. 17; Isidore of Seville, *Etymologiae* 11, i, 141, in William Sharpe, *Isidore of Seville: The Medical Writings*, Transactions of the American Philosophical Society, n.s., 54, no. 2 (1964). Cf. Charles T. Wood, "The Doctor's Dilemma: Sin, Salvation, and the Menstrual Cycle in Medieval Thought," *Speculum* 56 (1981): 710–27; Helen Lemay, trans., *Women's Secrets: A Translation of Pseudo-Albertus Magnus' "De secretis*

mulierum" with *Commentaries* (Albany: State University of New York Press, 1992), passim; and Cadden, *Meanings of Sex Difference*, pp. 173–76. See also the essays in the Buckley and Gottlieb volume (n. 90, above) and Chris Knight, *Blood Relations: Menstruation and the Origins of Culture* (New Haven: Yale University Press, 1991), for anthropologists' recent reassessments of the supposed universality of menstrual pollution beliefs.

92. Lemay, *Women's Secrets*; Monica H. Green, "'Traittié tout de mençonges': The *Secrés des dames*, 'Trotula,' and Attitudes Towards Women's Medicine in Fourteenth- and Early Fifteenth-Century France," in *Christine de Pizan and the Categories of Difference*, ed. Marilynn Desmond (Minneapolis: University of Minnesota Press, 1998), pp. 146–78 (reprinted in *Women's Healthcare*, essay 6); and Fernando Salmón and Montserrat Cabré i Pairet, "Fascinating Women: The Evil Eye in Medical Scholasticism," in *Medicine from the Black Death to the Great Pox*, ed. Roger French et al. (Aldershot: Ashgate, 1998), pp. 53–84.

93. One of the few instances where the Plinian tradition encroached upon the *Trotula*'s more positive view of menstruation is a Middle English translation entitled *The boke called Trotela*. See Monica H. Green, "A Handlist of Latin and Vernacular Manuscripts of the So-Called *Trotula* Texts. Part 2: The Vernacular Translations and Latin Re-Writings," *Scriptorium* 51 (1997): 80–104, at pp. 87–88; and "From 'Diseases of Women,'" p. 24.

94. For an incisive critique of modern assumptions about the Hippocratic "discovery" of the disease "hysteria" (advocated particularly by Ilza Veith in *Hysteria: The History of a Disease* [Chicago: University of Chicago Press, 1965]), see Helen King, "Once Upon a Text: Hysteria from Hippocrates," in *Hysteria Beyond Freud*, ed. Sander Gilman et al. (Berkeley: University of California Press, 1993), pp. 3–90; and idem, *Hippocrates' Woman*, chap. 11. As King shows, the noun "hysteria" was never used by ancient medical writers, nor did any of them conceive of the disease entity of "uterine suffocation" as having anything but a physical, organic cause. Ancient (and for the most part, medieval) concepts of uterine suffocation cannot be subsumed under modern psychiatric understandings of "hysteria" (a term which, significantly, has now been removed from the psychiatric etiological canon) without violence to the historical notions themselves.

95. Ann Ellis Hanson, "Hippocrates: *Diseases of Women* 1," *Signs* 1 (1975): 567–84, at p. 576.

96. King, *Hippocrates' Woman*, pp. 220–21, points out that although sex-as-therapy is usually mentioned in modern accounts of Hippocratic "hysteria," in the Hippocratic texts themselves the recommendation is only made infrequently.

97. King, *Hippocrates' Woman*, p. 215.

98. King suggests that it had coalesced by the second century B.C.E. (*Hippocrates' Woman*, p. 229).

99. Soranus of Ephesus, *Soranus' Gynecology*, trans. Owsei Temkin (Baltimore: Johns Hopkins University Press, 1956; reprint 1991), p. 149.

100. Heinrich von Staden, *Herophilus: The Art of Medicine in Early Alexandria* (Cambridge: Cambridge University Press, 1990).

101. *Soranus' Gynecology*, p. 153.

102. He allowed use of fragrant substances applied to the nose for uterine pro-

lapse on the belief that they had a relaxing effect; King, *Hippocrates' Woman*, p. 224.

103. Aside from two encounters with already decomposed corpses (from which he was able to discern skeletal anatomy only), Galen never dissected humans. His range of animal dissections, on the other hand, was truly remarkable.

104. Hanson and Green, "Soranus of Ephesus," pp. 1051–52.

105. Latin text edited by Werner Bernfeld, "Eine Beschwörung der Gebärmutter aus dem frühen Mittelalter," *Kyklos* 2 (1929): 272–74. Exorcisms of the womb can also be found in Copenhagen, Det Kgl. Bibliotek, Gamle Kgl. Samling, MS 1653, s. XI (Beneventan, perhaps at Monte Cassino), f. 216v; and in Anglo-Norman in a four-teenth-century English manuscript, London, British Library, MS Harley 273, f. 213r. For examples from German, see Britta-Juliane Kruse, *Verborgene Heilkünste: Geschichte der Frauenmedizin im Spätmittelalter*, Quellen und Forschungen zur Literatur- und Kulturgeschichte, 5 (Berlin: Walter de Gruyter, 1996), pp. 50–53. The existence of earlier, similar charms or exorcisms without the Christian elements confirms that these, too, have their source in pagan antiquity.

106. Bos, *Ibn al-Jazzār on Sexual Diseases*, pp. 274–75. These views were rendered into Latin by Constantine the African with no significant variation; see Green, "Transmission," p. 265.

107. *LSM 1*, ¶47: "Ex huiusmodi semine superhabundante et corrupto quedam frigida fumositas dissoluitur et ascendit ad quasdam partes que uulgo dicuntur cornelieis dicuntur, que quia uicine sunt pulmoni et cordi et ceteris instrumentis uocum, inde contingit loquele fieri impedimentum, et huiusmodi morbi principium solet oriri ex defectu menstruorum." On this peculiar term *corneliei*, see note to ¶47 in the edition.

108. *TEM*, ¶60: "Aliquando matrix de loco suo ita quod ascendit ad cornices pulmonis, id est pennas, et descendit ita quod exeat, et tunc fit dolor in synistro latere. Et ascendit ad stomachum et ita inflat quod non potest aliquid transglutire. Et uenter frigescit et patitur in eo tortiones et ructat." In the source text, *Liber de muliebria*, this condition was described simply as "Signs when the womb is not in its place" (*De signa matricis, quando loco suo non est*); there was no mention of the lungs or of complete extrusion, though all the remaining symptoms included in the *TEM* appear. See Ferdinand Paul Egert, *Gynäkologische Fragmente aus dem frühen Mittelalter nach einer Petersburger Handschrift aus dem VIII.–IX. Jahrhundert*, Abhandlungen zur Geschichte der Medizin und der Naturwissenschaften, Heft 11 (Berlin: Emil Ebering, 1936), p. 40.

109. *LSM 1*, ¶60: "Aliquando autem mouetur matrix tota de sede sua nec tamen sursum eleuatur uersus spiritualia, nec per orificium foras descendit, cuius signum est dolorem sentit in sinistro latere, distencionem membrorum, difficultatem transgluciendi, torsionem et rugitum uentris habet." Note that in the standardized ensemble edited here, the list of symptoms has changed slightly.

110. Green, "Transmission," pp. 263–68. On Johannes Platearius and his *Practica brevis*, see Tony Hunt, *Anglo-Norman Medicine*, 2 vols. (Cambridge: D. S. Brewer, 1995–97), 1: 149–62.

111. *Anothomia Mundini* (Pavia, 1478), as reproduced in Ernest Wickersheimer, *Anatomies de Mondino dei Luzzi et de Guido de Vigevano* (Paris: E. Droz, 1926), pp. 26b–27a: "Galienus vi° de interioribus, scilicet, quod suffocatio matricis non fit quia matrix corporaliter [*sic*] moueatur usque ad gulam uel pulmonem, quia hoc est impossibile. Sed hoc contingit siue accidit quia ipsa non potens expellerit uapores per

partes inferiores propter aliquam causam mouetur et constringitur in parte inferiori ut expellat ad superiora . . . et tunc mulieres dicunt quod habent matricem in stomacho . . . dicunt mulieres quod habent matricem in gula . . . dicunt tunc mulieres quod matrix ad earum cor peruenit." Mundino takes care to explain that women's perceptions are not far from the truth, since, by sympathetic action, the womb can in fact affect all these organs.

112. Men needed it, too, though the pathological consequences of abstinence were less dire for them.

113. One text, the *De passionibus mulierum* B, omitted all discussion of general physiology and anatomy. The second adaptation, *Non omnes quidem*, deliberately omitted reference to virginity when it compressed Muscio's original discussion of sexuality. The salubriousness of virginity was also actively suppressed in two later renderings of the *Gynecology*, one a late-twelfth-century Hebrew translation and the other a late-thirteenth-century Latin abbreviation called *De naturis mulierum*. On all these adaptations of Muscio, see Hanson and Green, "Soranus of Ephesus."

114. Johannes Platearius, *Practica*: "Si ex corrupto spermate fiat, si virum habeat. Si virgo est vel vidua consilium . . . ut nubat, si voto castitatis vel continentie teneatur, fiat hoc remedium: salgemma, nitrum pulverizentur et distemperentur cum aceto et aqua salsa, et bombix intincta imponatur, ex hoc enim fit quedam morditio." Other texts likewise had recommended masturbation or remarriage along with medicinal remedies; see Green, "Transmission," pp. 146–47.

115. On the formal vow of chastity, see Mary C. Erler, "English Vowed Women at the End of the Middle Ages," *Mediaeval Studies* 57 (1995): 155–203. See also the discussion of *Treatments for Women*, below.

116. These remedies consist of medicated pessaries intended to cause the corrupted seed to issue forth.

117. Oxford, Bodleian Library, MS Ashmole 399, f. 33r–v; the manuscript contains a copy of the *Trotula* proto-ensemble (*LSM* only) and a fragment of the *DOM*. The main body of the manuscript can be dated to ca. 1292; the *Trotula* and several other texts were added somewhat later. The images on ff. 33–34, however—although clearly of English provenance, like the rest of the manuscript—are on a separate bifolium whose origin and date of insertion into the manuscript are uncertain. This series of pictures has elicited considerable interest among historians. Charles Talbot was the first to recognize these figures as referring to the disease of uterine suffocation; see C. H. Talbot, *Medicine in Medieval England* (New York: Science History Publications, London: Oldbourne, 1967), pp. 81–82. See Green, "Handlist. Part 1," p. 158, for further bibliography. My interpretation of these scenes differs from that proposed by Laurinda Dixon, *Perilous Chastity: Women and Illness in Pre-Enlightenment Art and Medicine* (Ithaca, N.Y.: Cornell University Press, 1995); in particular, I consider the four additional scenes of f. 34r–v to be unrelated to uterine suffocation.

118. Platearius, *Practica*: "nisi ex flosculo lane naribus apposito vel ex ampulla vitrea super pectus posita ut dicit Galenus." Like the wool test, the water test also had ancient precedents; see King, *Hippocrates' Woman*, p. 227.

119. *LSM 1*, ¶48: "Let there be applied to the nose anything which has a strong odor, such as castoreum, pitch, burnt wool, burnt linen cloth or burnt leather, and similar things" (*Naribus apponantur aliqua que sunt grauis odoris, ut castoreum, galbanum, pix, lana combusta, lineus pannus combustus uel pellis combusta, et similia*).

120. Hanson and Green, "Soranus of Ephesus," p. 1055.

121. *LSM* I, ¶53: "Let good-smelling spices be applied to the nose, such as balsam, spikenard, clove, storax and sweet-smelling things of this kind. And below, let
her be suffumigated with things of foul odor, such as a burnt cloth, and other things
which were mentioned above [i.e., in ¶48]" (*apponantur naribus species bene redolentes,
ut balsamum, spica, folium, storax et huiusmodi bene olencia. Et inferius subfumigetur
rebus graui odoris, ut pannus combustus, et cetera que supradicta sunt*).

122. Brain, *Galen on Bloodletting*.

123. Pedro Gil-Sotres, "Derivation and Revulsion: The Theory and Practice of
Medieval Phlebotomy," in García-Ballester et al., *Practical Medicine*, pp. 110–55.

124. Unlike the references to phlebotomy and cupping, all of which derive from
the *Viaticum*, no textual source for ¶27 has yet been found. The absence of phlebotomy from *Treatments for Women* is one of its notable points of contrast with *Conditions
of Women*, though it does employ cupping glasses on one occasion (¶179) and leeches
twice (¶¶179 and 195). Hildegard of Bingen addresses the three techniques of phlebotomy, cupping, and scarification at length in her *Causes and Cures*; see Hildegard of
Bingen, *On Natural Philosophy and Medicine: Selections from "Cause et cure,"* trans.
Margret Berger (Rochester, N.Y.: D. S. Brewer, 1999), pp. 88–95.

125. This Dutch manuscript and the two others that contain this rendition of the
Trotula are the only ones out of over 180 extant manuscripts of the *Trotula* (Latin and
vernacular) to have any technical illustrations.

126. Note that the term "pessary" in modern medical usage refers most commonly to devices used to support a prolapsed uterus or pelvic floor, and only rarely to
a vehicle for applying medicines.

127. Roger de Baron, *Practica minor*: "Sicut predictis clisteribus suppositoriis et
siringa utendum tantum in causis inferiorum sic et pessariis in causis tantum matricis;
nec mirum. Ista enim loca remota sunt a nutritivis et ita in vigore debilitantur venien-
tia ad inferiora tamquam remota tum longitudine vie tum meatuum angustia debilitat
prorsus nullam habent efficatiam."

128. To date I have not found any obvious source for ¶74.

129. See Green, "Development," table 1, ¶¶75a (= ¶82 of this edition), 76, 78,
78a, and 78b (= ¶77).

130. I have found only two exceptions. The earliest is in a late antique or early
medieval text, *De passionibus mulierum* A, which offers the instruction that, in order to
conceive a female, the two partners together should drink the dried vagina of a hare
(*Vt feminam concipiat. Vuluam leporis siccam tere et ambo bibant et coeant*). The other
exception is a recipe in the Middle English text *Sekenesse of Wymmen 2*, which translates ¶76 from *Conditions of Women*. Whereas the Latin had given separate instructions for the man and woman for the single purpose of conceiving a male child, the
English misinterprets the woman's procedure as being a separate prescription for conceiving a female child. See Beryl Rowland, *Medieval Woman's Guide to Health: The
First English Gynecological Handbook* (Kent, Ohio: Kent State University Press, 1981),
p. 168, ll. 30–33. On the history of this text, see Monica H. Green, "Obstetrical and
Gynecological Texts in Middle English," *Studies in the Age of Chaucer* 14 (1992):
53–88; reprinted in Green, *Women's Healthcare*, essay 4.

131. Constantine's name was changed to Galen at the proto-ensemble stage (see
note to the edition). There is a certain irony in this reference to Constantine, for the

one chapter of the *Viaticum* not rendered into Latin (or at least not found in any extant manuscripts) is that on abortifacients. Other than this suppression, there is almost nothing in the Constantinian corpus to suggest that he attempted to impose Christian condemnations of sexuality or birth control on the medical texts he was translating. See Green, "Constantinus Africanus."

132. See Riddle, *Contraception and Abortion*.

133. *LSM 1*, ¶92: "Mulieres que assistunt ei non respiciant eam in uultu, quia multe mulieres solent esse ut uerecunde in ipso partus uisu." Cf. note to the edition.

134. On the *Sator arepo*, see Ernst Darmstaedter, "Die Sator-Arepo-Formel und ihre Erklärung," *Isis* 18 (1932): 322–29; and R. Bader, "Sator Arepo: Magik in der Volksmedizin," *Medizinhistorisches Journal* 22 (1987): 115–34. Most interesting is the fact that the *Sator arepo* here replaces a Christian charm that had been in the rough draft of the text, the *Treatise on the Diseases of Women*.

135. *LSM 1*, ¶2: "Earum ergo miseranda calamitas et maxime cuiusdam mulieris gratia animum meum sollicitat ut contra predictas egritudines earum prouideam sanitati. Vt ergo ex libris Ypocratis, Galieni, Constantini pociora decerperem labore non minimo mulierum gratia desudaui, ut et causas egritudinum et curas exponerem cum causis."

136. The compound medicines employed in *Treatments for Women* are *potio sancti Pauli*, *rosata novella*, *trifera magna*, and *trifera saracenica*. *Conditions of Women* recommends the use of *diathesseron*, *hierapigra*, *hieralogodion*, *trifera saracenica*, *rosata novella*, *diaciminum*, and *oxizaccara*. *Diathesseron*, *hierapigra*, *diaciminum*, and *oxizaccara* derive from *Conditions of Women*'s source text, the *Viaticum*; the other three are novel additions. Another distinctive characteristic of *Treatments for Women* is that, aside from its possible use in two compound medicines (themselves of Muslim origin), this text does not employ sugar as an ingredient (see the note accompanying ¶187 in the edition), which would, in the twelfth century, still have to have been brought to the mainland from Sicily or imported from Muslim countries. *Conditions of Women*, in contrast, adopts from the *Viaticum* and another source four different uses of sugar (¶¶79, 81, 91, and 101); see also the uses of sugar in the excerpts from Rhazes' *Liber ad Almansorem* (¶¶124 and 127). Sugar was already well incorporated into the pharmacopeia of other Salernitan practitioners by the second quarter of the twelfth century. On the availability of sugar in the twelfth century, see William D. Phillips, Jr., "Sugar Production and Trade in the Mediterranean at the Time of the Crusades," in *The Meeting of Two Worlds: Cultural Exchange Between East and West During the Period of the Crusades*, ed. Vladimir P. Goss (Kalamazoo, Mich.: Medieval Institute Publications, 1986), pp. 393–406.

137. Only two passages in *Treatments for Women* give any direct indication of the anatomical views underlying the physiology. The first is in ¶139, where the beneficial effects of sneezing in childbirth are explained. The author adds, "For as Copho says, the organs are shaken by the sneezing to such a degree that the cotyledons are broken, that is, the ligaments by which the infant is tied to the womb" (*Nam ut dicit Copho, quassantur membra sternutione in tantum ut rumpantur chotilidones, id est ligamenta quibus alligatur infans matrici*). In ¶141, in discussing a remedy for women who suffer from their chastity, the author remarks, "And it should be noted that a pessary ought not be made [for this condition] lest the womb be injured, for the mouth of the

womb is tied to the vagina just as the lips of the mouth are joined to each other (except when conception occurs for then the womb is pulled back)" (*Et est notandum quod non debet fieri pessarium ne ledatur matrix, quoniam os matricis uulue iungitur ut oris labia inter se iunguntur, nisi fiat conceptio, quoniam tunc retrahitur matrix*).

138. *DCM 1*, ¶132: "Ut de cura mulierum nobis compendiosa fiat traditio, uidendum est que calide, que frigide fuerint mulieres, ad quod tale facimus experimentum."

139. *DCM 1*, ¶132: "Licinium oleo pulegino inungimus uel oleo muscellino, uel laurino uel alio aliquo oleo calido, et licinium illinitum uulue in quantitate parui digiti imponimus cum dormitum in nocte ierit, alligando cum forti filo cruribus ut si cum euigilauerit, sit intus attractum, detur nobis indicium quoniam de frigiditate laborat. Si uero expulsum, datur indicium quoniam laborat ex caliditate."

140. Hans Wölfel, ed., *Das Arzneidrogenbuch "Circa instans" in einer Fassung des XIII. Jahrhunderts aus der Universitätsbibliothek Erlangen: Text und Kommentar als Beitrag zur Pflanzen- und Drogenkunde des Mittelalters* (Berlin: A. Preilipper, 1939).

141. *DCM 1*, ¶134: "et sic a pessima habundantia mundate et ad conceptionem apte inueniuntur."

142. As I shall argue more fully in *Women and Literate Medicine in Medieval Europe: Trota and the "Trotula"* (forthcoming), the ultimate source of ¶135 is the *Practica* of Trota (see below). There, this recipe for an emmenagogue is explicitly introduced as a fertility measure: "[A recipe] according to Trota for provoking the menses, on account of whose retention the woman is unable to conceive" (*Secundum Trotam ad menstrua prouocanda, propter quorum retentiones mulier concipere non potest*).

143. For other evidence for dieting in this period, see Skinner, *Health and Medicine*, pp. 20–21.

144. While some might argue, following Riddle (n. 83, above), that all the emmenagogues and fetal expulsives could be *used* as contraceptives and abortifacients, the manner in which they are presented here gives no indication that a double purpose was intended. (Compare this with the frankness with which other sexual matters are discussed.) Whether the seemingly pronatalist stance of *Treatments for Women* suggests demographically determined attitudes toward contraception similar to those proposed for Roman times (i.e., that contraception would be largely limited to extramarital encounters) remains to be seen. On the Roman period, see Bruce W. Frier, "Natural Fertility and Family Limitation in Roman Marriage," *Classical Philology* 89 (1994): 318–33.

145. *DCM 1*, ¶141: "Item sunt quedam mulieres quibus non permittitur habere carnale commercium, quia uoto tenentur, tum quia religiose, tum quia uidue, quoniam quibusdam non licet ad secunda uota migrare, que cum uoluntatem coeundi habeant immodicam et non coheunt, sicut non explent uoluntatem, sic grauem inde incurrunt passionem."

146. *DCM 1*, ¶203: "Quedam puelle uidentur quasi morbo caduco laborantes quod contingit ex suffocatione matricis compressis spiritualibus."

147. *DCM 1*, ¶140: "For the womb, made as if it were a wild beast because of the sudden evacuation, falls this way and that as if it were wandering" (*Matrix namque quasi facta siluestris propter subitam euacuationem quasi uagando huc et illuc se declinat*). This whole sentence is typical of the kind of theoretical additions to the original cures

of Trota assembled in *Treatments for Women*. I will discuss this further in *Women and Literate Medicine*.

148. *DCM 1*, ¶170: "Iterum sunt quedam quibus a matrice dependet frustrum carnis. Sed est notandum quod istud eis contigit ex spermate recepto et intus inuiscato, quia post coitum se non mundificant."

149. See Jacquart and Thomasset, *Sexuality and Medicine*; and Cadden, *Meanings of Sex Difference*.

150. See n. 145 above.

151. Drell, "Marriage, Kinship, and Power," p. 210.

152. See Skinner, "Women, Wills and Wealth," at p. 151.

153. ¶192 in the present edition was not originally part of the *DCM*.

154. A more detailed treatment for genital hygiene in the original version of *Women's Cosmetics* (see below) is similarly said to "constrict the vagina."

155. *DCM 1*, ¶193: "Sunt quedam immunde meretrices et corrupte que plusquam uirgines inueniri cupiunt, faciunt quod constrictorium ad istud, sed nimis inconsulte quoniam et se ipsas reddunt sanguinolentas et uiri membrum uulnerant. Accipiunt uitrum et nitrum et redigunt in puluerem et uulue inponunt." The reading *uitrum et* (glass and) dropped out in later versions of the text (see note to the edition), yet it is the use of ground glass that best explains why this procedure was originally thought to have been so dangerous. *Nitrum* is described by the Salernitan text on pharmacology, the *Circa instans*, as "having the power to dissolve and cleanse." Unlike ground glass, however, which is prescribed in the *Circa instans* for removing scabies and causing scarification and corrosion (i.e., it is normally used only externally), *nitrum* is prescribed in several instances for normal internal use (see also *DOM* ¶¶253, 302, and 310 below for cosmetic uses).

156. One copy of the revised ensemble (Vatican, Biblioteca Apostolica, MS Pal. lat. 1253, s. XIII ex., f. 174v) interestingly deletes this harsh reference to prostitutes, saying only that these are "deflowered and corrupted women" (*quedam deflorate et corrupte*). This unique alteration says nothing, of course, about twelfth-century Salernitan attitudes, though it may be an interesting hint of at least one scholar's attitudes in late-thirteenth-century Montpellier, where this manuscript may have been composed.

157. Very little is known about prostitution in southern Italy in this period, though there is enough to suggest that the practice was not rare. See Salvatore Tramontana, "La meretrice," in *Condizione umana e ruoli sociali nel Mezzogiorno normanno-svevo. Atti delle none giornate normanno-sveve, Bari, 17–20 ottobre 1989*, ed. Giosuè Musca (Bari: Centro di Studi Normanno-Svevi della Università degli Studi di Bari, Edizioni Dedalo, 1991), pp. 79–101. Studies of medieval France suggest that women who became prostitutes often did so because their family ties had been broken after they lost their virtue. See Kathryn L. Reyerson, "Prostitution in Medieval Montpellier: The Ladies of Campus Polverel," *Medieval Prosopography* 18 (1997): 209–28, at p. 212.

158. Salernus, *Catholica*, in *Magistri Salernitani nondum editi*, ed. Piero Giacosa (Turin: Fratelli Bocca, 1901), pp. 147–48. An extensive collection of vaginal constrictives would later appear in the thirteenth-century *Compendium medicine* of the English writer Gilbertus Anglicus.

159. Cf. *Conditions of Women* which limits its discussion of postpartum condi-

tions to removing the afterbirth (§§104–5, 107–10), bringing on the lochial flow (§111), and vague "uterine pain" (§112). These remedies involve the administration of oral substances or the use of suffumigations, never any hands-on intervention.

160. The one passage similar to it is in the Salernitan compendium *On the Treatment of Illnesses*. This will be discussed in Green, *Women and Literate Medicine*.

161. Although uterine prolapse is mentioned at least in passing in most Salernitan texts, *Treatments for Women* is the only one that recognizes that coughing produces a threat to the pelvic floor.

162. Compare the comments of the late-fourth-century writer Theodorus Priscianus, who in closing his brief text on gynecology admits some limits to theoretical knowledge. His goal has been merely to lay out the causes and remedies of the principal gynecological disorders; for matters relating to childbirth, he concedes that "you ought to refer to experience rather than reading" (Valentin Rose, ed., *Theodori Prisciani Euporiston libri III* [Leipzig: Teubner, 1894], p. 248). The one major exception to this normative omission of routine obstetrical care is Muscio's *Gynaecia*, which was to serve as the principal source for obstetrical material in later medieval texts. See Hanson and Green, "Soranus of Ephesus," pp. 1056–59.

163. Note that §§254, 256–59, 261–71, 286–88, and 290 of the third part of the present edition were originally part of *Treatments for Women*.

164. *DCM 1*, §167: "Item unguentum satis ualens contra solis adustionem et fissuram quamlibet et maxime ex uento, et pustulas ex aere, et contra maculas in facie quas faciunt salernitane pro mortuis."

165. William of Apulia, *De rebus gestis*, 5.292–300, p. 252.

166. Cf. Diane Owen Hughes, "Mourning Rites, Memory, and Civilization in Premodern Italy," in *Riti e rituali nelle società medievali*, ed. Jacques Chiffoleau, Lauro Martines, and Agostino Paravicini Bagliani, Collectanea, 5 (Spoleto: Centro Italiano di Studi sull'Alto Medioevo, 1994), pp. 23–38.

167. §§230–31, however, specifically address hemorrhoids consequent to childbirth.

168. See note to §154 in the edition. Male practitioners also addressed genital conditions, of course; Petrus Musandinus, for example, noted that gonorrhea (flow of the seed) happened to both men and women, and he offered a remedy that could take away the itching "in either sex, men or women." For an instance where a fourteenth-century French female practitioner treats a male patient for a genital injury but does not herself touch the wound, see Joseph Shatzmiller, *Médecine et justice en Provence médiévale: Documents de Manosque, 1262–1348* (Aix-en-Provence: Publications de l'Université de Provence, 1989), pp. 150–51; and Monica H. Green, "Documenting Medieval Women's Medical Practice," in García-Ballester et al., *Practical Medicine*, pp. 322–52, at p. 346.

169. §173a: "Item ad inpetiginem fricamus locum satis cum radice lapacii acuti, et puluerem de Copho factum superspargimus." This recipe would later be deleted from the *Trotula* ensemble.

170. Already in *DCM 2*, these two references to "M. F." and "J. F." were interpreted simply as "Ferrarius."

171. Anthropologists have in recent years raised the question of whether menstruation is always the regular, monthly phenomenon that has come to be expected in modern Western societies. Pregnancy, prolonged lactation, and malnutrition would

all combine to make menstruation a fairly *ir*regular event for many women of child-bearing age in many traditional societies. See, for example, Barbara B. Harrell, "Lactation and Menstruation in Cultural Perspective," *American Anthropologist* 83 (1981): 796–823.

172. For example, frankincense (which would have been imported from East Africa or the Arabian peninsula) is employed thirteen times in *DCM 1*; nutmeg, cloves, and dragon's blood (all of which would be imported from Indonesia) are employed five, four, and one time, respectively; galangal (from India or southeast Asia) is employed three times.

173. The cosmetic text attributed to the late- twelfth-century medical writer Richardus Anglicus, in contrast, offers etiologies for most conditions discussed.

174. *DOM 1*, ¶305f: "Sunt nonnulle mulieres que propter magnitudinem sui instrumenti et eiusdem grauem odorem ad opus uenereum plurimum rudes reperiuntur et inepte, adeo ut uiris coeuntibus tamen generent fastidium quod opus inceptum semiplenum relinquant, nec ad eas amplius affectant accedere."

175. This chapter (¶305f) was deleted from the revised ensemble (see below), hence it does not appear in the present edition. For a Middle English translation (derived in this case from the intermediate *Trotula* ensemble), see Alexandra Barratt, ed., *Women's Writing in Middle English*, Longman Annotated Texts (London: Longman, 1992), pp. 35–37.

176. The author of the leading Salernitan text on materia medica, the so-called *Circa instans*, listed several cosmetic uses of white lead (i.e., carbonate of lead). He also noted lead's toxicity, though he did not attribute it to the lead itself: "It should be noted that those who make white lead often incur apoplexy, epilepsy, paralysis, and wheezing because of the dissolving and mortifying frigidity of the vinegar [used in its production]" (*Notandum quod hii qui cerusam faciunt sepius incurrent apoplexiam, epilepsiam, paralisim, artheticam propter frigiditatem aceti dissolventem et mortificantem*; ed. Wölfel, p. 29). Copho, in his *Practica*, simply noted that white lead sometimes corroded the gums of women who used it to anoint the face (ed. Creutz, p. 302).

177. Cf. ¶296.

178. The iconography of fig. 8 merits further analysis. On the one hand, the two horned and horn-bearing figures resemble personified representations of the winds as found in contemporary manuscripts of Byzantine origin. (My thanks to William Tronzo of Tulane University and Colum Hourihane of the Index of Christian Art, Princeton University, for their considered advice on possible parallels.) More prosaically, it is also possible that the two attendants are meant to be eunuchs. The use of eunuchs was common in both Byzantine and Islamic culture at this time, and the Normans adopted this practice in the royal court in Sicily as well as in their private households. See Pasquale Corsi, "L'eunuco," in Musca, *Condizione umana e ruoli sociali*, pp. 251–77.

179. *DOM 1*, ¶242: "First, let her go to the baths, and let her steam herself so that she sweats. But if she has no access to baths, let steambaths be made thus, just like the women beyond the Alps [do] who lack baths of this kind" (*In primis eat ad balnea, et stuphet se ut sudet. Si autem balnea defuerint, cum stuphis sicut transmontane mulieres que huiusmodi carent balneis fiant stuphe sic*).

180. Although originally attributed to Muslim women, in the revised ensemble this was changed to "noble Salernitan women." See note to ¶245 in the edition.

181. The so-called *cerusa saracenica* was first omitted from the transitional ensemble; see Green, "Development," p. 199. Employing sowbread, wild nep, red and white bryony, sweet woodruff, Aaron's beard, dragon arum, squirting cucumber, florentine iris, rose water, and, of course, lead, this face whitener involved a complicated preparation, demanding multiple mixings, strainings, and dryings in the sun.

182. *DOM 1*, ¶304a: "Vidi quandam sarracenam in Sicilia hac medicina sola infinitos de huiusmodi egritudine curantem." In the standardized ensemble, this sentence was transposed to the beginning of the following paragraph (¶305).

183. *DOM 1*, ¶241a: "Huius in circuitu rationis ego regulis mulierum quas in artificiali decore faciendo facetas inueni meam rationem muniui, ut in singulis tam ad ornatum faciei quam ceterorum membrorum mulierum doctus reperiar, ita ut cuilibet mulieri nobili seu etiam gratcie de huiusmodi artificio aliquid a me querenti iuxta sui qualitatem et modum conuenientis suum adhibere[m] consilium ut et ego laudem et ipsa exoptatum ualeat consequi effectum." Unlike *Conditions of Women* and *Treatments for Women*, the gender of the author of *Women's Cosmetics* is grammatically established in the text itself.

184. A recent example of how potent the idea of female authorship is can be found in Laurie Finke, *Women's Writing in English: Medieval England* (London: Longman, 1999). Less concerned with the historical question of whether the author was a woman than with the literary question of how the "author-function" works, Finke does not mention that in the three manuscripts of Middle English *Trotula* translations she examines that supposedly bear "a woman's signature" (p. 119), there is no reference anywhere to a woman Trota or "Trotula" as author: two have no authorial name attached, while the third uses the masculine or neuter form of "Trotula" as a title (*Liber Trotuli*).

185. Ordericus Vitalis, *The Ecclesiastical History*, ed. and trans. Marjorie Chibnall, 6 vols. (Oxford: Clarendon Press, 1969–80), 2: 28 and 74–76; Marie de France, *Les Deux Amanz*, in *The Lais of Marie de France*, trans. and intro. Glyn S. Burgess and Keith Busby (Harmondsworth: Penguin Books, 1986), p. 83. On Marie's depictions of women healers more generally, see Peggy McCracken, "Women and Medicine in Medieval French Narrative," *Exemplaria: A Journal of Theory in Medieval and Renaissance Studies* 5, no. 2 (1993): 239–62.

186. I have collected all the evidence for the *mulieres Salernitane* in a forthcoming essay: "*Mulieres Salernitane*: The Medical Practices and Reputation of the Women of Twelfth-Century Salerno." Certain of these references to "the Salernitan women" may, it is true, ultimately have to be rejected from our historical documentation. Right here in the *Trotula* standardized ensemble, for example, the claim that the "Salernitan women" make the facial ointment described in ¶167 reflects a corruption of the original text of *Treatments for Women*, where it is only said that Salernitan women are accustomed to scratch their faces in mourning; the author of *Treatments for Women* claims credit for the ointment itself. In the cosmetic section of the ensemble (¶245), a depilatory that had originally been credited to Muslim noblewomen (*nobiles Sarracene*) has now been attributed to Salernitan noblewomen (*nobiles Salernitane*).

187. Four other Salernitan women are said by a seventeenth-century writer, Antonio Mazza, to have composed medical texts, but thus far no medieval evidence can be found for their existence, let alone their *oeuvres*. See Monica H. Green, "In

Search of an 'Authentic' Women's Medicine: The Strange Fates of Trota of Salerno and Hildegard of Bingen," *Dynamis: Acta Hispanica ad Medicinae Scientiarumque Historiam Illustrandam* 19 (1999): 25–54.

188. See Green, "Development," p. 153, n. 101, for citations. I have adopted the form "Trota" here because it was this form that was given currency by northern European scribes who were chiefly responsible for the dissemination of her work outside of Salerno.

189. An edition will be included in Green, *Women and Literate Medicine*.

190. Conrad Hiersemann reedited all the excerpts attributed to "Trot" (which he assumed was an abbreviation for a hypothetical masculine name "Trottus") in *Die Abschnitte aus der Practica des Trottus in der Salernitanischen Sammelschrift De Aegritudinum Curatione: Breslau Codex Salern. 1160–1170*, inaugural dissertation (Leipzig: Institut für Geschichte der Medizin, 1921).

191. An edition of the story in ¶151 from the original *DCM* will be included in the appendix of *Women and Literate Medicine*. As the notes to the text of the standardized ensemble below make clear, the anecdote in ¶151 underwent considerable change as the text developed.

192. The sole complete extant copy of the first version of *Treatments for Women* ends, "All these things here noted have been proved, with Trota as witness" (*Probata hec omnia hic notata teste Trota*). This phrase seems to be in the metrical form known as iambic senarius (my thanks to Francis Newton for pointing this out to me) and so may deliberately have been intended as a rhythmical chant. It does, in any case, resemble other legal formulae of the period. It may therefore indicate that Trota herself certified the accuracy of the original transcription and so could guarantee its authenticity. I will discuss Trota's relationship to *Treatments for Women* at greater length in *Women and Literate Medicine*.

193. See notes to ¶¶176 (*gladene*), 204 (*chinke*), and 218 (*digge*) in the text below. All three terms are documented in Middle English; see Hans Kurath et al., eds., *The Middle English Dictionary* (Ann Arbor: University of Michigan Press, 1952–), s.v. *chinke, dikking,* and *gladen*. All three terms are also documented in Old English, though not in every case with precisely the same medical meanings. (My thanks to Pauline A. Thompson of the *Dictionary of Old English* for her advice on this matter.) There is not a single extant copy of *Treatments for Women* that does not bear traces of the English synonyms. Later manuscripts show that Continental scribes misunderstood the English forms, which must have been unfamiliar to them; even the corruptions, however, are vestiges of the original English terms. See also ¶227 on use of the French (?) term *multe*.

194. Since these practices were likely to have been widespread in Mediterranean areas and not confined to Salerno, it seems unlikely that a Salernitan woman herself would consider this merely a local practice. See Hughes, "Mourning Rites," for other instances where these Mediterranean practices shocked visitors.

195. Some copies of *Conditions of Women* bear either the title or the author's name "Trotula," but these are all late manuscripts (fourteenth century and after) and have probably been identified as component parts of the *Trotula* ensemble by their scribes. Neither "Trota" nor "Trotula" is found with earlier manuscripts of the Latin text, nor with any vernacular translations of the independent *Conditions of Women*. See Green, "Development," pp. 152–53.

196. Trota's virtually complete lack of bookishness suggests an informal training. Here we may contrast her with her contemporary, Hildegard of Bingen (1098–1179), the only other documented medieval female medical writer before the fourteenth century. Hildegard's medicine is unique in many respects, but it is clear that she is drawing heavily on literate medical traditions, particularly the recently translated *Pantegni* of Constantine the African.

197. I thus disagree with Benton (Benton, "Trotula") who, not recognizing the debt of *Treatments for Women* to Trota, asserted that all three *Trotula* texts were undoubtedly male-authored and were only attributed to a woman to hide this fact. I do agree with him, however, that in identifying Trota (later "Trotula") as "an expert on women," the *Trotula* attribution considerably narrowed the achievements of the historical Salernitan practitioner, whose medical expertise was clearly so much broader than gynecology and cosmetics alone.

198. For example, of some twenty-three Latin copies known from medieval library catalogs, only nine still exist. Since books donated to institutional libraries had a better chance of surviving than those in private circulation, the actual rate of loss was probably significantly higher than this ratio suggests.

199. See Hanson and Green, "Soranus of Ephesus," pp. 1056–61.

200. This section summarizes arguments laid out more fully in Green, "Development." Readers will also find there concordances comparing all the different versions of the independent texts and the ensembles. For the convenience of the reader using the present translation, I have added an asterisk (*) at the head of all paragraphs that are *not* original to the three independent Salernitan texts.

201. See n. 75, above.

202. There is a third version of *Women's Cosmetics*, but this was probably not redacted until the latter half of the thirteenth century.

203. See the notes to ¶¶242 and 244 in the text for instances where this process of abbreviation caused substantive changes.

204. This collation from the two versions explains why the paragraphs on prenatal care (here ¶¶79–81) appear in a different place in the ensemble than they originally had in *Conditions of Women*. See the notes to the text.

205. On the *Liber ad Almansorem*, see Danielle Jacquart and Françoise Micheau, *La médecine arabe et l'occident médiéval* (Paris: Maisonneuve et Larose, 1990), pp. 63–64 and 150; and Danielle Jacquart, "Note sur la traduction latine du *Kitāb al-Manṣūrī* de Rhazes," *Revue d'Histoire des Textes* 24 (1994): 359–74. The version used for the *Trotula* ensemble is Version A, i.e., that predating the revision of Gerard of Cremona (d. 1187); my thanks to Danielle Jacquart for her confirmation of this point.

206. See Green, "Development," pp. 153–54, for full citations.

207. This is preserved particularly well in manuscripts of the Harley Group of the proto-ensemble (a branch of the *Trotula* ensemble that has several "early" features). These end either *Explicit hec Trota multum mulieribus apta* (Here ends this Trota, very useful for women) or more simply *Explicit Trotta* (Here ends Trotta). The former phrase is in dactylic hexameter, a metrical form which, by its rhythmical nature, may have been meant to ensure authenticity (see n. 192 above).

208. This use of the third person in ¶151 should have seemed all the more incongruous since the first person plural ("we") is regularly used throughout *Treatments for Women*.

209. See the note to ¶289 in the text.

210. The editor apparently did not notice, however, that s/he had duplicated the instruction for the emmenagogues, hence the redundancy in the present text of ¶¶106 and 110.

211. The term "Lombard" had by the thirteenth century come into general use in northern Europe to refer to any Italian merchant. On negative attitudes toward "Lombards," see Lilian M. C. Randall, "The Snail in Gothic Marginal Warfare," *Speculum* 37 (1962): 358–67. However, since it is not known where the standardized ensemble was redacted, the exact connotations of the usage here remain unclear. Nine of the twenty-one copies of the standardized ensemble that include ¶124 lack the reference; one manuscript (Paris, Bibliothèque Nationale de France, MS lat. 6988) replaces *sicut Lombardis* with *sicut prouincialibus* (like people from Provence). Since this latter manuscript comes from southern France, the local referent was probably meant to be quite cutting.

212. A fifteenth-century French translator may have recognized the problem, which s/he skirts by leaving the passage in Latin (Paris, Bibliothèque Nationale de France, MS fr. 1327, f. 115r).

213. Jacqueline Marie Musacchio, *The Art and Ritual of Childbirth in Renaissance Italy* (New Haven: Yale University Press, 1999); and Green, "Transformation."

214. If we add the manuscripts of the standardized ensemble to those of its near cousin, the revised ensemble (of which there are thirteen copies extant), the total constitutes more than a quarter of the total 146 copies of all versions of the Latin texts.

215. The two extant manuscripts are, respectively, Paris, Bibliothèque Nationale de France, MSS lat. 16222, and lat. 16191. On copies of the *Trotula* available in France in this period, see Green, "'Traittié.'"

216. Paris, Bibliothèque Nationale de France, MS lat. 6964.

217. On all the vernacular translations, see Green, "Handlist," Part 2; and the appendix to *Women's Healthcare*.

218. Kremsmünster, Stiftsbibliothek, MS 72, ff. 159r–184r (s. XV med., Austria): *Explicit tractatus bonus qui intitulatur vetula de doloribus.*

219. Salzburg, Erzabtei St. Peter, MS b V 22, ff. 149r–162v (ca. 1456, Leipzig): *Incipit liber de passionibus mulierum secundum Trotulam* and *Explicit Arnaldus de noua uilla.*

220. Munich, Bayerische Staatsbibliothek, Clm 3875 (an. 1478–79 at Klattau [Bohemia]), ff. 194ra–204rb, was copied by Johannes Rudolt of Klattau. The anonymous English scribe/editor of Oxford, Bodleian Library, MS Bodley 682 (s. XV², England), ff. 172r–196r, interjected into the *Trotula* material from other authors. Notably, s/he returned to the older interpretation of "Trotula" as being the title of the work (*tractatus intitulatus Trotula mulierum*).

221. See tables 1–3 in Green, "Development," for Kraut's rearrangements of the standardized ensemble.

222. Kraut, p. 22: "Ideo si illarum quaedam ob periculum mortis non auderet concipere . . ."

223. Kraut, p. 34: "Nisi de restrictione amplitudinis uuluae, propter honestam causam liceret tractare, nullam de ea mentionem faceremus; sed cum per hanc impediatur aliquando conceptio, necesse est tali impedimento sic subuenire."

224. Kraut omitted ¶¶190–93, 195, and 308–9, retaining only ¶¶194 and 307.

225. Kraut, pp. 23–24.

226. Quite a few new errors or misreadings crept in (e.g., *bombardis* [guns] for *Lombardis* in ¶124), though whether they were due to Kraut or the printer is uncertain.

227. In addition to the controversy over the author's gender (see the Preface, above), Kraut's alterations led to a controversy in the sixteenth and seventeenth centuries over whether the text was ancient or modern. See Green, "Search."

228. On the Laon manuscript, see the Latin edition, p. 63. On the Middle English translations, see Green, "Obstetrical and Gynecological Texts."

229. The Glasgow and Wrocław (Poland) manuscripts are collated in my edition of the standardized ensemble as MSS **G** and **W**, respectively. The only other manuscripts where the *Trotula* appears as a pamphlet are fifteenth-century copies, and in every case it seems that it was quickly bound with other, technical literature. For documented cases of women owning (or having addressed to them) works on diet and regimen, see Monica H. Green, "The Possibilities of Literacy and the Limits of Reading: Women and the Gendering of Medical Literacy," in Green, *Women's Healthcare*, essay 7.

230. Excerpts from this translation, called in one manuscript *The Knowyng of Womans Kynde in Chyldyng*, have been edited by Barratt, *Women's Writing*, pp. 29–35; Professor Barratt has a complete edition of the text forthcoming. On the question of slander and gynecology, see Green, "'Traittié.'"

231. I will address this question of users of the text at length in *Women and Literate Medicine*. In "Possibilities of Literacy," I note that vernacular cosmetic literature was more regularly directed to female audiences than were gynecological texts.

232. For an excellent survey of the wide array of medieval scientific theories of sex difference, see Cadden, *Meanings of Sex Difference*. For practical matters of gynecological therapeutics, Latinate physicians could and did turn to the sections on reproductive diseases in such massive medical encyclopedias as Avicenna's *Canon*.

233. For a full comparison of the component parts of the standardized ensemble vis-à-vis other versions of the texts, see tables 1–3 in Green, "Development."

234. Green, "Development."

235. I will discuss the significance of these modes of address in Green, *Women and Literate Medicine*.

236. I include at the beginning of the list of *materia medica* the sources I have used for identification purposes.

237. For example, Tony Hunt, *Plant Names of Medieval England* (Cambridge: D. S. Brewer, 1989), identifies *aff(r)odilus* as ramsons, wild garlic/crow garlic (*Allium ursinum* L./*vineale* L.), or sweet woodruff (*Asperula odorata* L.). Willem F. Daems, *Nomina simplicium medicinarum ex synonymariis Medii Aevi collecta: Semantische Untersuchungen zum Fachwortschatz hoch- und spätmittelalterlicher Drogenkunde*, Studies in Ancient Medicine, 6 (Leiden: E. J. Brill, 1993), in contrast, identifies it as either yellow asphodel (*Asphodeline lutea* [L.] Rchb.), white asphodel (*Asphodelus albus* Mill.), Turk's cap lily (*Lilium martagon* L.), or field gladiolus (*Gladiolus italicus* Mill.).

238. Grains of wheat are at the basis of this system of calculation.

239. Van den Berg, *Eene Middelnederlandsche Vertaling*, p. 191.

Book on the Conditions of Women

1. This is the beginning of *Conditions of Women*, which in some copies of the ensemble would be called the *Trotula major*. For explanation of the genesis of the authoress "Trotula" and the ascription of the *Trotula* ensemble to her, see the Introduction above.

2. The Latin term used here is *gremium*. In classical Latin, it literally meant "lap" (as I have translated it here), though it was also used euphemistically to refer to the female genitalia in general. See J. N. Adams, *The Latin Sexual Vocabulary* (Baltimore: Johns Hopkins University Press, 1982), pp. 77, 92, 218–20. It is used nowhere else in any of the *Trotula* texts, which instead employ the prosaic but unambiguous *matrix* (womb, uterus) and *uulua* (vagina) and, in the *DCM* in reference to the external genitalia, the *pudenda* (the shameful parts, the privates).

3. The Latin term *medicus* is masculine. It is conceivable that the author was using *medicus* in a generic, not specific, sense—i.e., that he was implying that women were too embarrassed to expose their diseases to *any* healer, male or female (a usage that is quite allowable in Latin grammar). The author stated later in the treatise that women are ashamed in front of other women during birth, though this was changed to a masculine pronoun in the standardized ensemble; see ¶92 below.

4. "And so with God's help" (literally, "God willing," *deo prestante*) is a corruption of an earlier reading "Cleopatre" found in *LSM 3* and carried forward into the ensemble. The reference, of course, was to the *Gynaecia Cleopatrae*, still widely circulating in the twelfth century. This reading, in its turn, had also been a corruption: the original name in *LSM 1* had been that of the Cassinese monk Constantine the African, translator of the *Viaticum*.

5. See the Introduction on the significance of this analogy.

6. The average age of menarche in *LSM 1* was thirteen, though already by the beginning of the thirteenth century copies of *LSM 3* were giving readings varying from twelve, to eleven, to even nine. Since these would all have been written in Roman numerals, changes (whether deliberate or inadvertent) would have been easy. *LSM 1* had listed "sixty or forty" (.lx. uel .xl.; the Arabic original had had "fifty or sixty") as the average age of menopause; a copy of *LSM 2* changes this to "sixty or sixty-five" (.lx. uel .lxv.) and says that the age for fat women is seventy-five (.lxxv.) instead of thirty-five. According to the basic logic behind this theory of menstruation, one would think that fat women would menstruate *longer* than women of normal or thin build because they would have the greatest excess of waste matter. Yet the particular logic in this case seems to be that fat women convert their excess matter into fat, thereby storing instead of excreting it. Presumably, their earlier onset of menopause is considered normal and healthy. On these ages of menarche and menopause more generally, see the Introduction.

7. See the Introduction regarding these alternate modes of egress for the menstrual blood.

8. I.e., the saphenous vein, a major vessel. See also ¶¶10 and 66.

9. The length of this woman's amenorrhea was to prove remarkably unstable. The *TEM* and *LSM 1* read 4 months, as had the *Viaticum* itself (whence this anecdote derives). *LSM 2* reads 9, *LSM 3* reads 10. The ensembles' readings range from 20 days

to 4, 9, 10, 11, or even 20 months. Most copies of the revised ensemble have 4 months, though readings of 10, 11, and 20 months are also found. It is unclear why the standardized ensemble editor reverted to 9 months, though there may have been concern that 4 months was too short a period to confidently distinguish between amenorrhea due to pregnancy and pathological amenorrhea.

10. See also ¶¶8 and 66.

11. See the Appendix for descriptions of these compound medicines.

12. This last phrase, "And let her be given one dose of one scruple" (*et detur una uice scrupulum .i.*), is unique to the standardized ensemble. It is superfluous and contradictory, of course, since the amount to be given has already been stated.

13. In *LSM 1–3*, the reading was *regine Francorum* (for the queen of the Franks). Rather than a woman in the area we now call France, this may have referred to one of the few Norman women who joined their male compatriots in southern Italy, where *Normanni* were not always differentiated from the *Franci* who also emigrated there. On the few Norman women who did emigrate, see Graham A. Loud, "How 'Norman' was the Norman Conquest of Southern Italy?" *Nottingham Medieval Studies* 25 (1981): 13–34, at p. 23. In all versions of the ensemble up through the revised redaction, the predominant reading was *regine Francie* (for the queen of France). The substance of the recipe derives from *Viaticum*, chap. 9.

14. The original reading, instead of *dyabrosim* (ulceration), was *aborsum* (miscarriage). Different terms (*anabrosin, dyabrosim*) first appear in some copies of the proto-ensemble.

15. On these compound medicines, see the Appendix.

16. A class of compound medicines; for *hieralogodion* and *hierapigra*, see the Appendix.

17. The reading *secundum alios* (according to others) was first introduced into the text in the proto-ensemble. The original reading in *LSM 1* had been "let her put [it] in wine or ale" (*ponat in uino uel ceruisia*); the alternate "or ale" does not appear in *LSM 2* or in any other version of the text. At some point between the redaction of the proto-ensemble and the transitional ensemble, "warm water" was added as an alternative. The phrase *secundum alios* may, then, refer not to other people's opinions but to the readings of other codexes. I suspect, however, that by the time of the standardized ensemble, the original meaning may have no longer been recognized.

18. "Dragon's blood" is a commonly used red gum or resin from a tree that grows in Malaysia and Indonesia.

19. Burning cupping glasses are small glass cups applied to the skin. A small burning object is placed inside so that the air (or, in our terms, oxygen) is consumed, thereby producing a vacuum. This suction then draws blood to the area. The logic behind the use of cupping glasses here, therefore, is that they will draw the excessively flowing menstrual blood away from the uterus upward in the body.

20. This recipe came into being through several layers of misreadings. See Monica H. Green, "The Development of the *Trotula*," *Revue d'Histoire des Textes* 26 (1996): 119–203, at p. 184, n. l.

21. This paragraph and the previous are corrupted from the original reading in *LSM 1–3*: "Make two plasters of horsemint ground with grease and put one on the belly, the other on the loins. ¶Also good for this is fresh nettle ground with grease and tied upon the belly and placed on the loins, and [if] with this [you put] delicate elm leaves, so much the better" (*Fiant duo emplastra de sisimbrio trito cum anxugia et*

unum super uentrem, alterum super renes pone. ¶Valent ad idem uiridis urtica trita cum axungia et ligata super uentrem et renes posita, et [si] cum ea folia ulmi tenera tanto melius). The editor of the proto-ensemble introduced several new readings, including adding wormwood (*absinthium*) alongside horsemint (*sisimbrium*) to the recipe in ¶41 and duplicating the final phrase of ¶42 (*et si . . . tanto melius*) in ¶41, though here substituting leaves of myrtle (*folia mirte*) for elm leaves. The editor of the transitional ensemble deleted the second recipe, presumably because of its seeming redundancy, though the standardized ensemble editor put it back in. The similarity of the two sentences in ¶42 is thus the product of a long process of corruption.

22. Note that the author is referring here to the woman's own seed. See the Introduction.

23. The term "collaterals" (*collaterales*) is a late attempt to make sense of a word that had troubled scribes ever since the original composition of the *LSM*. In the *TEM* (the *LSM* "rough draft"), the fume rose to the lobes of the lungs "which are joined on one side to the heart and on the other are near to the womb; it [the fume] also touches the other organs pertaining to the voice" (*ascendit fumus ad pennas pulmonis in una parte iunctas cordi et in alia uicinas matrici; tangit etiam cetera instrumenta ad uocem pertinencia*). In *LSM 1*, the organs affected were called the *cornelieis*, "which are close to the lung and the heart and the other organs of the voice" (*Ex huiusmodi semine superhabundante et corrupto quedam frigida fumositas dissoluitur et ascendit ad quasdam partes que uulgo dicuntur cornelieis, que quia uicine sunt pulmoni et cordi et ceteris instrumentis uocis, inde contigit fieri impedimentum loquele*). In the transitional ensemble, the term had become *conlidones*; in the intermediate ensemble, forms such as *coralles, thorales*, and *cornelles* occur. The reading stabilized as *collaterales* in the revised ensemble.

24. A compound medicine; see the Appendix.

25. In the *TEM*, this name appeared as *Justus*. In *LSM*, it was *Justinus*. I have not yet been able to trace the source of this recipe.

26. The plural is used here perhaps in reference to both the opening of the vagina and the cervix.

27. The fruit "quinces" appears twice here because of a textual corruption. In the original *LSM*, the recommended fruits were *mespila, sorbas, et citonia et acria poma* (medlars, service-berries, quinces, and bitter apples). *Coctana*, which is a synonym for *citonia* (quinces), seems to have entered the text first as a substitution for *citonia* (it is found thus in the Erfurt Group of the proto-ensemble). In the transitional ensemble, *coctana* becomes incorporated as the first of now five fruits, a reading that persists in all later versions of the text. The elimination of *citonia* in two manuscripts used for the Latin edition (GW) suggests an alert scribe who noticed the redundancy.

28. The original reading *cornu cerui* (buck's-horn plantain, i.e., an herb, not an animal part) had been corrupted to *corde cerui* (deer heart) in some copies of the proto-ensemble. It was perhaps understood to be a reference to deer heart bone (*os de corde cerui*), the bone found in the hearts of certain large animals, esp. deer, which was used medicinally.

29. In *LSM 1–3*, this had read "of a different kind" (*diuersi generis*). The change to *coloris* occurred in the intermediate ensemble.

30. In *LSM 1*, the reading had been "or because the menses are always deficient" (*ex eo non numquam menstrua deficiunt*). The *non* dropped out in the version of *LSM 2* that was used as the basis of the proto-ensemble.

31. Difficult or painful urination.

32. The logic of this is that bloodletting is intended to move blood to different parts of the body; by reason of the suction, the blood moves to the area around the site of the incision of the vein. Because the uterus is in the lower part of the body, it is usually necessary to induce the blood to flow *down* in the body, not up (as venesection in the hand would cause).

33. Medicaments that encourage the production of sanies and pus and, in consequence, the dissolution of the tumor.

34. The *Zād al-musāfir/Viaticum*, the original *LSM*, and most versions of the ensemble have Dioscorides' name here, not Galen's; cf. Bos, *Ibn al-Jazzār on Sexual Diseases*, p. 279. The name drops out in most copies of the revised ensemble, so that it is not clear who is speaking (*dicit*). The editor of the standardized ensemble then fills in the lacuna with Galen's name.

35. The reference is to Paul of Aegina and derives from the *Zād al-musāfir/Viaticum*. Cf. Bos, *Ibn al-Jazzār on Sexual Diseases*, pp. 279–80.

36. *LSM 1* had prescribed only veal marrow (*medulla uituli*) and fat of a badger/squirrel (*adeps melote*). Extant *LSM 3* manuscripts give variant readings for *melote* (*molete, anseris,* and *uituli*), but the word was incorporated in its correct form into the proto-ensemble. It was at that point, apparently, that the gloss *id est, taxi* (that is, of a *taxus*), was added, though only one manuscript actually preserves that correct reading. Others, instead, have already corrupted it into *talpe* (of a mole), *tapsonis* (??), and *caponis* (of a capon). All these variants are found in the intermediate ensemble, where the *id est* (that is) has been replaced by *et* (and), with the result that the emphasis on synonymy was lost. In the revised ensemble, *adipem caponis* becomes stabilized (now placed consistently right after *medullam uituli*), while *talponis* or, in one case, *taxonis,* is retained as the fourth of the string of ingredients. *Taxonis* stabilizes as the reading of the standardized ensemble.

37. The addition of the word *ceroti* (a wax-based compound, cf. ¶278) was an error introduced at the stage of the standardized ensemble. *LSM 1* had had *croci* (saffron), which, to judge from Bos's edition of the *Zād al-musāfir* (*Ibn al-Jazzār on Sexual Diseases*, pp. 279–80), must have been the correct reading. *Croci* dropped out in *LSM 2* and some copies of *LSM 3*, and thus was never incorporated into the ensemble. The standardized ensemble editor collated his text with a copy of *LSM 1* (see Green, "Development," p. 168), and either he misread the abbreviation for *croci* as *ceroti* or the error had already crept into the copy of the *LSM* from which he was working.

38. A thin, blood-stained, purulent discharge.

39. Again (cf. ¶67), Galen's name has replaced that of Dioscorides; the change was first introduced in the revised ensemble. As with the other citations to Dioscorides, this comes directly out of the *Viaticum/Zād al-musāfir*. See Bos, *Ibn al-Jazzār on Sexual Diseases*, p. 283.

40. From the original *LSM* up through the intermediate ensemble, the phrase "just as Hippocrates attests" (*sicut testatur Ypocras*) was found at the beginning of ¶74 on impediments to conception, not, as here, at the end of ¶73.

41. Literally, "her man."

42. ¶¶79–81 had originally appeared after ¶88 in *LSM 1–2* (cf. Green, "Development," table 1, ¶¶88a–c). Thus, the original order followed the natural chronology of reproduction: aids to conception (¶¶74–75, 75a, 78, and 78a-b), contraceptives (¶¶83–87), risk factors for miscarriage and its prevention (¶88), a regimen for pregnancy and treatment of its common disorders (¶88a–c), the process of birth (¶89),

and finally difficulties of birth (¶90 and following). The disorder of the ensemble came about because the proto-ensemble editor reinserted the contraceptive and fetal development chapters (¶¶83–88, which had been dropped from *LSM 3*) in the wrong place. See the Introduction.

43. This recipe was displaced here in the proto-ensemble (it had originally appeared between ¶¶75 and 76), and it was never restored to its original, more logical position.

44. In the *TEM* and *LSM 1–2*, the name of Constantine appeared here, in reference to Constantine the African, *Pantegni, Practica* 1: 18, "On women who have small vaginas" (*De mulieribus paruas vuluas habentibus*, printed in *Opera omnia Ysaac*, Lyons 1515, pars 2, f. 62va). Constantine's name was changed to "Galyenus" in the proto-ensemble.

45. The addition of the phrase "or even tasted" (*uel etiam gustatus*) is another instance where the editor of the revised ensemble has incorporated a variant reading into the text instead of resolving the discrepancy.

46. This reference to Hippocrates' views on phlebotomy does not derive from the *Viaticum* nor, apparently, from the Galenic commentary on the *Aphorisms* (my thanks to Ann Ellis Hanson for checking the latter text for me). Since recommendations of phlebotomy are very rare in the Hippocratic corpus (cf. Helen King, *Hippocrates' Woman: Reading the Female Body in Ancient Greece* [London: Routledge, 1998], p. 199), it is most likely that this passage derives from a late antique, pseudo-Hippocratic source.

47. A compound medicine; see the Appendix.

48. In *LSM 1*, this had read "on inclined areas" (*per decliuia*). It was changed to "through the house" (*per domum*) in Group B of the transitional ensemble and is found thereafter in all later forms of the ensemble. (It is also found in one branch of the proto-ensemble, the Erfurt Group.) This change seems a subtle suggestion that childbirth was to be confined within the home and not paraded publicly in the streets.

49. It is not clear whether the reading should be "those men" or more broadly "those people." The Latin masculine plural (*qui*) can encompass women among a group of men. Either way, however, the use of the masculine pronoun assumes the inclusion of men in the birthing process, an interesting change from the original text. In the *TEM*, the author specifically said it was the midwives (*obstetrices*) who were not to look at the woman. In the *LSM*, this was changed to the less specific but still clearly feminine "those women who assist her" (*Mulieres que assistunt ei*). *Mulieres* dropped out in the proto-ensemble, leaving only the feminine pronoun *que*. Whether the change from the feminine to the masculine pronoun (*qui*) in some copies of the transitional ensemble—a reading that became fixed in the revised ensemble—was deliberate is impossible to determine.

50. The strings of letters and syllables in this recipe and in ¶100 reflect corruptions first introduced into the text in the proto-ensemble. Presumably, they were allowed to stand because editors and scribes assumed the gibberish was part of the magical formula, which by its very nature was not meant to be understood. For the original magical formula of the *LSM*, see the Introduction.

51. Unlike the previous string of magical syllables (see note above), this recipe had no magic component in the original *LSM*. The phrase from *bibat* to the end read simply, "let her drink woman's milk with oil and she will give birth immediately" (*bibat lac muliebre cum oleo et statim pariet* [or *liberabitur* in some manuscripts]). As

with the *Sator arepo* formula, these nonsensical syllables first appear in some copies of the proto-ensemble.

52. The reason for the caution was that the root of gourd was thought to have such a powerful expulsive faculty that, if not taken away immediately after the fetus's exit, it would draw out the womb as well.

53. ¶106 is a later addition, essentially repeating ¶111 below (an original component of the *LSM*). ¶¶107–10 were omitted from most copies of the proto-ensemble, so that the text moved directly from ¶105 to the discussion of the lochial flow in ¶111. When the editor of the revised ensemble reinserted the omitted material, she or he inadvertently reintroduced the "original" passage on the lochial flow (the "new" ¶106), which now differed slightly in phrasing from ¶111.

54. This passage (like the rest of ¶¶104–8) is drawn directly from the *Viaticum*, chap. 17. If we can accept the Arabic original of Ibn al-Jazzār's text, "horse's hoof" (*ungula caballina*) is here meant literally (Bos, *Ibn al-Jazzār on Sexual Diseases*, p. 294). However, there was in the Latin pharmacopeia an herb called *ungula caballina* (coltsfoot [*Tussilago farfara* L.]), and it may well be that this was what later readers of the text understood.

55. The citation of Hippocrates is a reference to *Aphorisms*, book 5. Aphorism 5:42 reads "A pregnant woman is of good complexion if the child be male; of ill complexion if the child be female" (G. E. R. Lloyd, ed., *Hippocratic Writings* [Harmondsworth: Penguin, 1978], at p. 225). The association of male fetuses with the right breast and females with the left is made, although with a different emphasis, in Aphorism 5:38: "If, in a woman who is carrying twins, one breast becomes thin, a miscarriage will occur of one of the children. If the right breast is affected, the male child will be lost; if the left, the female" (ibid., p. 224). The *TEM* ends with this recipe; the two extant copies of *LSM 1* add two brief obstetrical recipes that, with the exception of one copy of *LSM 3*, are found in no other versions of the text.

56. The following eight paragraphs (¶115–22) were added by the redactor of *LSM 2*.

57. On the preparation of *diathessaron*, see ¶11 above; on *theriac*, see the Appendix.

58. A kind of round, flat lozenge, to be dissolved slowly in the mouth.

59. The following reflects an ancient formula for describing fetal development. See, for example, the so-called *Gynaecia* attributed to the fourth-century writer Avianus Vindicianus.

60. In much medieval medical parlance, *nervi* could mean nerves in our modern sense, but also tendons and ligaments.

61. The following four paragraphs (¶¶124–27) derive from the fourth book of the *Liber ad Almansorem* (The Book for al-Mansur), a long regimen of health by the Persian physician Abū Bakr Muḥammad ibn Zakariyā ar-Rāzī (ca. 865–925, known in Latin as Rhazes), which was translated from Arabic into Latin in Spain probably in the third quarter of the twelfth century. This material was added to the *LSM* by the redactor of the proto-ensemble. See the Introduction.

62. This apparently refers to an earlier section of Rhazes's book that is not included here.

63. For *dialtea*, see the Appendix. *Diaceraseos* is presumably some kind of com-

pound medicine made with wax, as is *ceroneum*. *Oxicroceum* is presumably a compound of vinegar and saffron.

64. I have not yet determined the source of the following paragraph.

65. These last three paragraphs in the *LSM* portion of the ensemble (¶129–31) come from the Salernitan physician Copho, to whom they are attributed in the compendium of Salernitan writings entitled *On the Treatment of Illnesses* (*De egritudinum curatione*); see Salvatore De Renzi, *Collectio Salernitana ossia documenti inediti, e trattati di medicina appartenenti alla scuola medica salernitana*, 5 vols. (Naples: Filiatre-Sebezio, 1852–59; repr. Bologna: Forni, 1967), 3: 342–43. The same material was also incorporated into the *Practica* of Trota.

66. A compound medicine; see the Appendix.

67. In Copho's *Practica*, we find passages that similarly link the uterus to disorders of the brain. See Rudolf Creutz, "Der Magister Copho und seine Stellung im Hochsalerno: Aus M. p. med. Q 2 (saec. XIII), fol. 85ᵃ–103ᵃ Würzburg," *Sudhoffs Archiv für Geschichte der Medizin und der Naturwissenschaften* 31 (1938), 51–60, and 33/5 and 6 (July 1941), 249–338, at pp. 292, 334.

68. On these compound medicines, see the Appendix.

69. According to traditional Hippocratic theory (which as explained in the Introduction was quite vague in its anatomy), there was a direct channel between a woman's nose and mouth and her womb and genitals. For an odor to pass directly from the genitals to the nose or mouth was proof that the channel was "open" and that the woman had no blockage that would impede conception.

70. A compound medicine; see the Appendix.

On Treatments for Women

1. This is the beginning of *Treatments for Women* (*De curis mulierum*). In many copies of the intermediate and revised ensembles, the *LSM* was referred to as *Trotula major*, and the *DCM* as *Trotula minor*. *Trotula major* disappeared as a rubric from the standardized ensemble, while *Trotula minor* became infrequent, being found in only five manuscripts. The rubric *Cura* (Treatment) is more common, and offers an explicit link between the preceding discussion of infertility that had closed the *LSM* (¶¶129–31) and the *DCM*'s opening section on treatment of infertility. In other words, the ensemble has now lost the last explicit indicator that the *DCM* is a different text from the *LSM*.

2. The reading *feminis* is a change introduced by the editor of the standardized ensemble; in the original *DCM* and all other versions of the ensemble, it had read *frigidis*, i.e., "a fumigation for cold women."

3. This is a cross-reference to ¶134 above.

4. *DCM 1–2* had not indicated that this procedure was only for women giving birth "with difficulty" (*difficulter*).

5. Sternutatives are substances that induce sneezing.

6. In *DCM 1*, this passage had had a slightly different reading: "For as Copho says, the members are shaken by the sneezing to such a degree that the cotyledons (that is, the ligaments by which the infant is tied to the womb) are broken" (*Nam ut dicit Copho, quassantur membra sternutione in tantum ut rumpantur chotilidones, id est*

ligamenta quibus alligatur infans matrici). Copho recommends sternutatives for difficult labor in his *Practica* (Rudolf Creutz, "Der Magister Copho und seine Stellung im Hochsalerno: Aus M. p. med. Q 2 [saec. XIII], fol. 85ª–103ª Würzburg," *Sudhoffs Archiv für Geschichte der Medizin und der Naturwissenschaften* 31 [1938]: 51–60, and 33, nos. 5 and 6 [July 1941]: 249–338, at p. 333), but makes no mention there of the cotyledons. In the *Anatomy of the Pig* attributed to Copho, however, the cotyledons are described as "the channels by which the fetus is tied to the womb" (*illi meatus quibus foetus alligatur, dicuntur cotyledones*); see George W. Corner, *Anatomical Texts of the Earlier Middle Ages: A Study in the Transmission of Culture* (Washington, D.C.: Carnegie Institution of Washington, 1927), p. 50.

7. The alternate readings *fecunda* (fecund/fertile/fruitful) and *secunda* (second) are also found in the revised ensemble. The original (and more plausible) reading was *secunda*, i.e., "because to certain women it is not permitted to pass to a second vow."

8. A compound medicine; see Appendix.

9. Instead of "phlegmatic and fat" (*fleumatica et grossa*) this should have read "phlegmatic and thin" (*fleumatica et gracilis*), as it did in *DCM 1*, in order to set up the proper contrast between the two different regimens. The error entered the text in the revised ensemble.

10. The original reading in *DCM 1* had been clearer: "we make for her a bath of seawater or water in which salt has been placed in an equal amount, or of rainwater" (*facimus ei balneum de aqua marina uel aqua cui sal sit impositum ad moderationem tantum, uel de aqua pluuiali*).

11. A compound medicine; see Appendix.

12. A cross-reference to ¶139.

13. This obscure passage reflects a significant alteration of the original text. In *DCM 1*, the reading had been "But let this thing of ours [this observation of ours?] be a secret/be hidden with women" or even "But let this be our secret with women" (*Sed istud nostrum cum mulieribus sit secretum*). This apparent *entre nous* of female author and audience was immediately altered in *DCM 2*: "But this thing, you know, is hidden with women" (*Sed istud nosti quod cum mulieribus sit secretum*). Further alterations occurred in various versions of the ensemble.

14. The inclusion of daisy here is due to a textual corruption. *DCM 1* had read "from comfrey, that is, consolida major or anagallus, which is the same thing" (*ex simphito, id est consolida maiori uel anagalli quod idem est*). *Consolida maiori* was later misread as *consolida minori*, which is an altogether different plant (*Bellis perennis* L.).

15. The phrase *continuitatis solutio* is a common technical term of medieval medicine. It can refer to various kinds of wounds or lesions.

16. I.e., the therapy just described in ¶149.

17. This may be a reference to appendicitis. In *DCM 1–2*, the woman is described as *yliose*, indicating that she suffered from the "iliac disease" (*passio iliaca*). This refers to the ileum, the last section of the small intestine. The ileum joins the cecum (the first section of the large intestine), which is where the vermiform appendix is found. *Passio iliaca* was described by a later twelfth-century writer, Roger de Baron, as follows: "The iliac disease is so called from the ylion intestine [which is] delicate and very sensitive. Because of its extreme sensitivity, it causes intolerable pain. On the first or second day, it kills." Roger de Baron, *Practica maior*, in *Cyrurgia*

Guidonis de Cauliaco, et Cyrurgia Bruni, Teodorici, Rolandi, Lanfranci, Rogerii, Berta-palie (Venice, 1519), f. 216rb.

18. In *DCM 1–2*, Trota's name appeared correctly. It was first changed to "Trotula" in the transitional ensemble. See Introduction.

19. The original *DCM* and early versions of the ensemble stated simply that Trota was called in "as a master" (*uocata fuit quasi magistra*). The qualifier *operis* (of this procedure/operation) was added in the intermediate ensemble. I have chosen to employ the masculine form "master" in the translation because "mistress" is not strong enough to convey the intended sense: i.e., that in being called in for this case, Trota/"Trotula" was being accorded the same respect as a fully acknowledged male master of medicine.

20. In *DCM 1–2*, reference was made only to an unspecified "swelling" (*inflatione*), not, as here, to a "swelling of the womb" (*inflatione matricis*). This addition distorts the story, of course, because it was Trota who conceived of a uterine diagnosis, whereas the original diagnosis (by whom is unspecified) was limited to an intestinal causation.

21. It is possible that this refers to any generic caustic substance rather than ink specifically.

22. The pronoun is a masculine plural, which in Latin can refer either to a group of males or to males and females together.

23. A remedy very similar to this is attributed to the *mulieres Salernitane* in the *Practica brevis* of Johannes Platearius II (d. 1161). In Platearius's text, however, the cabbage leaf is used for pustules of the penis, not swelling. See *De egritudinum curatione*, in Salvatore De Renzi, *Collectio Salernitana ossia documenti inediti, e trattati di medicina appartenenti alla scuola medica salernitana*, 5 vols. (Naples: Filiatre-Sebezio, 1852–59; repr. Bologna: Forni, 1967), 2: 330; and Tony Hunt, *Anglo-Norman Medicine*, 2 vols. (Cambridge: D. S. Brewer, 1994–97), 1: 241.

24. Again, the pronoun is masculine plural.

25. Difficulty urinating.

26. I have translated *simplex benedicta* as "uncompounded hemlock" on the interpretation that the modifier *simplex* is used precisely in order to distinguish the "simple" (i.e., the herb alone) from a compound medicine also named *Benedicta*; see the Appendix.

27. In *DCM 1*, he was identified as master Mattheus Ferrarius. I have not yet been able to trace this treatment in any known writings of Ferrarius.

28. Some manuscripts of the revised and standardized ensembles give the feminine pronoun here, presumably by force of the subject matter of the treatise as a whole. The later reference to treatment of the penis, however, clarifies the patient's sex.

29. A special kind of unguent; see Appendix.

30. The phrase "or of semen" (*uel spermatis*) was added in the standardized ensemble.

31. In *DCM 1–2*, the author explicitly said that the menses ought not be provoked in old women who have a sanious flux, since they are sterile, i.e., postmenopausal (*quedam ueterane fluxum saniosum continue educentes, quibus in menstrua prouocando non est subueniendum cum sint steriles*). These women are to be distin-

guished from the women described in the next paragraph, who (presumably still in their childbearing years) also are sterile and who also suffer from the same sort of sanious flux, but for whom, this time, a treatment is offered. This underscores the general view of the *DCM* that menstruation is more a prerequisite for conception than a vital purgation necessary for overall health. The negative was retained in some copies of the proto-ensemble and in one copy each of the transitional and intermediate ensembles. It disappears totally in the revised ensemble. Conceivably, the last clause here could be read "even though they are sterile."

32. Presumably a cross-reference to the "hot" herbs prescribed in ¶134.

33. See ¶151 above.

34. The phrase "This remedy is decent" (*hoc remedium est honestum*) was not in *DCM 1*. It originated in *DCM 2*, presumably to indicate that the main indicated use, for genital itching, did not compromise a woman's virtue.

35. Cf. ¶290 below.

36. This paragraph underwent considerable deformation as the ensemble developed. The final sentence in particular has two peculiarities. First, it is not found at all in *DCM 1*. It originated in a version of *DCM 2*, which essentially repeated the information in the first sentence of the paragraph. Second, in the proto-ensemble, it was specified that the Salernitan women use this unguent *contra crustulas pro mortuis factas* (for the scabs made [in mourning] for the dead). In the transitional ensemble, *crustulas* became *cataractas* (cataracts, floods; see also ¶290). Finally, in the word doubling characteristic of the standardized ensemble, the obscure *coraculas* (rivulets) is added as a gloss to *catharactas*.

37. In the *DCM* and early versions of the ensemble, this had read "before the ninth day" (*ante nouem diem* or *dies*). The "nine" was changed to "twenty" in one branch of the revised ensemble tradition and in the standardized ensemble.

38. The original reading of the *DCM* and all versions of the ensemble had been "redness" (*ruborem*), not "swelling" (*tumorem*). The Basel manuscript used for the base text of the Latin edition is unique in this misreading.

39. The Latin text here reads *ceruse, gerse et olibani ana unciam .i. Gersa* is often used a synonym for *cerusa* and had been the original reading throughout *DCM 1*. With one exception (see ¶211), *gersa* was systematically changed to *cerusa* in *DCM 2*. The use of *gerse* here seems to have been a reintroduction by the revised ensemble editor, who was collating his/her text with *DCM 1*. I have omitted it, however, in the translation since it is redundant.

40. A skin condition characterized by intense itching.

41. In *DCM 1*, this had read *equis*, i.e., "this unguent is good for horses [*equis*] which scratch themselves because of itching." *Equis* was changed to *eis* (for them) in *DCM 2*, with *illis* (for those) appearing later in the ensemble tradition. The reference to horses is also found in the ultimate source of this remedy, the chapter *De scabie* in Trota's *Practical Medicine According to Trota*. It is thus ironic that in some copies of the standardized ensemble the rubric stresses that humans were the intended recipients of this therapy.

42. The Latin pronoun is masculine.

43. In *DCM 1*, the English term *gladene* had been given. It was changed to the Latin *gladiolum* in *DCM 2*. On the use of English in the *DCM*, see the Introduction.

44. See ¶167 above.

45. The Latin text reads *et puluis cutim extrahendo*. In *DCM 1–2* and all versions of the ensemble up through the intermediate ensemble, this had read "first" (*prius*) instead of "powder" (*puluis*). Confusion is first evident in the revised ensemble, with *plus* and *post* occasionally appearing. I have restored the original reading in the translation, since it is impossible to render any sense out of the Latin as it stands.

46. *DCM 1* had had a clearer reading: "Mix these powders with a little water in the hand and you should anoint the face, rubbing sufficiently" (*Istos pulueres misce cum aqua pauca in manu et faciem illinias satis fricando*). In later versions this was changed to "and with the same, you should anoint the hands and face, rubbing" (*et eodem manus et faciem illinias fricando*). "And the face" (*et faciem*) dropped out in the revised ensemble. The standardized ensemble editor restores the phrase "mix with a little water" (*cum pauca aqua misce*) but fails to correct "on the hands" (*manus*) back to "in the hand" (*in manu*) or to restore *et faciem*.

47. In his *Practica* (in Rudolf Creutz, "Der Magister Copho und seine Stellung im Hochsalerno: Aus M. p. med. Q 2 (saec. XIII), fol. 85ª–103ª Würzburg," *Sudhoffs Archiv für die Geschichte der Medizin und der Naturwissenschaften* 31 [1938]: 51–60, and 33, nos. 5 and 6 [July 1941]: 249–338, at p. 299), the Salernitan physician Copho specified that whereas phlebotomy or cupping glasses were to be used on the (normatively) male patient for redness or blemishes of the face, leeches were to be used on women.

48. The phrase "and we cure this in the above-mentioned manner" (*et predicto modo sanamus*) apparently referred to what had been the preceding chapter in *DCM 1–2* for removing warts (¶179a, *Ad uerrucas cum acu circumquaque eleuamus*). This recipe was moved to a later position in the transitional ensemble, where it was to remain (¶199, below).

49. In *DCM 1–2*, the substance had been *alumen rotundum* (round alum). It was changed to *oleum rosaceum* (rose oil) in the transitional ensemble.

50. It is, of course, the exterior rind that is green in walnuts. In the *DCM*, this had originally (and correctly) been "cleaned of the exterior that is green" (*mundatam ab illo exteriori quod uiride est*).

51. In *DCM 1*, the powder was to be made from cinnabar (*de minio*). In *DCM 2*, the reading was expanded to "from cumin and cinnabar" (*de cimino et minio*). The reading *et minio* dropped out in the proto-ensemble.

52. See ¶167 above.

53. In *DCM 1*, this was attributed to "M. J. F." In *DCM 2*, this appears as "master Ferrarius" (*magistrum Ferrarium*). Although it is possible that the original abbreviation referred to a Johannes Ferrarius, no such individual has yet been documented from other sources. There was, however, a Johannes Furias, who is mentioned in Trota's *Practica*.

54. The phrase "with sugar" (*cum zucchara*) was not in *DCM 1–2*, where sugar is never employed (see the Introduction). It was first added in the revised ensemble.

55. There was no mention of prolapse (*exitus*) in *DCM 1–2*, which had begun the paragraph simply "For the vagina after birth" (*Ad uuluam post partum*). How the corruption *in exitu*, which first enters the text in the revised ensemble, came about is unclear.

56. This chapter went through a series of very interesting corruptions from its

original form in *DCM 1*. There, it had been a general postpartum regimen. The first two sentences survived transmission with no substantive deformation. The third sentence, however, had originally referred not to the care of the woman but to that of the child. "We have [someone] blow into the backsides of male as well as female children and through the mouth and through the nose so that, the breath having been received, they revive" (*Puerorum etiam femininorum posterioribus inflare facimus, et per os et per nares ut spiritu recepto reuiuiscant*). In other words, this was an instruction for stimulating respiration in the newborn. Already in *DCM 2*, this was corrupted to "And we also have a powder of the above-mentioned [ingredients] blown into [the woman] through her backside and through her mouth and nose in order that, the spirit having been received, she revives" (*Et puluerem etiam predictorum insufflare per posterioribus [sic] facimus, per os et per nares ut spiritu recepto reuiuiscat*). In the transitional ensemble, it had changed to "We have the powders mentioned above in later [chapters?] blown through the mouth and nose lest they [the mouth and nose?] swell up" (*Pulueres predictos posterioribus facimus insufflare per os et nares ne intumescant*).

57. In *DCM 1*, this had read *alumen album* (white alum), not *albumina ouorum* (whites of eggs). It had already changed to the latter in some copies of the proto-ensemble and became permanently fixed as "whites of eggs" in the transitional ensemble. The constrictive properties of alum were, needless to say, undoubtedly greater than those of egg whites.

58. This recipe was first added to the proto-ensemble.

59. As noted in the Introduction, this recipe had originally employed both powdered natron and powdered glass (*uitrum et nitrum*). Vitrum dropped out in *DCM 2*, though the similarity of "v" and "n" in most scripts allowed the reading *uitrum* occasionally to be reintroduced.

60. In *DCM 1*, this had read "the vagina might swell up because of coitus" (*vulva . . . infletur ex coitu*), the difference being that the cause of the swelling was stressed, not simply (as it is found here) the fact of it happening.

61. See ¶167 above.

62. What is presented as a single statement here in ¶203 had in *DCM 1* been two separate assertions: that breast pain in young women was transitory, being caused by the (first) eruption of the menses; and that some young women seem to be suffering from "the falling sickness," which is caused by the compression of the respiratory organs by uterine suffocation. The two statements were first linked by the phrase "because also" (*quod etiam*) in *DCM 2*; the present corruption is first found in the transitional ensemble.

63. Instead of saying that the cough was very severe (*acerrima*), *DCM 1* had offered the synonym "and it is called *chinke* in English" (*et dicitur anglice chinke*). Scribes of *DCM 2* already show that the English term itself needed to be glossed (one manuscript adds the incorrect French gloss *id est, sire*) or, more conveniently, omitted altogether. The phrase disappears from the transitional ensemble. The editor of the revised ensemble apparently was trying to make sense of some remnant of the phrase in whatever copy of the *DCM 1* s/he was using; some manuscripts have the reading "and it is called 'very harsh'" (*et dicitur acerrima*). The phrase "and it is called" (*et dicitur*) was clearly extraneous, however, and was soon deleted.

64. In the original *DCM*, this recipe had been for redness (*ruborem*), not pain (*dolorem*), of the eyes.

65. *DCM 1* had read "of white lead" (*gerse*) instead of "of plaster of Paris" (*gipsi*). The error was introduced very early in the transmission. Cf. the note on ¶172 above.

66. The referent (*terram campanie*) could also be more specific, "earth of Campania," that is, the region of southern Italy in which Salerno was situated. On "blacking" (*atramentum*), see also ¶256.

67. In *DCM 1*, this had read *camphoratam* (southernwood), not *camphoram* (camphor).

68. In *DCM 1*, this had read, "Our Lord Jesus Christ was born, and he was pierced by the lance, and he paid no heed to the wind or pain or any misfortune" (*Dominus noster Jesus Christus natus fuerit, et lancea lanceatus, non curabat nec de uento, nec de dolore, nec de ulla occasione*). The reading *uento* (wind) was corrupted to *unguento* (unguent) in *DCM 2*. The editor of the revised ensemble changed *occasione* (misfortune) to *unctione* (unction).

69. The Latin terms here are *cythare uel uigelle*. Given the difficulty of identifying precisely what instruments were meant in this historical context, I have translated them loosely. My thanks to Professor Lex Silbiger of Duke University for advice on this matter.

70. See the Introduction regarding the presence of Middle English terms in this text. This is the only one of the three original English terms (cf. ¶¶176 and 204) to survive intact into the later versions of the ensemble.

71. This recipe, which essentially repeats the previous one, is first found in the intermediate ensemble.

72. Two different terms for "marsh mallow" (*Althaea officinalis* L.) are used here: *malva* and *bismalva*. In *DCM 1*, they were *malva* and *malviscum*, the latter perhaps referring to mayweed, stinking chamomile (*Anthemis cotula* L.).

73. In *DCM 1*, this had read *faucium* (glandules of the throat), not *faciei* (of the face). The corruption *faciei* appears in one copy each of the proto- and the transitional ensemble, while in the intermediate ensemble the usual reading is *cum fascia* (with a bandage). The reading *faciei* was reintroduced in the revised ensemble.

74. The reading here is strained due to the misplacement of *quandoque* in the first line. *DCM 1* had read, "Pain of the womb happens from miscarriage before its time, sometimes from retention of the menses, which happens more often because of frigidity. Rarely [does it happen] from excessive heat" (*Dolor matricis contingit ex aborsu ante tempus, quandoque ex retentione menstruorum que sepius fit ex frigiditate. Raro autem ex calore nimio*).

75. On both these compound medicines, see Appendix.

76. Sexual intercourse.

77. A compound medicine; see Appendix.

78. Instead of *policariam, DCM 1* read *herbam etnam, id est multe*. This phrase never appears again in *DCM 2* or any version of the ensemble, all of which replace it with *policariam minorem*. The original phrase is striking in two respects: first, the name *herba etna* (which thus far I have found documented nowhere else) is in obvious reference to the volcano on Sicily. Second, the synonym *multe* would seem to be a vernacular term, since, if it were Latin, it would have an accusative case ending. One possibility is that, as in ¶¶176, 204, and 218, this is an English word. Tony Hunt, *Plant Names of Medieval England* (Cambridge: D. S. Brewer, 1989), finds *molde* or *melde* offered as the English equivalent of *hermodactila*. *Hermodactila* (= ramsons,

wild garlic; crow garlic; or meadow saffron) is not, however, related to *policaria minor* (small fleabane). An alternate possibility is suggested by the term *herba etna*, which may be an error for *herba emma*; the latter term is given as the synonym for *policaria minor* in ¶231 in a collection of excerpts from *DCM 1*. If so, this might suggest that *multe* is an alternate spelling (or simply misspelling) of the Old French *mul(l)et* (flea-bane). Thus, the substitution in *DCM 2* of *herba etna [emma?]*, *id est multe* with *policaria minor* would reflect a correct understanding of the herbal referent.

79. *DCM 1* had had "cumin, ginger" (*cimini, zinziberis*) instead of "frankincense, cinnamon" (*thuris, cinamoni*).

80. Literally, "go to the chair."

81. *DCM 1* had said "on the wound" (*in uulneri*), not "in the vagina" (*in uulua*). The latter first appears in *DCM 2*.

82. As in ¶216 above, this had originally been a reference to *camphorata* (south-ernwood), not *camphoram* (camphor).

83. In *DCM 1*, the final sentence, rather than referring to the whole remedy for hemorrhoids just described, was instead an aside stating another use for white alum alone: "And you should know that alum alone thus pulverized and inserted as a sup-pository renders a violated woman tighter than a virgin" (*et scias quia alumen solum sic puluerizatum et suppositum uiolatam strictiorem reddit quam uirginem*).

84. This had read "for [aiding] the woman's birth" (*Ad partum mulieris*) in *DCM 1–2*, not "for birth of the womb" (*partum matricis*). The change first appeared in one branch of the revised ensemble and stabilized in the standardized ensemble.

85. In *DCM 1–2*, this had read "place vinegar in a pot beneath her" (*mitte acetum in olla inferius*), not "into the vagina" (*in uuluam*). The change occurred in the transi-tional ensemble (Group B). Presumably, in its original form a suffumigation was intended.

86. On the cotyledons, see ¶139 above.

87. Rather than reading "Likewise in another fashion" (*Item aliter*), this chapter had originally been introduced in the proto-ensemble with the heading "A test to see if a woman has been corrupted or not" (*Si mulier sit corrupta an non, experimentum*). If the woman urinated, she was sexually experienced; if she did not, she was still a vir-gin (*Si non, non*). Already in some copies of the transitional ensemble the correct heading was lost. The corruption became permanent in the intermediate ensemble, hence this rather strange procedure for getting rid of scabies.

88. When this recipe was first introduced into the transitional ensemble (Group B), it was attributed to "the wife of Petrus Vivianus" (*Vnguentum uxoris Petri Viu-iani ad faciem dealbandam*). The attribution dropped out in the revised ensemble.

On Women's Cosmetics

1. This is the beginning of the third *Trotula* text, *On Women's Cosmetics* (*De ornatu mulierum*). As an independent text, the *DOM* had originally opened with a preface (see the Introduction); this, however, was incorporated only into the transi-tional ensemble, and thereafter lost entirely. *Women's Cosmetics* was amplified in the ensemble by the addition of ¶¶254, 256–59, 261–71, 286–88, and 290 from *Treatments for Women*, and by completely new material; the order of the original *Women's Cos-metics* was nevertheless maintained. The rubric most commonly found here in the

standardized ensemble, *De palliandis mulieribus*, literally means "On covering up women."

2. *DOM 1*, in a fuller reading, had specified that steambaths were for those women who lacked access to formal baths, "just like women beyond the Alps" (*Si autem balnea defuerint, cum stuphis sicut transmontane mulieres que huiusmodi carent balneis fiant stuphe sic*). This statement both implies the Italian origin of the *DOM* and demonstrates the author's awareness of the habits of women outside his own region. Indeed, his assumption that the needs of northern European women should be taken into account suggests his concern to make his text "marketable" beyond a local audience. The reference to "women beyond the Alps" was deleted from *DOM 2* (the direct source of the ensemble text of the *DOM*).

3. The Latin term *fovea* normally refers to a small storage space for storing grain. On this practice generally, see David Andrews, "Underground Grain Storage in Central Italy," in *Medieval Lazio*, ed. David Andrews et al. (Oxford: B.A.R., 1982), pp. 123–35.

4. *Populeon*, a compound medicine, was not included in this recipe in *DOM*. It was added by the intermediate ensemble editor.

5. See the Appendix for descriptions of both *populeon* and *unguentum album*.

6. The ensemble here follows *DOM 2*, which, in abbreviating the original passage of *DOM 1*, had completely contradicted it. *DOM 1* had read, "If, however, this depilatory is too thick, when the woman wishes to be anointed let her dilute it with her own urine. For the addition of more water would make it worse" (*Si autem hec pilatoria nimis fuerit spissa, quando mulier uult inungi liquefaciat ea mulier cum urina sua. Nam alia aqua imposita ea peioraret*).

7. In all versions of the *DOM* and in early versions of the ensemble, this reference had been to "noble Saracen women" (*nobiles Sarracene*). The change to "noble Salernitan women" (*nobiles Salernitane*) occurred in the revised ensemble.

8. It is possible that what I have here and in ¶254 translated as "henna" (for the Latin *alcanna*) should instead be rendered as "alkanet." Both plants (*Lawsonia inermis* L., and *Alkanna tinctoria* [L.] Tsch., respectively) produce a red dye.

9. This last sentence is found in only one copy of *DOM 2*, Vatican, Biblioteca Apostolica, MS Pal. Lat. 1165 (s. XIII in., Germany); and one copy of the proto-ensemble, Paris, Bibliothèque Nationale de France, MS lat. 6988A (s. XV in., E. France). In both cases, the reading is *furculos* (little forks [or furrows]), not *fusculos*. In the translation, I have employed the original reading since it is impossible to render any sense out of *fusculos*, which is only documented in dictionaries of medieval Latin as an alternate spelling for *flosculus*, a kind of garment worn by monks.

10. The reference to "the above-mentioned little sack," ostensibly a cross-reference to ¶244 above, in fact reflects a textual error. In *DOM 1*, this sentence had read, "Afterward you should again wet the hair with the above-mentioned strained liquid, then you should wrap the head thus prepared with a small bandage" (*Postea madefacias iterum capillos cum predicta colatura, tunc inuoluas capud sic paratum faseolo*). The reference to the bandage dropped out in *DOM 2*. When the editor of the transitional ensemble incorporated selected readings from *DOM 1*, *faseolo* was misread as *saccello*. The addition of the adjective *predicto* is that editor's attempt at cross-referencing to the *saccellus* mentioned in ¶244.

11. In *DCM 1*, from whence this remedy derives, after "for two days" (*duos dies*)

there had been a new sentence, "You will also be able to color the eyebrows [with this]" (*Supercilia etiam colorare poteris*). *Supercilia etiam* dropped out in the transitional ensemble.

12. See note to ¶33 above.

13. *Cerotum* is a wax-based ointment. A description of its preparation can be found in ¶278 below.

14. In *DCM* 1, what now reads as "which . . . [is] made in Gaul" (*quod fit in Gallia*) had been "which is made by shoemakers" (*quod fit a sutoribus*). In *DCM* 2, *in Gallia* was added, and in the transitional ensemble *a sutoribus* was dropped.

15. Meerschaum is a soft, white, claylike, heat-resistant mineral, a hydrous magnesium silicate ($H_4Mg_2Si_3O_{12}$).

16. In *DCM* 1–2 (¶207f) and in the early versions of the ensemble, this recipe had been for "falling hair" (*capillos cadentes*), not "whitening the hair" (*capillos candendos*). The corruption entered the text in the revised ensemble.

17. The first half of this paragraph was originally part of the *DCM* (¶207o). The latter half (from "Let cabbage stalks") is the novel addition of the transitional ensemble (Group B) editor. It is found in all later versions of the ensemble.

18. In *DCM* 1 (where this recipe had originally appeared), root of oak gall (*radix gallarum*) had been called for, not root of marsh mallow (*altea*).

19. The instructions for preparing the wax had been considerably more detailed in *DOM* 1: "Let wax be dissolved in a clay vessel. Then let a glass jug full of cold water be taken and another vessel likewise full of cold water. Let the jug be fully immersed in the boiling wax, and having quickly extracted it let it be immersed in the other vessel full of cold water. And thus all the wax will be extracted fine and delicate like the leaf of a tree" (*Resoluatur cera in uase fictili. Tunc habeatur ampulla uitrea plena aqua frigida et aliud uas similiter plenum aqua frigida. Inmergatur ampulla ita plena in cera bullienti, et cito extracta mergatur in alio uase pleno aqua frigida, et sic extrahetur tota cera subtilis et tenuis quemadmodum folium arbori*).

20. This phrase is nonsensical, since no powders have been mentioned. The phrase *misce hos pulueres* first appeared in *DCM* 2 and was incorporated unchanged into the transitional ensemble.

21. The Latin term is *serpigo*. The Salernitan writer, Master Salernus, in his *Catholica*, defines it as "an intense, extremely itchy form of scabies" (*grossa scabies pruriginosa et scabiosa*); Piero Giacosa, ed., *Magistri Salernitani nondum editi* (Turin: Fratelli Bocca, 1901), p. 103

22. This should have referred to the vinegar prepared with elecampane (*radix enule*) described in the middle of the paragraph, not a separate preparation made with spurge root (*radix esule*).

23. This recipe was a later addition to the text. It derives from Bernard de Provence, *Commentarium super Tabulas Salerni*, in *Collectio Salernitana ossia documenti inediti, e trattati di medicina appartenenti alla scuola medica salernitana*, ed. Salvatore De Renzi, 5 vols. (Naples: Filiatre-Sebezio, 1852–59; reprint Bologna: Forni, 1967), 5:273. It was added by the editor of the transitional ensemble, together with another ascribed to the Salernitan women, which employed gladden (*spatula fetida*) for wrinkles; this latter recipe (¶293c) was later deleted by the revised ensemble editor.

24. The opening sentences of this paragraph conflate the two versions of this recipe originally found in *DCM* 1 (cf. Monica H. Green, "The Development of the *Trotula*," *Revue d'Histoire des Textes* 26 (1996): 119–203, Table 2, ¶¶167 and 232g). In

its entirety, the second occurrence had read: "For burn of the face due to the heat of the sun. Take root of domestic lily, wash it with warm [water], and cook it in water. Once cooked, grind it. Then take powder of mastic, frankincense, borax, and camphor—some of each—and fresh pork grease, and mix them with rose water" (*Ad ustionem faciei per calorem solis. Accipe radicem lilii domestici, laua calida, et in aqua coque. Coctam pista. Post accipe puluerem masticis, olibani, boracis, camphore ana, et anxugiam recentem porcinam, et cum aqua rosacea conficias*). From the first occurrence of the recipe (i.e., ¶167), the editor of the proto-ensemble drew the exact amounts of mastic, etc., and the additional ingredient of white lead (*gersa*). The rest of the paragraph then repeats the preparation instructions from ¶167 in full.

25. This phrase, "women only" (*mulieres solum*), had originally been "Salernitan women" (*mulieres Salernitane*). The abbreviation for "Salernitan," *sal'*, was misread as *sol'* by the revised ensemble editor, hence the reading *mulieres solum* here.

26. On the genesis of the peculiar usage of "floods" (*cataractas*), see the note to ¶167.

27. The masculine pronoun is used.

28. Interestingly, Trota seems to have been one of the people who believed that fistulas near the eyes could be cured, though she did not employ agrimony. See Conrad Hiersemann, *Die Abschnitte aus der Practica des Trottus in der Salernitanischen Sammelschrift De Aegritudinum Curatione: Breslau Codex Salern., 1160–1170*, inaugural diss. (Leipzig: Institut für Geschichte der Medizin, 1921), p. 13.

29. Or possibly "at the end of the root."

30. In *DOM 1–3*, this passage had read "Take the marine plant with which the Saracens dye leather skins a violet color" (*in colore uiolaceo* or *uiole*). The corruption *uiridi* (green) appears first in the revised ensemble. A green dye would not make much sense for a cosmetic intended to redden the skin, yet not a single scribe or annotator ever corrected this error.

31. This paragraph (which repeats the latter part of ¶304) is the product of a scribal error. See the note to ¶304, below.

32. The correct reading should have been, "Let there be made a powder which is wrapped in cut wool or a fine linen cloth" (*fiat puluis, qui in lana succida inuolutus, uel in panno lineo subtili*).

33. In *DOM 1–3*, this sentence had concluded the previous paragraph.

34. The Salernitan textbook on *materia medica* called *Circa instans* distinguishes between *sulphur uiuum* and *sulphur mortuum* as follows: "One kind [of sulfur] is 'live,' which is produced by the earth; the other is 'extinguished' or 'dead,' which is prepared artificially and is found in bronze or lead pipes." Hans Wölfel, ed., *Das Arzneidrogenbuch "Circa instans" in einer Fassung des XIII. Jahrhunderts aus der Universitätsbibliothek Erlangen. Text und Kommentar als Beitrag zur Pflanzen- und Drogenkunde des Mittelalters* (Berlin: A. Preilipper, 1939), p. 107.

35. The last part of this paragraph (from "From all these dried things" to the end) and the paragraph that should have followed it (¶304a, here ¶301) were misplaced above in the revised ensemble, hence the "creation" of ¶300.

36. The approbation in the first sentence of ¶305 had concluded the previous paragraph for alleviating bad breath in the independent *DOM*, where it had stood in the position of ¶304a (displaced forward in this edition as ¶301). In the original text, the author had specified that he had seen this Muslim woman in Sicily (*Vidi quandam sarracenam in Sicilia*). In the second sentence (originally a separate recipe), a generic

woman (*mulier*) was clearly expressed as the subject of the remedy, hence my use of the feminine pronoun here.

37. A compound medicine. See the Appendix for a description.

38. Scribal invocations of the Lord's blessing at the close of a text were common medieval practice.

Appendix: Compound Medicines

1. There is as yet no critical edition of the *Antidotarium Nicholai*. I have used the Latin text published in W. S. van den Berg, *Eene Middelnederlandsche Vertaling van het Antidotarium Nicolai (Ms. 15624–15641, Kon. Bibl. te Brussel)* (Leiden: E. J. Brill, 1917); portions of his edition are conveniently reproduced in Tony Hunt, *Anglo-Norman Medicine*, 2 vols. (Cambridge: D. S. Brewer, 1995–97), 1: 316-28. I have listed the compound medicines alphabetically here under the standardized spellings used in my translation of the *Trotula*; the second heading reflects the orthography in van den Berg's edition. For a recent account of the influence of the *Antidotarium Nicolai*, see Gundolf Keil, "Nicolaus Salernitanus," in *Die deutschen Literatur des Mittelalters: Verfasserlexikon*, gen. ed., Kurt Ruh, 2d ed. (Berlin: Walter de Gruyter, 1978–   ), 6: 1134–51.

2. Reading *tetanum* for *teranum*.

3. This formula is used in most recipes here to indicate the expected yield. Rarely, however, do all the ingredients add up in total weight to the amounts claimed.

4. I have translated both *litosperma* and *granum solis* as "gromwell," following the identifications in Tony Hunt, *Plant Names of Medieval England* (Cambridge: D. S. Brewer, 1989).

5. The Latin introduces a negative in this passage (*non ponantur*), which makes no sense since elder and sowbread are not otherwise mentioned.

6. Latin: *domina medicinarum*.

7. A fourfold ingredient list is, in fact, described in the *LSM*, ¶11.

8. *Esdra magna* is another compound medicine. It is named after the prophet Esdra, who supposedly invented it while he was in exile in Babylon. It contains over one hundred ingredients.

9. A resinous excrescence from mummies; see Michael Camille, "The Corpse in the Garden: *Mumia* in Medieval Herbal Illustrations," *Micrologus* 7. *The Corpse* (1999): 297–318.

10. Reading *densitatem* (per editorial note) for *diversitatem*.

11. The term used here is *stagnum*, which could either refer to a compound of silver and lead or to tin.

12. See note 8 above.

13. See note on *silfium* in the Index Verborum. It is not clear to what plant the present term refers.

14. The Latin term here is *emotoici*. Cf. Master Salernus, *Catholicon*: "Emotoici are those who spit blood" (*Emotoici sunt qui sanguinem spuunt*); Piero Giacosa, ed., *Magistri Salernitani nondum editi* (Turin: Fratelli Bocca, 1901), p. 112.

15. Conditions characterized by *calculi* (i.e., kidney and bladder stones).

16. A compound medicine made from coral.

17. In the preceding list of ingredients, of course, only half an ounce of fresh violets had been called for.

Bibliography

This bibliography includes works cited as well as other studies relating to women's health care in the Middle Ages.

Adams, J. N. *The Latin Sexual Vocabulary*. Baltimore: Johns Hopkins University Press, 1982.

Amarotta, Arcangelo R. "Pourquoi Salerne?" In *From Epidaurus to Salerno: Symposium held at the European University Centre for Cultural Heritage, Ravello, April 1990*, ed. Antje Krug. *PACT* 34 (1992): pp. 11–18.

———. *Salerno romana e medievale: Dinamica di un insediamento.* Società Salernitana di Storia Patria, Collana di Studi Storici Salernitani, 2. Salerno: Pietro Laveglia, 1989.

Amundsen, Darrel W., and Carol Jean Diers. "The Age of Menarche in Medieval Europe." *Human Biology* 45 (1973): 363–69.

———. "The Age of Menopause in Medieval Europe." *Human Biology* 45 (1973): 605–12.

André, J. *Lexique des termes de botanique en latin*. Paris: Klincksieck, 1956.

———. *Les noms de plantes dans la Rome antique*. Paris: Belles Lettres, 1985.

Andrews, David. "Underground Grain Storage in Central Italy." In *Medieval Lazio*, ed. David Andrews, John Osborne, and David Whitehouse, pp. 123–35. Oxford: B.A.R., 1982.

Aymar, Alphonse. "Contributions à l'étude du folklore de la Haute-Auvergne: Le sachet accoucheur et ses mystères." *Annales du Midi* 38 (1926): 273–347.

Bader, R. "Sator Arepo: Magik in der Volksmedizin." *Medizinhistorisches Journal* 22 (1987): 115–34.

Baldwin, John W. *The Language of Sex: Five Voices from Northern France Around 1200*. Chicago: University of Chicago Press, 1994.

Barkaï, Ron. *A History of Jewish Gynaecological Texts in the Middle Ages*. Leiden: Brill, 1998.

———. *Les infortunes de Dinah: Le livre de la génération. La gynécologie juive au Moyen-Age*. Trans. Jacqueline Barnavi and Michel Garel. Paris: Cerf, 1991.

———. "A Medieval Hebrew Treatise on Obstetrics." *Medical History* 33 (1989): 96–119.

Barratt, Alexandra, ed. *Women's Writing in Middle English*. Longman Annotated Texts. London: Longman, 1992.

Bayon, H. P. "Trotula and the Ladies of Salerno." *Proceedings of the Royal Society of Medicine* 33 (1939–40): 471–75.

Beccaria, Augusto. *I codici di medicina del periodo presalernitano (secoli IX, X, e XI)*. Rome: Edizioni di Storia e Letteratura, 1956.

Benjamin of Tudela. *The Itinerary*. Intros. Michael A. Signer, Marcus Nathan Adler, and A. Asher. Malibu, Cali.: Joseph Simon/Pangloss Press, 1983.

Bennett, Judith, and Amy Froide, eds. *Singlewomen in the European Past, 1250–1800*. Philadelphia: University of Pennsylvania Press, 1999.

Benson, Robert L., and Giles Constable, with Carol D. Lanham, eds. *Renaissance and Renewal in the Twelfth Century*. Cambridge: Harvard University Press, 1982.

Benton, John F. "Trota and Trotula." In vol. 12 of *Dictionary of the Middle Ages*, Joseph R. Strayer, editor-in-chief, pp. 213–14. 13 vols. New York: Charles Scribner's Sons, 1982–89.

———. "Trotula, Women's Problems, and the Professionalization of Medicine in the Middle Ages." *Bulletin of the History of Medicine* 59 (1985): 30–53.

Berg, W. S. van den. *Eene Middelnederlandsche Vertaling van het Antidotarium Nicolai (Ms. 15624–15641, Kon. Bibl. te Brussel)*. Leiden: E. J. Brill, 1917.

Bernard of Provence. *Commentarium Magistri Bernardi Provincialis super Tabulas Salerni*. In vol. 5 of *Collectio Salernitana ossia documenti inediti, e trattati di medicina appartenenti alla scuola medica salernitana*, ed. Salvatore De Renzi, 5 vols. Naples: Filiatre-Sebezio, 1852–59; reprint Bologna: Forni, 1967.

Bernfeld, Werner. "Eine Beschwörung der Gebärmutter aus dem frühen Mittelalter." *Kyklos* 2 (1929): 272–74.

Biller, Peter. "Birth-Control in the West in the Thirteenth and Early Fourteenth Centuries." *Past and Present*, no. 94 (February 1982): 3–26.

Bloch, Herbert. *Monte Cassino in the Middle Ages*. 3 vols. Cambridge: Harvard University Press, 1986.

Blondiaux, Joël. "La femme et son corps au haut moyen-âge vus par l'anthropologue et le paleopathologiste." In *La femme au moyen âge*, ed. Michel Rouche and Jean Heuclin, pp. 115–37. Maubeuge: Publication de la Ville de Maubeuge, Diffusion Jean Touzot, 1990.

Blumenfeld-Kosinski, Renate. *Not of Woman Born: Representations of Caesarean Birth in Medieval and Renaissance Culture*. Ithaca, N.Y.: Cornell University Press, 1990.

Boggi Cavallo. *See* Cavallo Boggi.

Bos, Gerrit, ed. *Ibn al-Jazzār on Sexual Diseases and Their Treatment*, Sir Henry Wellcome Asian Series. London: Kegan Paul, 1997.

———. "Ibn al-Jazzār on Women's Diseases and Their Treatment." *Medical History* 37 (1993): 296–312.

Brain, Peter. *Galen on Bloodletting: A Study of the Origins, Development, and Validity of His Opinions, with a Translation of the Three Works*. Cambridge: Cambridge University Press, 1986.

Buckley, Thomas. "Menstruation and the Power of Yurok Women." In *Blood Magic: The Anthropology of Menstruation*, ed. Thomas Buckley and Alma Gottlieb, pp. 187–209. Berkeley: University of California Press, 1988.

Bullough, Vern. "Medieval Medical and Scientific Views of Women." *Viator* 4 (1973): 485–501.

Bullough, Vern, and Cameron Campbell. "Female Longevity and Diet in the Middle Ages." *Speculum* 55 (1980): 317–25.

Burnett, Charles S. F. *The Introduction of Arabic Learning into England*. Panizzi Lectures, 1996. London: British Library, 1997.

Burnett, Charles, and Danielle Jacquart, eds. *Constantine the African and Alī ibn al-Abbās al-Magūsī: The "Pantegni" and Related Texts*. Leiden: E. J. Brill, 1994.

Cabré, Montserrat. "Kate Campbell Hurd-Mead (1867–1941) and the Medical Women's Struggle for History." *Collections. The Newsletter of the Archives and Special Collections on Women in Medicine. The Medical College of Pennsylvania*, Philadelphia, no. 26 (February 1993): 1–4, 8.

Cadden, Joan. *Meanings of Sex Difference in the Middle Ages: Medicine, Science, and Culture*. Cambridge: Cambridge University Press, 1993.

Camille, Michael. "The Corpse in the Garden: *Mumia* in Medieval Herbal Illustrations." *Micrologus 7. The Corpse* (1999): 297–318.

Cassese, L. *Pergamene del monastero benedettino di S. Giorgio (1038–1698)*. Salerno: Archivio di Stato, 1950.

Cavallo Boggi, Pina, ed.; Matilde Nubié and Adriana Tocco, trans. *Trotula de Ruggiero: Sulle malattie delle donne*. Turin: La Rose, 1979.

Cavallo Boggi, Pina, ed.; Piero Cantalupo, trans. *Trotula de Ruggiero: Sulle malattie delle donne*. Palermo: La Luna, 1994.

Chaucer, Geoffrey. *Canterbury Tales*. In *The Riverside Chaucer*, ed. Larry D. Benson, 3d ed. Boston: Houghton Mifflin, 1987.

Citarella, Armand O. "Amalfi and Salerno in the Ninth Century." In *Istituzioni civili e organizzazione ecclesiastica nello Stato medievale amalfitano: Atti del Congresso internazionale di studi Amalfitani, Amalfi, 3–5 luglio 1981*, pp. 129–45. Amalfi: Centro di Cultura e Storia Amalfitana, 1986.

———. "Merchants, Markets, and Merchandise in Southern Italy in the High Middle Ages." In *Mercati e mercanti nell'alto medioevo: L'area euroasiatica e l'area mediterranea, 23–29 aprile 1992*, pp. 239–84. Settimane di Studio del Centro Italiano di Studi sull'Alto Medioevo, 40. Spoleto: Centro Italiano di Studi sull'Alto Medioevo, 1993.

Constantinus Africanus. *Viaticum*. In *Opera omnia Ysaac*. Lyons, 1515.

Corner, George Washington. *Anatomical Texts of the Earlier Middle Ages: A Study in the Transmission of Cultures*. Washington, D.C.: Carnegie Institute of Washington, 1927.

Corsi, Pasquale. "L'eunuco." In *Condizione umana e ruoli sociali nel Mezzogiorno normanno-svevo. Atti delle none giornate normanno-sveve, Bari, 17–20 ottobre 1989*, ed. Giosuè Musca, pp. 251–77. Bari: Centro di Studi Normanno-Svevi della Università degli Studi di Bari, Edizioni Dedalo, 1991.

Creutz, Rudolf. "Der Magister Copho und seine Stellung im Hochsalerno: Aus M. p. med. Q 2 (saec. XIII), fol. 85ᵃ–103ᵃ Würzburg." *Sudhoffs Archiv für Geschichte der Medizin und der Naturwissenschaften* 31 (1938): 51–60, and 33, nos. 5 and 6 (July 1941): 249–338.

Cuna, Andrea. *Per una bibliografia della Scuola medica Salernitana (secoli XI–XIII)*. Milan: Guerini e Associati, 1993.

Daems, Willem F. *Nomina simplicium medicinarum ex synonymariis Medii Aevi collecta: Semantische Untersuchungen zum Fachwortschatz hoch- und spätmittelalterlicher Drogenkunde*. Studies in Ancient Medicine, 6. Leiden: E. J. Brill, 1993.

Darmstaedter, Ernst. "Die Sator–Arepo-Formel und ihre Erklärung." *Isis* 18 (1932): 322–29.

Deegan, Marilyn. "Pregnancy and Childbirth in the Anglo-Saxon Medical Texts: A Preliminary Survey." In *Medicine in Early Medieval England*, ed. Marilyn Deegan and D. G. Scragg, pp. 17–26. Manchester: Centre for Anglo-Saxon Studies, University of Manchester, 1989.

Delaney, Janice, Mary Jane Lupton, and Emily Toth. *The Curse: A Cultural History of Menstruation*. Rev. ed. Urbana: University of Illinois Press, 1988.

Delva, Anna. *Vrouwengeneeskunde in Vlaanderen tijdens de late middeleeuwen*. Brugge: Vlaamse Historische Studies, 1983.

De Renzi, Salvatore. *Collectio Salernitana ossia documenti inediti, e trattati di medicina appartenenti alla scuola medica salernitana*. 5 vols. Naples: Filiatre-Sebezio, 1852–59; reprint Bologna: Forni, 1967.

Dixon, Laurinda. *Perilous Chastity: Women and Illness in Pre-Enlightenment Art and Medicine*. Ithaca, N.Y.: Cornell University Press, 1995.

Drell, Joanna H. "Family Structure in the Principality of Salerno during the Norman Period, 1077–1154." *Anglo-Norman Studies: Proceedings of the Battle Conference* 18 (1995): 70–103.

———. "Marriage, Kinship, and Power: Family Structure in the Principality of Salerno under Norman Rule, 1077–1154." Ph.D. diss., Brown University, 1996.

Drew, Katherine Fischer, trans. *The Lombard Laws*. Philadelphia: University of Pennsylvania Press, 1973.

Du Cange, Charles Du Fresne, et al. *Glossarium mediae et infimae latinitatis*. Rev. ed., 10 vols. Niort: L. Favre, 1883–87.

Egert, Ferdinand Paul. *Gynäkologische Fragmente aus dem frühen Mittelalter nach einer Petersburger Handschrift aus dem VIII.–IX. Jahrhundert*. Abhandlungen zur Geschichte der Medizin und der Naturwissenschaften, Heft 11. Berlin: Emil Ebering, 1936.

Erler, Mary C. "English Vowed Women at the End of the Middle Ages." *Mediaeval Studies* 57 (1995): 155–203.

Finke, Laurie. *Women's Writing in English: Medieval England*. London: Longman, 1999.

Frier, Bruce W. "Natural Fertility and Family Limitation in Roman Marriage." *Classical Philology* 89 (1994): 318–33.

Galante, Maria. *Nuove pergamene del monastero femminile di S. Giorgio di Salerno*. Vol. 1 (993–1256). Edizioni Studi Storici Meridionali, 7. Salerno: Edizioni Studi Storici Meridionali, 1984.

García-Ballester, Luis. "Introduction: Practical Medicine from Salerno to the Black Death." In *Practical Medicine from Salerno to the Black Death*, ed. Luis García-Ballester, Roger French, Jon Arrizabalaga, and Andrew Cunningham, pp. 1–29. Cambridge: Cambridge University Press, 1994.

Garufi, A. "Di un stabilimento balneare in Salerno nel secolo XII." *Studi medievali* 1 (1904–5): 276–80.

Giacosa, Piero, ed. *Magistri Salernitani nondum editi*. Turin: Fratelli Bocca, 1901.

Gil, Moshe. "Sicily, 827–1072, in Light of the Geniza Documents and Parallel Sources." In *Italia Judaica: Gli ebrei in Sicilia sino all'espulsione del 1492. Atti del V convegno internazionale Palermo, 15–19 giugno 1992*, pp. 96–171. Pubblicazioni degli Archivi di Stato, Saggi 32. Palermo: Ministero per i Beni Culturali e Ambientali, 1995.

Gil-Sotres, Pedro. "Derivation and Revulsion: The Theory and Practice of Medieval Phlebotomy." In *Practical Medicine from Salerno to the Black Death*, ed. Luis García-Ballester, Roger French, Jon Arrizabalaga, and Andrew Cunningham, pp. 110–55. Cambridge: Cambridge University Press, 1994.

Glare, P. G. W. *Oxford Latin Dictionary*. Oxford: Clarendon Press, 1982.

Glaze, Florence Eliza. "Medical Writer: 'Behold the Human Creature.'" In *Voice of the Living Light: Hildegard of Bingen and Her World*, ed. Barbara Newman, pp. 125–48. Berkeley: University of California Press, 1998.

———. "The Perforated Wall: The Ownership and Circulation of Medical Books in Medieval Europe, ca. 800–1200." Ph.D. diss., Duke University, 1999.

Godefroy, Frédéric. *Dictionnaire de l'ancienne langue française, et de tous ses dialectes du IXe au XVe siècle*. 10 vols. Paris: F. Vieweg, 1881–1902.

Goitein, S. D. *A Mediterranean Society: The Jewish Communities of the Arab World as Portrayed in the Documents of the Cairo Geniza*. 6 vols. Vol. 6 with Paula Sanders. Berkeley: University of California Press, 1967–1993.

Goltz, Dietlinde. *Mittelalterliche Pharmazie und Medizin*. Stuttgart: Wissenschaftliche Verlagsgesellschaft, 1976.

———. *Studien zur Geschichte der Mineralnamen in Pharmazie, Chemie und Medizin von den Anfängen bis Paracelsus*. Sudhoffs Archiv, Beihefte 14. Wiesbaden: Franz Steiner, 1972.

Gottlieb, Alma. "Menstrual Cosmology among the Beng of Ivory Coast." In *Blood Magic: The Anthropology of Menstruation*, ed. Thomas Buckley and Alma Gottlieb, pp. 55–74. Berkeley: University of California Press, 1988.

Grauer, Anne L. "Life Patterns of Women from Medieval York." In *The Archaeology of Gender: Proceedings of the Twenty-Second Annual Conference of the Archaeological Association of the University of Calgary*, ed. Dale Walde and Noreen D. Willows, pp. 407–13. Calgary: University of Calgary Archaeological Association, 1991.

Green, Monica H. "Books as a Source of Medical Education for Women in the Middle Ages." *Dynamis: Acta Hispanica ad Medicinae Scientiarumque Historiam Illustrandam* 20 (2000): 331–69.

———. "Constantinus Africanus and the Conflict Between Religion and Science." In *The Human Embryo: Aristotle and the Arabic and European Traditions*, ed. G. R. Dunstan, pp. 47–69. Exeter: Exeter University Press, 1990.

———. "The *De genecia* Attributed to Constantine the African." *Speculum* 62 (1987): 299–323; reprinted in Green, *Women's Healthcare*, essay 3.

———. "The Development of the *Trotula*." *Revue d'Histoire des Textes* 26 (1996): 119–203; reprinted in Green, *Women's Healthcare*, essay 5.

———. "Documenting Medieval Women's Medical Practice." In *Practical Medicine from Salerno to the Black Death*, ed. Luis García-Ballester, Roger French, Jon Arrizabalaga, and Andrew Cunningham, pp. 322–52. Cambridge: Cambridge University Press, 1994; reprinted in Green, *Women's Healthcare*, essay 2.

———. "From 'Diseases of Women' to 'Secrets of Women': The Transformation of Gynecological Literature in the Later Middle Ages." *Journal of Medieval and Early Modern Studies* 30 (2000): 5–39.

———. "A Handlist of the Latin and Vernacular Manuscripts of the So-Called *Trotula* Texts. Part 1: The Latin Manuscripts." *Scriptorium* 50 (1996): 137–75.

———. "A Handlist of the Latin and Vernacular Manuscripts of the So-Called *Trotula* Texts. Part 2: The Vernacular Translations and Latin Re-Writings." *Scriptorium* 51 (1997): 80–104.

———. "In Search of an 'Authentic' Women's Medicine: The Strange Fates of Trota of Salerno and Hildegard of Bingen." *Dynamis: Acta Hispanica ad Medicinae Scientiarumque Historiam Illustrandam* 19 (1999): 25–54.

———. "Obstetrical and Gynecological Texts in Middle English." *Studies in the Age of Chaucer* 14 (1992): 53–88; reprinted in Green, *Women's Healthcare*, essay 4.

———. "The Possibilities of Literacy and the Limits of Reading: Women and the Gendering of Medical Literacy." In Green, *Women's Healthcare*, essay 7.

———. "'Traittié tout de mençonges': The *Secrés des dames*, 'Trotula,' and Attitudes Towards Women's Medicine in Fourteenth- and Early Fifteenth-Century France." In *Christine de Pizan and the Categories of Difference*, ed. Marilynn Desmond, pp. 146–78. Minneapolis: University of Minnesota Press, 1998; reprinted in Green, *Women's Healthcare*, essay 6.

———. "The Transmission of Ancient Theories of Female Physiology and Disease Through the Early Middle Ages." Ph.D. diss., Princeton University, 1985.

———. *Women and Literate Medicine in Medieval Europe: Trota and the "Trotula."* Forthcoming.

———. *Women's Healthcare in the Medieval West: Texts and Contexts.* Aldershot: Ashgate, 2000.

———. "Women's Medical Practice and Health Care in Medieval Europe." *Signs: Journal of Women in Culture and Society* 14 (1989): 434–73. Reprinted in *Sisters and Workers in the Middle Ages*, ed. J. Bennett et al., pp. 39–78. Chicago: University of Chicago Press, 1989. Reprinted in Green, *Women's Healthcare*, essay 1.

Grierson, Philip. "The Salernitan Coinage of Gisulf II (1052–1077) and Robert Guiscard (1077–1085)." *Papers of the British School of Rome* 24, n.s. 2 (1956): 40–46.

Grubmüller, Klaus, et al., ed. *"Vocabularius Ex quo": Uberlieferungsgeschichte Ausgabe.* Tübingen: Max Niermeyer, 1989.

Hallaert, M.-R. *The "Sekenesse of wymmen": A Middle English Treatise on Diseases in Women (Yale Medical Library, MS. 47 fols. 60r–71v).* Scripta: Mediaeval and Renaissance Texts and Studies, 8. Brussels: Omirel, UFSAL, 1982.

Hanson, Ann Ellis. "Hippocrates: *Diseases of Women 1.*" *Signs: Journal of Women in Culture and Society* 1 (1975): 567–84.

———. "The Medical Writers' Woman." In *Before Sexuality: The Construction of Erotic Experience in the Ancient Greek World*, ed. David Halperin et al., pp. 309–37. Princeton: Princeton University Press, 1990.

Hanson, Ann Ellis and Monica H. Green. "Soranus of Ephesus: *Methodicorum princeps.*" In *Aufstieg und Niedergang der römischen Welt*, general ed., Wolfgang Haase and Hildegard Temporini. Teilband 2, Band 37.2, pp. 968–1075. Berlin: Walter de Gruyter, 1994.

Harrell, Barbara B. "Lactation and Menstruation in Cultural Perspective." *American Anthropologist* 83 (1981): 796–823.

Hiersemann, Conrad. *Die Abschnitte aus der Practica des Trottus in der Salernitanischen Sammelschrift De Aegritudinum Curatione: Breslau Codex Salern. 1160–1170.* Inaugural diss. Leipzig: Institut für Geschichte der Medizin, 1921.

Hildegard of Bingen. *Causae et curae.* Ed. Paul Kaiser. Leipzig: Teubner, 1903. Reprint Basel: Basler Hildegard-Gesellschaft, 1980.

———. *On Natural Philosophy and Medicine: Selections from "Cause et cure."* Trans. Margret Berger. Rochester, N.Y.: D. S. Brewer, 1999.

Hughes, Diane Owen. "Mourning Rites, Memory, and Civilization in Premodern Italy." In *Riti e rituali nelle società medievali*, ed. Jacques Chiffoleau, Lauro Martines, and Agostino Paravicini Bagliani, pp. 23–38. Collectanea, 5. Spoleto: Centro Italiano di Studi sull'Alto Medioevo, 1994.

Hughes, Muriel Joy. *Women Healers in Medieval Life and Literature*. New York: Columbia University Press, 1943. Reprint Freeport, N.Y.: Books for Libraries Press, 1968.

Hultsch, Friedrich. *Metrologicorum scriptorum reliquiae*. Vol. 1: *Scriptores Graeci*. Leipzig: Teubner, 1864.

Hunt, Tony. *Anglo-Norman Medicine*. 2 vols. Cambridge: D. S. Brewer, 1994–97.

———. *Plant Names of Medieval England*. Cambridge: D. S. Brewer, 1989.

Hurd-Mead, Kate Campbell. *A History of Women in Medicine*. Haddam, Conn.: Haddam Press, 1938. Reprint New York: AMS Press, 1977.

al-Idrisi. *L'Italia descritta nel "Libro del Re Ruggero" compilato da Edrisi*. Trans. (into Italian) Michele Amari and Celestino Schiaparelli. In *Atti della Reale Accademia dei Lincei* 274. 2d ser., vol. 8, 1876–77. Rome: Salviucci, 1883.

Jacquart, Danielle. "Note sur la traduction latine du *Kitab al-Manṣūrī* de Rhazes." *Revue d'Histoire des Textes* 24 (1994): 359–74.

Jacquart, Danielle, and Françoise Micheau. *La médecine arabe et l'occident médiéval*. Paris: Maisonneuve et Larose, 1990.

Jacquart, Danielle, and Claude Thomasset. *Sexuality and Medicine in the Middle Ages*. Trans. Matthew Adamson. Cambridge: Polity Press; Princeton: Princeton University Press, 1988.

Jiménez Brobeil, Sylvia A. "A Contribution to Medieval Pathological Gynaecology." *Journal of Paleopathology* 4 (1992): 155–61.

Johnson, Willis. "The Myth of Jewish Male Menses." *Journal of Medieval History* 24 (1998): 273–95.

Jordan, Mark D. "The Construction of a Philosophical Medicine: Exegesis and Argument in Salernitan Teaching on the Soul." *Osiris*, 2d ser., 6 (1990): 42–61.

———. "Medicine as Science in the Early Commentaries on 'Johannitius.'" *Traditio* 43 (1987): 121–45.

Jubayr, Muhammad ibn Ahmad ibn. *The Travels of Ibn Jubayr, being the chronicle of a mediaeval Spanish Moor concerning his journey to the Egypt of Saladin*. Trans. R. J. C. Broadhurst. London: J. Cape, 1952.

Keil, Gundolf. "Nicolaus Salernitanus." In vol. 6 of *Die deutschen Literatur des Mittelalters: Verfasserlexikon*, coll. 1134–51. 2d ed., Kurt Ruh, general ed. Berlin: Walter de Gruyter, 1978–.

King, Helen. *Hippocrates' Woman: Reading the Female Body in Ancient Greece*. London: Routledge, 1998.

———. "Medical Texts as a Source for Women's History." In *The Greek World*, ed. A. Powell, pp. 199–218. London: Routledge, 1995.

———. "Once Upon a Text: Hysteria from Hippocrates." In *Hysteria Beyond Freud*, ed. Sander Gilman, Helen King, Roy Porter, George Rousseau, and Elaine Showalter, pp. 3–90. Berkeley: University of California Press, 1993.

Knight, Chris. *Blood Relations: Menstruation and the Origins of Culture*. New Haven: Yale University Press, 1991.

Kraut, Georg, ed. *Trotulae curandarum Aegritudinum Muliebrium, ante, in & post partum liber unicus, nusquam antea editus.* In *Experimentarius medicinae.* Strasbourg: Joannes Schottus, 1544.

Kristeller, Paul Oskar. "The School of Salerno: Its Development and Its Contribution to the History of Learning." *Bulletin of the History of Medicine,* 17 (1945): 138–94. Reprinted in Italian translation with further revisions as *Studi sulla Scuola medica Salernitana.* Naples: Istituto Italiano per gli Studi Filosofici, 1986.

Kruse, Britta-Juliane. *Verborgene Heilkünste: Geschichte der Frauenmedizin im Spätmittelalter.* Quellen und Forschungen zur Literatur- und Kulturgeschichte, 5. Berlin: Walter de Gruyter, 1996.

Kurath, Hans, et al., eds. *The Middle English Dictionary.* Ann Arbor: University of Michigan Press, 1952–.

Kusche, Brigitte. *Frauenaufklärung im Spätmittelalter: Eine philologisch-medizinhistorische Untersuchung und Edition des gynäkologisch-obstetrischen GKS 1657 Kopenhagen.* Acta Universitatis Umensis. Stockholm: Almqvist & Wiksell International, 1990.

Latham, R. E. *Dictionary of Medieval Latin from British Sources.* London: Published for the British Academy by Oxford University Press, 1975– .

Laurent, Sylvie. *Naître au moyen âge de la conception à la naissance: La grossesse et l'accouchement (XIIe–XVe siècle).* Paris: Le Léopard d'Or, 1989.

Lawn, Brian. *The Prose Salernitan Questions.* London: British Academy/Oxford University Press, 1979.

———. *The Salernitan Questions: An Introduction to the History of Medieval and Renaissance Problem Literature.* Oxford: Clarendon Press, 1963.

Lehmann, Volker. *Die Geburt in der Kunst: geburtshilfliche Motive in der darstellenden Kunst in Europa von der Antike bis zur Gegenwart.* Braunschweig: Braunschweiger Verlagsanstalt, 1978.

Lemay, Helen. "Anthonius Guainerius and Medieval Gynecology." In *Women of the Medieval World: Essays in Honor of John H. Mundy,* ed. Julius Kirshner and Suzanne F. Wemple, pp. 317–36. Oxford: Blackwell, 1985.

———. "Women and the Literature of Obstetrics and Gynecology." In *Medieval Women and the Sources of Medieval History,* ed. Joel T. Rosenthal, pp. 189–209. Athens: University of Georgia Press, 1990.

———, trans. *Women's Secrets: A Translation of Pseudo-Albertus Magnus' "De secretis mulierum" with Commentaries.* Albany: State University of New York Press, 1992.

Leone, Simeone and Giovanni Vitolo. *Codex diplomaticus Cavensis IX: 1065–1072.* Cava dei Tirreni: Badia di Cava, 1984.

Lloyd, G. E. R., ed. *Hippocratic Writings.* Harmondsworth: Penguin Books, 1978.

Loud, Graham A. "How 'Norman' Was the Norman Conquest of Southern Italy?" *Nottingham Medieval Studies* 25 (1981): 13–34.

Mabberley, D. J. *The Plant-Book: A Portable Dictionary of the Vascular Plants.* 2d ed. Cambridge: Cambridge University Press, 1997.

MacKinney, Loren. "Childbirth in the Middle Ages, as Seen in Manuscript Illustrations." *Ciba Symposium* 8, nos. 5–6 (December 1960): 230–36.

Maclean, Ian. *The Renaissance Notion of Woman: A Study in the Fortunes of Scholasticism and Medical Science in European Intellectual Life.* Cambridge: Cambridge University Press, 1980.

Mancini, Clodomiro, trans. *Il De mulierum passionibus di Trocta salernitana*. Scientia Veterum 31. Genoa: n.p., 1962.

Marie de France. *Les Deux Amanz*. In *The Lais of Marie de France*, trans. and intro. Glyn S. Burgess and Keith Busby. Harmondsworth: Penguin Books, 1986.

Marland, Hilary, ed. *The Art of Midwifery: Early Modern Midwives in Europe*. London: Routledge, 1993.

Mason-Hohl, Elizabeth, trans. *The Diseases of Women by Trotula of Salerno: A Translation of "Passionibus mulierum curandorum."* Hollywood, Calif.: Ward Ritchie Press, 1940.

Matthew, Donald. *The Norman Kingdom of Sicily*. Cambridge: Cambridge University Press, 1992.

McCracken, Peggy. "Women and Medicine in Medieval French Narrative." *Exemplaria: A Journal of Theory in Medieval and Renaissance Studies* 5, no. 2 (1993): 239–62.

Menjot, Denis, ed. *Les Soins de beauté: Moyen Age, début des temps modernes. Actes du IIIe Colloque International Grasse (26–28 avril 1985)*. Nice: Faculté des Lettres et Sciences Humaines, Université de Nice, 1987.

Mews, Constant. "Religious Thinker: 'A Frail Human Being' on Fiery Life." In *Voice of the Living Light: Hildegard of Bingen and her World*, ed. Barbara Newman, pp. 52–69. Berkeley: University of California Press, 1998.

Mittellateinisches Wörterbuch bis zum ausgehenden 13. Jahrhundert. Munich: Beck, 1967–.

Mørland, Henning, ed. *Oribasius latinus*. Symbolae Osloenses, fasc. suppl. 10. Oslo: A. W. Brogger, 1940.

Morpurgo, Piero. *Filosofia della natura nella Schola salernitana del secolo XII*. Pref. Enrique Montero Cartelle. Bologna: CLUEB, 1990.

Müller, Erwin, ed. *Der Traktat "Liber iste" (die sogenannten Glossae Platearii) aus dem Breslauer Codex Salernitanus*. Würzburg: Konrad Triltsch, 1942.

Mundino de' Luzzi. *Anothomia Mundini*. Pavia, 1478. Reproduced in Ernest Wickersheimer, *Anatomies de Mondino dei Luzzi et de Guido de Vigevano*. Paris: E. Droz, 1926.

Münster, Ladislao. "Women Doctors in Mediaeval Italy." *Ciba Symposium* (English edition) 10, no. 3 (1962): 136–40.

Musacchio, Jacqueline Marie. *The Art and Ritual of Childbirth in Renaissance Italy*. New Haven: Yale University Press, 1999.

Newton, Francis. *The Scriptorium and Library at Monte Cassino, 1058–1109*. Cambridge Studies in Palaeography and Codicology, 7. Cambridge: Cambridge University Press, 1999.

Nirenberg, David. *Communities of Violence: Persecution of Minorities in the Middle Ages*. Princeton, N.J.: Princeton University Press, 1996.

Nutton, Vivian. "Continuity or Rediscovery: The City Physician in Classical Antiquity and Mediaeval Italy." In *The Town and State Physician in Europe from the Middle Ages to the Enlightenment*, ed. A. W. Russell. Wolfenbüttel: Herzog August Bibliothek, 1981.

———. "Velia and the School of Salerno." *Medical History* 15 (1971): 1–11.

O'Neill, Ynez Violé. "Another Look at the 'Anatomia Porci'." *Viator* 1 (1970): 115–24.

Ordericus Vitalis. *The Ecclesiastical History*. Ed. and trans. Marjorie Chibnall. 6 vols. Oxford: Clarendon Press, 1969–80.

Ovid. *Amores, Medicamina faciei femineae, Ars amatoris, Remedia amoris.* Ed. E. J. Kenney. Oxford: Clarendon Press, 1961.

Park, Katharine. "Medicine and Society in Medieval Europe, 500–1500." In *Medicine in Society: Historical Essays*, ed. Andrew Wear, pp. 59–90. Cambridge: Cambridge University Press, 1992.

PDR for Herbal Medicines. Montvale, N.J.: Medical Economics Company, 1998.

Phillips, William D., Jr. "Sugar Production and Trade in the Mediterranean at the Time of the Crusades." In *The Meeting of Two Worlds: Cultural Exchange Between East and West During the Period of the Crusades*, ed. Vladimir P. Goss, pp. 393–406. Kalamazoo, Mich.: Medieval Institute Publications, 1986.

Pliny. *Natural History.* Ed. and trans. W. H. S. Jones. 10 vols. Cambridge: Harvard University Press, 1963.

Post, J. B. "Ages of Menarche and Menopause: Some Medieval Authorities." *Population Studies* 25 (1971): 83–87.

Prou, Maurice, and Alexandre Vidier, eds. *Recueil des chartes de l'Abbaye de Saint-Benoit-sur-Loire.* 2 vols. Documents publiés par la Société historique et archéologique du Gatinais, 5. Paris: 1900–1907.

Ramseyer, Valerie. "Ecclesiastical Power and the Restructuring of Society in Eleventh-Century Salerno." Ph.D. diss., University of Chicago, 1996.

Randall, Lilian M. C. "The Snail in Gothic Marginal Warfare." *Speculum* 37 (1962): 358–67.

Resnick, Irven. "On the Roots of the Myth of Jewish Male Menses in Jacques de Vitry's *History of Jerusalem*." *International Rennert Guest Lecture Series* 3. Ramat Gan: Bar-Ilan University, 1998.

Reyerson, Kathryn L. "Prostitution in Medieval Montpellier: The Ladies of Campus Polverel." *Medieval Prosopography* 18 (1997): 209–28.

Riddle, John M. *Contraception and Abortion from the Ancient World to the Renaissance.* Cambridge: Harvard University Press, 1992.

———. *Eve's Herbs: A History of Contraception and Abortion in the West.* Cambridge, Mass.: Harvard University Press, 1997.

Robertson, Eugenia. "*Circa instans* and the Salernitan *Materia medica*." Ph.D. diss., 3 vols., Bryn Mawr College, 1982.

Roger de Baron. *Practica maior.* In *Cyrurgia Guidonis de Cauliaco, et Cyrurgia Bruni, Teodorici, Rolandi, Lanfranci, Rogerii, Bertapalie.* Venice, 1519.

Rowland, Beryl, ed. *Medieval Woman's Guide to Health: The First English Gynecological Handbook.* Kent, Ohio: Kent State University Press, 1981.

Rufinus. *The Herbal of Rufinus, edited from the Unique Manuscript.* Ed. Lynn Thorndike, with Francis S. Benjamin, Jr. Chicago: University of Chicago Press, 1946.

Salernus. *Catholica.* In *Magistri Salernitani nondum editi*, ed. Piero Giacosa, pp. 69–162. Turin: Fratelli Bocca, 1901.

Salmón, Fernando, and Montserrat Cabré i Pairet. "Fascinating Women: The Evil Eye in Medical Scholasticism." In *Medicine from the Black Death to the Great Pox*, ed. Roger French, Jon Arrizabalaga, Andrew Cunningham, and Luis García-Ballester, pp. 53–84. Aldershot: Ashgate, 1998.

Sharpe, William. *Isidore of Seville: The Medical Writings. Transactions of the American Philosophical Society*, n.s., 54, no. 2 (1964).

Shatzmiller, Joseph. *Médecine et justice en Provence médiévale: Documents de Manosque, 1262–1348*. Aix-en-Provence: Publications de l'Université de Provence, 1989.

Siraisi, Nancy G. *Medieval and Early Renaissance Medicine: An Introduction to Knowledge and Practice*. Chicago: University of Chicago Press, 1990.

Skinner, Patricia. "'And Her Name Was . . .?' Gender and Naming in Medieval Southern Italy." *Medieval Prosopography* 20 (1999): 23–49.

———. "Disputes and Disparity: Women at Court in Medieval Southern Italy." *Reading Medieval Studies* 22 (1996): 85–105.

———. *Health and Medicine in Early Medieval Southern Italy*. The Medieval Mediterranean, 11. Leiden: Brill, 1997.

———. "The Possessions of Lombard Women in Italy." *Medieval Life* 2 (spring 1995): 8–11.

———. "Urban Communities in Naples, 900–1050." *Papers of the British School at Rome* 49, n.s. 62 (1994): 279–99.

———. "Women, Literacy and Invisibility in Southern Italy, 900–1200." In *Women, the Book and the Godly: Selected Proceedings of the St Hilda's Conference, 1993*. Ed. Lesley Smith and Jane H. M. Taylor, pp. 1–11. Cambridge: D. S. Brewer, 1995.

———. "Women, Wills and Wealth in Medieval Southern Italy." *Early Medieval Europe* 2 (1993): 133–52.

Solinus, C. Julius. *Collectanea rerum memorabilium*. Ed. Theodor Mommsen. Berlin: Weidmann, 1864.

Soranus of Ephesus. *Soranus' Gynecology*. Trans. Owsei Temkin. Baltimore: Johns Hopkins University Press, 1956. Reprint 1991.

Squatriti, Paolo. *Water and Society in Early Medieval Italy, A.D. 400–1000*. Cambridge: Cambridge University Press, 1998.

Stannard, Jerry. "Identification of the Plants Described by Albertus Magnus, *De vegetabilibus*, lib. VI." *Res Publica Litterarum* 2 (1979): 281–318. Reprint *Pristina Medicamenta: Ancient and Medieval Medical Botany*. Aldershot: Ashgate, 1999, essay 15.

Stuard, Susan Mosher. "Dame Trot." *Signs: Journal of Women in Culture and Society* 1 (1975): 537–42.

Sudhoff, Karl. "Die erste Tieranatomie von Salerno und ein neuer salernitanischer Anatomietext." *Archiv für Geschichte der Mathematik, der Naturwissenschaften, und der Technik* 10 (1927): 136–47.

———. "Die vierte Salernitaner Anatomie." *Archiv für Geschichte der Medizin* 20 (1928): 33–50.

Talbot, C. H. *Medicine in Medieval England*. New York: Science History Publications; London: Oldbourne, 1967.

Talbot, C. H., and E. A. Hammond. *The Medical Practitioners in Medieval England: A Biographical Register*. London: Wellcome Historical Medical Library, 1965.

Taviani-Carozzi, Huguette. *La principauté lombarde de Salerne (IX–XI siècle): Pouvoir et société en Italie lombarde méridionale*. 2 vols. Collection de l'école française de Rome, 152. Rome: École Française, 1991.

Theodorus Priscianus. *Theodori Prisciani Euporiston libri III*. Ed. Valentin Rose. Leipzig: Teubner, 1894.

Tramontana, Salvatore. "La meretrice." In *Condizione umana e ruoli sociali nel Mezzogiorno normanno-svevo. Atti delle none giornate normanno-sveve, Bari, 17–20 ottobre*

1989. Ed. Giosuè Musca, pp. 79–101. Bari: Centro di Studi Normanno-Svevi della Università degli Studi di Bari, Edizioni Dedalo, 1991.

Udovitch, Abraham. "New Materials for the History of Islamic Sicily." In *Giornata di Studio: Del nuovo sulla Sicilia musulmana (Roma, 3 maggio 1993)*, pp. 183–210. Rome: Accademia Nazionale dei Lincei, 1995.

Vázquez Bujan, Manuel Enrique. *El "De mulierum affectibus" del Corpus Hippocraticum. Estudio y edición crítica de la antigua traducción latina*. Monografías de la Universidad de Santiago de Compostela, 124. Santiago de Compostela, 1986.

Veith, Ilza. *Hysteria: The History of a Disease*. Chicago: University of Chicago Press, 1965.

von Staden, Heinrich. *Herophilus: The Art of Medicine in Early Alexandria*. Cambridge: Cambridge University Press, 1990.

Wack, Mary F. *Lovesickness in the Middle Ages: The "Viaticum" and Its Commentaries*. Philadelphia: University of Pennsylvania Press, 1990.

William of Apulia. *De rebus gestis Roberti Wiscardi*. Ed. and tr. (into French) Marguerite Mathieu, *La Geste de Robert Guiscard*. Istituto Siciliano di Studi Bizantini e Neoellenici, Testi e Monumenti, 4. Palermo: Istituto Siciliano di Studi Bizantini e Neoellenici, 1961.

Wolf, Hans Kaspar, ed. *Gynaeciorum, hoc est de Mulierum tum aliis, tum gravidarum, parientium et puerperarum affectibus et morbis libri veterum ac recentiorem aliquot, partim nunc primum editi, partim multo quam ante castigatiores*. Basel: Thomas Guarinus, 1566.

Wolf, Kenneth Baxter. *Making History: The Normans and Their Historians in Eleventh-Century Italy*. Philadelphia: University of Pennsylvania Press, 1995.

Wölfel, Hans, ed. *Das Arzneidrogenbuch "Circa instans" in einer Fassung des XIII. Jahrhunderts aus der Universitätsbibliothek Erlangen. Text und Kommentar als Beitrag zur Pflanzen- und Drogenkunde des Mittelalters*. Berlin: A. Preilipper, 1939.

Wood, Charles T. "The Doctor's Dilemma: Sin, Salvation, and the Menstrual Cycle in Medieval Thought." *Speculum* 56 (1981): 710–27.

Index

CPSIA information can be obtained
at www.ICGtesting.com
Printed in the USA
JSHW031214250321
12900JS00001B/1